Complexity, Management and the Dynamics of Change

The structure of contemporary business organizations owe more to the ideas of Isaac Newton and the seventeenth century than many of us realize. Most are modelled on principles of cause and effect and linear chains of command structured around distinct departments. But modern science has moved on since Newtonian mechanics, and in this profoundly important text, Elizabeth McMillan shows how the insights of complexity science can allow today's managers to embrace the challenges and uncertainty of the twenty-first century, and successfully oversee organizational change and development.

Complexity science refers to the study of complex adaptive systems. These can absorb information, learn and then intelligently adapt in response to environmental changes. This book brings these ideas into an important new arena by:

- outlining the historical relationship between science and organizations
- reviewing current perspectives on organizational change and best practice
- citing real-life examples of the use of complexity science ideas
- discussing issues which may arise when using ideas from complexity

Written in an accessible style to bridge the gap from scientific theory to commercial applicability, this ground-breaking text shows how organizations can become more effective, democratic and sustainable through complexity science. It is a key text for all students of business and management, and all practitioners working in the field.

Elizabeth McMillan is a Senior Research Fellow at the Open University, and an experienced consultant with extensive management experience. She is a co-founder and Director of the UK Complexity Society, and a Fellow of the Chartered Institute of Personnel and Development.

Complexity, Management and the Dynamics of Change

Challenges for practice

Elizabeth McMillan

LONDON AND NEW YORK

First published 2008
by Routledge
2 Park Square, Milton Park, Abingdon, Oxon OX14 4RN

Simultaneously published in the USA and Canada
by Routledge
711 Third Avenue, New York, NY 10017

*Routledge is an imprint of the Taylor & Francis Group,
an informa business*

© 2008 Elizabeth McMillan

Typeset in Times New Roman by
RefineCatch Limited, Bungay, Suffolk

British Library Cataloguing in Publication Data
A catalogue record for this book is available from the British Library

Library of Congress Cataloging in Publication Data
McMillan, Elizabeth M., 1953–
    Complexity, management and the dynamics of change : challenges
for practice / Elizabeth McMillan.
        p. cm.
    Includes bibliographical references and index.
    ISBN 978–0–415–41721–1 (hardback)—ISBN 978–0–415–41722–8
(pbk.) 1. Organizational change. 2. Management. I. Title.
    HD58.8.M3648 2007
    658.4′06–dc22

                                                    2007035205

ISBN 10: 0–415–41721–X (hbk)
ISBN 10: 0–415–41722–8 (pbk)
ISBN 10: 0–203–50712–6 (ebk)

ISBN 13: 978–0–415–41721–1 (hbk)
ISBN 13: 978–0–415–41722–8 (pbk)
ISBN 13: 978–0–203–50712–4 (ebk)

Contents

Illustrations

Figures

Tables

Preface

I was very pleased and rather overwhelmed when it was agreed that I should write a textbook on complexity science and its application in organizations, especially in stimulating organizational change. My first book *Complexity, Organizations and Change* drew heavily on my doctoral thesis and inevitably had a strong academic flavour. This book is for managers and those who aspire to be managers – students. It is focused on using the ideas that flow from the science of complexity to challenge and change thinking and to stimulate new practices. It is a book about application and I have tried to fill it with rich case studies and examples of good practice from across the world.

For too long many of us have lived in our wealthy societies at the expense of the rest of the world and the biosphere. A change of thinking has been long overdue. As I am writing, huge swathes of the English countryside are deep in flood waters possibly brought on by climatic changes that our industrial past has engineered. The moving finger has written and we have to change our ways while we can. Complexity science can help us in many ways to learn to live in the new world that is emerging – and part of that world should be a new and more humane management science based on our complex adaptive natures.

I would welcome engagement with students, academics and managers who would like to join me in developing a new complexity-based management science. www.elizabethmcmillan.co.uk

Acknowledgements

There are many people I should thank for helping me to prepare and write this book. I should especially like to thank Ysanne Carlise and Peter Kelby for reading through different chapters and providing helpful comments; Janine Talley and Paul Argyle for their contributions; and the office team and particularly Gemma Walker, for their invaluable professional support. Last, but definitely not least, I should like to thank my family and friends for their patience and encouragement, without which I should probably have given up long ago!

1   Introduction

Key points

- Why I am writing this book
- What this book is about
- The structure of this book and how to use it
- Time to adapt and become up to date

Ostensibly this book is about management and the management of change in all its rich complexity. But it is not a book about the management of change. It is a book about managers and organizations seeking to exist in such a way that change is just part of the normal flow of process that should be organizational life. What I mean by these seemingly paradoxical statements should be explained and become apparent as you read through this book. It is no mystery. It is about taking organizations and their managers 'out of the laboratory' and into the real world. This is the complex world that has emerged from millennia of massive and sometimes cataclysmic upheavals and is today's living planet. In order to better understand this world and what it implies for organizations and managers this book uses as its guide science: complexity science.

Why I am writing this book

There are many books out there in bookshops and university libraries that cover the topics of change and management. Many are excellently written and well researched. So why should I be adding to this collection? There are a number of answers to this question.

First of all, many of these books were written some time ago and base their conclusions and their recommendations on research and consultancy that was carried out before then. A considerable number are still relevant and useful in a wide range of contexts and situations. But, in my opinion, far too many are based on a way of thinking that does not reflect the way the world actually works. This is especially unhelpful in the fast-paced globalized world of the twenty-first century. Additionally, and most significantly, this way of thinking has its roots in a world view that developed over 300 years ago in the West and which emanated from the Scientific Revolution. It is a way of thinking that led to the 'command and control' ethos in organizations and management. Times have changed and it is an ethos which is more reminiscent of management in the 1950s and 1960s than in the 2000s. Yet there is still plenty of evidence to show that the controlling mindset lingers on and has yet to be completely replaced. This book offers a set of ideas which aim to contribute towards a replacement.

Most existing management books on organizational change draw their materials on current best practice – and so they are only able to reflect what is already out there and happening. This is useful for the manager keen to discover and emulate best practice wherever it may be found. But how much good practice is there? In 1995 the *Harvard Business Review* published an article by John Kotter on organizational transformations. Kotter had studied over 100 organizations of varying sizes in the USA and Europe. Some were highly successful, others less so, but they had all been endeavouring to transform themselves into more successful companies. They had used a range of approaches that will be familiar: total quality management, de-layering, down-sizing, process re-engineering, cultural change and so on. But Kotter discovered that very few of these efforts towards major change had been completely successful and some had been outright failures. He concluded that on a scale of successful change initiatives most organizations came somewhere between successful and failing but with 'a distinct tilt to the lower end of the scale' (Kotter 1995: 59).

Clearly, in the 1990s a range of organizations, some with vast resources and all with capable and experienced managers, were not successfully implementing major organizational change. One possible reason for this, as Kotter pointed out, at the time, was that there was relatively little experience of introducing major transformatory change programmes. How much has changed since then? I suspect not a great deal. There are a number of factors that have contributed to this. One, I would suggest, is that the management literature on change and organization renewal continues to offer too many outdated and unrealistic models. For example, many of these models divorce planning from implementation and emphasize the importance of planning at the expense of making things happen. There are widespread assumptions made that if a strategic change intervention is carefully planned and resourced then the forecast outcomes will emerge as part of a predicted process – with perhaps the occasional but manageable hiccup. I would argue that this approach stems from a world view rooted in the past and a quasi-mechanistic mindset.

Also organizations still have a tendency to introduce major change initiatives as a response to some form of crisis or serious threat. Or sometimes it is the arrival of a new chief executive or senior manager with a powerful personal vision and a reputation to create or protect that forces changes upon an organization.

So if there are few organizations out there that are truly successful when it comes to managing change, authors and managers are not left with many role models to consider and possibly emulate. Is there a danger that we may be endlessly repeating ourselves? This appears to me to be a distinct possibility, particularly when many institutions still adhere to tried and tested models which are based on attitudes and approaches intrinsically grounded on established practice.

Generally speaking, change is not perceived by managers as an ongoing process that should constantly flow through all parts of an organization to sustain it and keep it competitive. Managers are not taught to think about change in this way; nor are they taught enough about adaptation and the human dynamics of change and changing. I am writing this book because it will offer some fresh thinking based on the latest ideas about how living systems, such as organizations, really work (combined with current best practice) and some key notions on adaptation and the dynamics of change. I happen to believe that many experienced managers know that the 'old ways' are not all that effective and their instincts suggest other approaches. But who are they to argue with the mainstream of management teaching? It is to be hoped that this book will encourage them to stand their ground and continue to trust in their intuition and their intelligent and insightful observations of human nature.

Another key reason why I am writing this book is that there are a limited number of books on the market which consider the dynamics of change, particularly the human dynamics of change as the key feature of any major change initiative. Furthermore there are very few books written on the management of change from a complexity science perspective. There are, of course, excellent books by Ralph Stacey and his colleagues at the University of Hertford in the UK and US authors such as Margaret Wheatley, T. Irene Sanders, Roger Lewin and Birute Regine, Richard Pascale, Mark Millemann and Linda Gioja, who write directly for students or practitioners. But given the number of books that have been published and continue to be published on management and change, these are but a small stream contributing to a huge river.

Complexity science is a new science that only emerged during the last half of the twentieth century and although it is now well accepted in the scientific community it has taken longer for it to make inroads into the thinking and practice of other non-scientific communities, including business and management. It is a complex science and the set of ideas it presents are not straightforward and easily reduced to neat catch phrases so that it has not readily been taken up by consultants eager for a quick new idea or by hectically busy managers looking for something simple to put into practice. It is difficult and time consuming to carry out research on large organizations and therefore to gather evidence from 'big' business on how these ideas are working. Thus examples and models have been slow to emerge in the management literature – but they are now appearing – and influencing others.

As this book will describe, there are organizations that have been trying out these ideas over a number of years. The managers in these companies have been true pioneers. They have been prepared to take risks and go into unknown territory. This book maps out some of the journeys they have taken in the hope that others will be encouraged to create their own trail.

Finally, I am writing this book because I am passionate about complexity science and the potential it offers not only organizations and managers, but society as a whole. Given that human beings are a socially organized species, then the way we organize ourselves and our societies has enormous implications for all of us. Complexity science-derived ideas can impact upon the way you work on a daily basis and the way that organizations function and survive, and expect to function and survive.

I write not as someone who is remote from the hurly-burly of organizational life, or as someone with very little experience of what it is to be managing in the modern world. I write as someone who has been a practising manager for many years and who has worked in a fast-moving retail environment and in local government and higher education administration – all rapidly transforming and transformed environments. I came across complexity science after struggling for many years to reconcile many aspects of modern management theory and recommended practice with my own experiences and my own practice. There always seemed to be a mismatch between much of the theory I found in textbooks and in taught environments. It was as if the things I was being recommended and taught came from another planet. This planet was an orderly place where it was possible to predict what would happen next. All things organizational were made possible if one managed carefully and put certain planning and implementation procedures into place. This was not the world I knew and it was a world where human dynamics appeared to have reduced relevance. Yet in conversations with managers about the really difficult challenges they encountered, I almost always found that human interactions were involved in one way or another.

I have been researching in the field of complexity science for over ten years now and involved in practically applying these concepts for even longer. Currently I am a full-time researcher so I keep up to date with developments in complexity and management studies through my own research undertakings and the work of other academics in institutions all over the world. I also carry out consultancy on a regular basis and have acted as an adviser on introducing complexity-based ideas to a number of organizations – this work keeps me on my toes – and I am constantly learning from these experiences. In this book I draw on all these activities and experiences in order to write a textbook that is informative, up to date and hopefully imaginative and inspiring!

What this book is about

This book is about complexity science and its application in management and organizations. It aims to simplify and make accessible complexity science concepts in such a way that students and managers may use them with confidence and understanding. It is about transforming the way we think about organizations, about their design, about the way they operate and most importantly about the roles of those who co-create them. It is about providing useful models that students and managers may use and adapt to develop a fresh approach to management based on complexity science principles.

Main themes

As I have indicated earlier, mainstream management practice in Western Europe and North America is still heavily influenced by ideas and approaches derived from an out-of-date world view: the classical, traditional, scientific world view. This is sometimes referred to as the Newtonian–Cartesian paradigm. This book argues that this is not sufficient in the fast changing world of the twenty-first century. Fresh management thinking is required at every level, as is fresh appraisals of management practice both strategic and operational – and complexity science offers this possibility.

This book seeks to explain and describe how viewing the world from a complexity paradigm perspective can shed fresh light on a range of organizational problems and issues associated with managing change. Complexity science is used to suggest innovative and ground-breaking ways of reshaping the organizational world so that it is more in tune with the times. It avers that understanding of complexity should help managers to cope more effectively with the waves of uncertainty and change that the twenty-first century is sure to bring and that these concepts are of more than metaphorical value to organizations.

I describe how organizations can move towards becoming more effective, democratic and sustainable by using knowledge of complexity science principles. This theme is supported by an in-depth case study of a traditional, complex and complicated organization that used ideas derived from complexity to challenge and change the predominant culture. From this approach emerged unexpected creative energies, complex learning and significant changes. Other case studies and examples are also provided throughout to demonstrate the powerful applicability of these ideas.

A number of useful complexity science models based on theory, research and practice are offered as useful materials. Students as they think and read about management studies in relation to change should find these models conceptually useful and insightful. It is hoped that students as prospective managers and also practising managers will be able to use these in such a way as to fine tune and develop their own complexity-based thinking and complexity-based approaches to management that are resonant with their own requirements and the demands of the twenty-first century.

The objectives of this book

The objectives of this book are as follows:

- To enable business and management students and others unfamiliar with the complexity paradigm to understand how it developed and its important features, without the need for a scientific education or background. Scientists have developed their own 'languages' with which they describe and explain phenomena and their terms are not always understood by others, including those from other disciplines. A physicist may not be understood by a chemist or by a biologist and vice versa. Thus within complexity science you will find many differing scientifically based explanations, some offering complex mathematical equations, for example. I am not a scientist by education and although I have read many scientific papers and I work closely with 'hard' scientists in order to better understand complexity, I do not 'speak' nor necessarily understand their esoteric 'language'. I have thought for some time that those working in complexity science need to develop a vocabulary that although rooted in verifiable science is understandable by all. We are a long way from achieving this. But this book will try to describe and explain complexity science concepts in a way that is widely accessible.
- To offer a choice on the depth of knowledge acquired about complexity science concepts. This is explained further in the section on structure.
- To further develop this understanding by briefly describing the relationship between organizations and classical science from an historical perspective and how this has influenced management studies and practice.
- To review attitudes and ideas on change and organizational change, in particular, in order to widen perspectives and set the context for modern management practice.
- To explore the possibilities and the unique capability complexity science offers when considering changing and reshaping organizations.
- To discuss some of the problems that may arise in organizations when working with ideas from complexity.
- To offer useful examples of the ways in which a wide variety of organizations have used ideas and insights from complexity to change or redefine themselves in some way.
- To encourage the reader who is new to complexity to want to learn more and to offer the 'experienced' reader some new theory and some new real-life insights based on original research.
- To provide a number of useful research-based models and guides that will enable managers, students and others to introduce complexity-based concepts into their organization and to critically consider their own practices.
- To offer a number of models or approaches to using complexity to encourage change or making a difference. These are multi-purpose and

may be used conceptually, analytically, diagnostically and to indicate possibilities for action.

- To encourage the reader to think with imagination and to speculate on future possibilities from a complex adaptive world perspective.

This book seeks to build a practical bridge between the world of science and the world of management. It offers a brief history of the development of complexity science and pulls together a wide range of essential, interlinked concepts and insights. It also considers the application of these to management and organizations in both theoretical and practical terms. Most complexity management texts do not offer such a comprehensive approach and all too often assume some knowledge of the science or refer to only a limited selection of key concepts. This book enables the reader to bypass the many scientific texts and to proceed directly to their own domain of interest. My own researches involve collaborations with biologists, physicists and mathematicians, and these have resulted in a rich understanding informed by scientific discovery and debate, unusual for the world of management.

The complexity paradigm is not always well understood by writers and consultants. Some proponents appear not to have grasped some of its essential or subtler aspects. For example, some still talk of the need for 'control' in organizations and construct complex linear models to represent non-linear systems. Some talk of 'complexity', using it as a smokescreen to put forward traditional thinking in a new guise. These misunderstandings hinder the development of new thinking and the emergence of a genuine new paradigm with significant application. This book points out these 'blind alleys' and aims to help the reader to differentiate and develop in-depth understanding.

The structure of this book

The book has been structured with the needs of readers in mind. Some students or managers may only wish to acquire a basic knowledge of complexity science. Others may be interested in acquiring more in-depth knowledge. Similarly some readers may have only a passing interest in the history of organizations and their relationship with science and its development, while others will take a keen interest. Accordingly, Chapters 2 and 3 have two parts. Part One gives the basic information and Part Two offers more in depth information and background. The reader should decide for himself or herself whether or not to read Part Two.

You will also find that each chapter begins with a list of key points. This will serve as a guide to the ground covered in the pages that follow. At the end of each chapter I have posed a number of key questions. These are designed to help you reflect on some of the concepts and ideas you have just encountered and also to stimulate your thoughts on practical, application issues and possibilities.

Thematically the book begins by arguing the case for updating management theory, and therefore practice and discusses the powerful influence classical science has had on the development of management studies and the prevalent paradigm. This sets the scene for the emergence of chaos theory and then complexity science and their impact on scientific thinking. Having set the context for the discussions in this book I then move on to consider our notions of change and how they have been affected by traditional, mechanistic views. This adds further to the context and alerts our minds to the journey ahead. The following chapters consider the application of complexity science concepts in organizations and management and include some important and detailed examples. It then focuses on a number or important principles and models for engendering successful organizational change. The journey taken by this book is reached with a final chapter which offers some final thoughts and possibilities.

The reader who has read my academic monograph *Complexity Organizations and Change*, which I wrote in 2003, will find that the structure of this book follows a similar pattern. However, this book is designed as a textbook and so it is written in a quite different way and with a strong focus on application. Further, it builds and expands upon many of the ideas presented in my earlier book and contains a substantial amount of completely new material much of it drawn from very recent research work and consultancy practice. I am indebted to a number of managers for their willingness to let me investigate their uses of complexity science concepts and to present their experiences in this book.

The contents of this book from Chapter 2 onwards are described briefly below.

Chapter 2. The clockwork manager – alive and well?

Part One: Time to move on

This chapter describes the need for a new science of management and explains why many aspects of modern management theory and practice are 300 years out of date. It considers the influence of classical science on organizations. There is a brief overview of mainstream management theory and practice – recognizing the impact of this and the need to develop new theory and practice that effectively blends the 'old' with the 'new' wherever possible.

Part Two: Classical science – a prestigious paradigm

This part of Chapter 2 describes the birth of classical science and the scientific tradition with reference to Galileo, Descartes, and Newton. It moves on to include the challenges to this paradigm that took place during the nineteenth and twentieth centuries. The relationship between science and society and how classical science affects western society as a whole is briefly discussed.

Chapter 3. Complexity science: understanding the science

Part One: The essential basics

The main theories and how they are being currently applied in many different domains are introduced in this chapter. It includes: chaos theory; the butterfly effect or sensitive dependence on initial conditions; notions of order and disorder; strange attractors; the 'edge of chaos'; fractals; complexity; self-organizing systems; complex adaptive systems; emergence; evolution and complexity.

Part Two: The basics plus

The second part of this chapter describes the history and development of those ideas and theories which have collectively become known as complexity science. It records how and when the first ideas emerged and describes the contributions of Edward Lorenz and sensitive dependence on initial conditions and strange attractors; Benoit Mandelbrot and the development of fractals; the emergence of complexity science with the work of scientists like John Holland and Murray Gell-Mann; Prigogine and dissipative structures; self-organization and the work of Stuart Kauffman and Brian Goodwin; and Chris Langton and emergence. This part of Chapter 3 aims to show how a new scientific paradigm was woven together by scientists working in different disciplines and on different continents.

Chapter 4. Change and the dynamics of change: thinking differently

The way organizations think about change and how this affects their ability to handle it is discussed in this chapter. It considers how perceptions of change have varied over time. Degrees of change are discussed and what we understand by first-order and second-order change. There is a section on approaches to change in organizations today and an exploration of some of the issues that arise. A comparison between traditional, mechanistic views on change with modern, dynamic complexity-inspired views of change is provided. Strategies for organizational change are briefly discussed before a comparison between some traditional approaches and a complexity-based approach is offered.

Chapter 5. Complexity in practice: doing things differently

This chapter focuses on the application of complexity principles to management and organizations and provides examples and case studies from the UK, Europe and the USA. It describes how some organizations are breaking out of the 'old' frameworks, doing things differently and managing without control. There are sections on: using the butterfly effect; using the 'edge

of chaos' to stimulate innovation and creativity; using fractals in organizations; and ways of applying self-organization to free up people and create
fresh energies. The organization as a complex adaptive organization is also
discussed.

Chapter 6. Complexity in action – a case study of the Open University

As the title of this chapter indicates, it is devoted to a single in-depth case
study of one organization. The chapter begins by setting the context for the
case study with some facts and figures about the Open University. It then
moves on to describe the threats the university faced and the strategic action
plan it developed in order to address these and change the institution. Then
the story of the four-year programme is provided. The main features of the
programme are described and discussed. These include: interactions and
the response dynamic; a people's movement; learning and change dynamics;
democracy and self-organization at work. Space in this chapter is given to the
creation of two important self-organizing teams and the impact this had on
the participants in the teams, their colleagues and the institution.

Chapter 7. Self-organizing change dynamics

Drawing on research derived from the case study of the Open University, this
chapter focuses on the use self-organizing principles in order to stimulate
self-organizing change dynamics. The contributions self-organizing teams
can make to strategic change processes and to the effective delivery of short-
term projects is described. Self-organizing teams, their operating principles
and practices are also discussed. This section also includes 'Team Working in
Organizations' – a model which considers team working and the development
of self-organizing teams within different organizational contexts. Finally, the
programme as a complex adaptive change process is discussed.

Chapter 8. Essential principles for introducing a complexity-based change process

This chapter too draws on the case study of the Open University and provides
twelve principles for introducing a complexity-based change process. Twelve
principles are provided for those managers who work at the strategic levels
and twelve are provided for more junior managers. These suggest the essential
actions and activities needed to stimulate changes at the micro- and macro-
levels in support of strategic action, engaging all employees in co-creating this
process.

Chapter 9. Innovating and changing: models for experimentation and adaptation

I have been researching and using complexity science and its application in organizations and management for well over a decade now and in this chapter I offer five models which I have developed during the last few years. They have emerged from a synthesis of hard thinking and research and in some instances from practical application of complexity concepts in organizations – and most importantly from the conversations I have had with practising managers. In my opinion, all the models are helpful conceptually. But they also offer useful possibilities for analysis and diagnosis and provide indicators of possible future actions and activities.

1 *The Transition Model for Strategy*. This model is designed to assist you in deciding where your organization is today in relation to classical management thinking and complexity thinking. It suggests how you may use the model to move an organization towards a complexity-style organization.

2 *The Complex Adaptive Learning Model of Strategy*. This model weaves together the concept of 'the edge of chaos' and our understanding of complex adaptive systems in the context of strategic thinking and aims to further support the learning school of strategy and learning organization notions. It is essentially a conceptual model.

3 *The Complex Adaptive Process Model*. This model is derived from knowledge and understanding of complex adaptive systems. This section describes the thinking underpinning the different features of the model and how to interpret and use them. This model may be used conceptually and as a practical model to introduce a complexity science-based approach to management thinking and practice at individual, team or organizational level. It is a multifaceted 'tool' that may be used as an analytical/diagnostic 'tool' at all levels; and as a 'tool' to suggest possibilities for action. It may also be used as a 'project' tool to help managers organize and effectively deliver projects using complexity science-based principles and approaches. Furthermore, it may also be used to monitor and evaluate activities.

4 *The Edge of Chaos Assessment Model*. This section takes the concept of 'the edge of chaos' and shows how it may be used in a number of different ways including as an analytical/diagnostic tool at the individual, team or organizational level. Examples of how to use the tool to provide an individual or an organizational 'health check' are provided.

5 *The Fractal Web*. This uniquely revolutionary model of organization design and structure challenges prevalent reductionist, linear ideas and approaches to organization design. The model was created via imagination and reflection and draws on fractal and biological concepts interwoven with self-organizing and complex adaptive systems principles.

Chapter 10. New perspectives, opportunities for innovation

This concluding chapter attempts to weave together the key ideas presented in this book and also offer some new ideas with radical possibilities for innovation and leadership.

Time to adapt

In 1965 the term 'future shock' was coined by the US writer, Alvin Toffler, to describe the shattering effects on people of experiencing too much change, happening far too fast. A few years later he wrote *Future Shock*, a prophetic and disturbing book, that was an eye opening social study of emerging trends and the implications for societies of rapid change and its attendant social, political, economic and ecological consequences. He wrote:

> I gradually became appalled by how little is actually known about adaptivity, either by those who call for and create vast changes in our society, or by those who supposedly prepare us to cope with these changes. Earnest intellectuals talk bravely about 'educating for change' or 'preparing people for the future'. But we know virtually nothing about how to do it. In the most rapidly changing environment to which man has ever been exposed, we remain pitifully ignorant of how the human animal copes.
>
> (Toffler 1983: 12)

Much has happened since the 1970s when Toffler wrote these words – but how much has really changed? How much have managers and students of management learnt about adaptation and how to cope with change? Systems thinking and notions of learning and the learning organization offer useful sets of ideas for handling change and uncertainty but how much has mainstream management thinking moved on? I would argue that this has been essentially an incremental change and that the bulk of management literature still draws too heavily on a preponderance of notions that were developed some 300 plus years ago.

How we think about management and the practice of management has a huge impact on organizations given that organizing is how we make things happen and how we make our societies function. Thus each and every manager and student of management has the collective potential to make an important contribution to the kind of society we live in. (See the later discussion on the butterfly effect.) Worryingly, there is considerable evidence to suggest that our westernized globally connected societies are experiencing many difficulties and some are struggling to avoid the shock and attendant dysfunction that Toffler warned us about.

Toffler was writing over forty years ago when complexity science had its genesis and it has taken the intervening years for the social sciences to recognize the huge potential that it offers. So on the plus side, we have learnt incrementally and are still learning a great deal about change and adaptation. Now, I believe, a leap forward is possible via utilization of the knowledge emanating from the new science of complexity. Toffler commented on how little was known about adaptation and how important it was for us to understand it and most importantly to be able to adapt and so cope with rapid changes. This book aims to add to our knowledge of adaptation and of change and its underpinning dynamics, especially those crucial human dynamics. In so doing it will try to bring you as up to date as possible with new approaches to the management of change from a complexity science perspective and to move management thinking into a new phase of understanding and action.

Key questions

- Do you think there is a need for fresh thinking in mainstream management studies about the management of change and organization renewal?
- Alvin Toffler coined the phrase 'future shock' in the 1960s – do you think organizations are currently experiencing this and why?
- Toffler was appalled by our lack of knowledge about change and how to cope with it describing us as 'pitifully ignorant'. What do you think of his views?

2 The clockwork manager – alive and well?

The world has moved on in our lifetime and more rapidly that at any other time within recorded human experience. Thus we are all trying to cope with a cataract of interwoven technological, economic, societal and ecological changes on a global scale. Sometimes this cataract is so strong that it threatens to overwhelm us. Cognitive psychologists state that as human beings we can effectively manage approximately (plus or minus two) seven chunks of information at any given time. Is it any wonder, therefore, that many managers are experiencing difficulties in handling organizational life and are keenly interested in uncovering useful ways of handling change in its many guises. I would argue that, unfortunately, traditional mainstream management studies have yet to keep pace with the needs of today's managers and are still offering too many ideas and prescriptions rooted in a view of the world that is now irrelevant. It is a view that arose out of a very exciting and challenging period of scientific discovery and experimentation: the late-sixteenth, the seventeenth and early-eighteenth centuries. This period is commonly referred to as the Scientific Revolution and it led to the development of classical science or the Newtonian–Cartesian paradigm. In Part One of this chapter I shall describe the origins of this view, its main features and how it came to be interwoven into our thinking about organizations and management. Part Two explores the birth of classical science and its development in more detail, briefly refers to challenges to its pre-eminence and offers a short discussion on the relationship between science and society.

PART ONE: TIME TO MOVE ON

Key points

- Classical science and a clockwork universe
- Industrialization and early organizations
- Organizations and management in the twentieth century
- The new millennium: challenges for organizations and management responses

Traditional thinking about organizations and how to manage them seemed to work well enough in the industrialized world of the late-nineteenth and early-twentieth centuries when life moved at a slower pace. Huge organizations benefited from economies of scale and traditional 'command and control' approaches to management. But as the last decades of the twentieth century showed, many of these traditional organizations struggled to survive. Why have they struggled? Why have they not kept pace with a rapidly changing world? In this chapter I shall endeavour to provide some answers to these questions by going back to the roots of modern organizations and some of the mainstream ideas that shaped them. In so doing I shall try to reveal how these 'roots' have continued to be influential right up to the present day, and how this influence has made it difficult for many organizations to respond and effectively adapt to the modern world. I have taken a roughly chronological route in tracing this development and considered some of the main theories of organization and management. But this is not meant to be an exhaustive study and I have referred only to those theories and practices that have become widespread and have relevance to the themes of this book.

Classical science and a machine world

In medieval Europe the world was seen as a living, spiritual place and the universe was viewed as a single organism with mankind at its centre. Everything existed in a scheme of timeless order called the 'Great Chain of Being', in which all living creatures had their place on an ascending scale of perfection which rose from the earth to the heavens. Each individual human being had his or her proper place in this great scheme of things and this provided status and meaning to his or her life. Thus this world view provided an explanatory framework for the way the world worked and spiritual and interpretative security. It was not without its drawbacks, however, as it placed limitations on the rights and freedoms of individuals and created absolute authorities in the shape of medieval kingship and ecclesiastical authority. But in the sixteenth and seventeenth centuries this world view was to undergo a series of radical challenges. These challenges came in the form of the great scientific discoveries and experiments of the period. This collectively became known as the Scientific Revolution. Out of this arose a new mechanistic view of the world and new scientific methods. The key figures in this period are Kepler, Copernicus, Galileo, Descartes, Bacon and Newton and their contributions are described in Part Two of this chapter.

The biologist Stuart Kauffman encapsulated the impact of this revolution when he wrote of Isaac Newton:

> What a giant step he took. Just imagine what it must have felt like to Newton as his new laws of mechanics took form in his mind. What wonder he must have felt. With a mere three laws of motion and a universal law

of gravitation in hand, Newton not only derived tides and orbits, but unleashed on the Western mind a clockwork universe.

(Kauffman 1996: 6)

So what are the main features of this new world view that arose out of the scientific discoveries of Newton and others and which epitomize classical science or the Newtonian–Cartesian paradigm?

The predictable clockwork universe

The influence of the scientific revolution was such that the universe was no longer thought of as a spiritual, living place but rather as a giant machine which could now be understood by careful and precise examination of its constituent parts. It was governed by universal laws and the continued working of these universal laws ensured that the 'clock' would eternally continue to function as predicted. Thus arose the accepted belief that the world is a predictable and stable place which, unless disturbed, operates like clockwork. This encouraged people to think that the future could be mapped out as part of some predictable plan, if one applied the correct universal laws.

T. Irene Sanders in her book *Strategic Thinking and the New Science* gives an insightful and very helpful explanation for the reason why the clock was chosen as a metaphor for this new world view. She writes:

> The clock, because of its central place in European society, became the metaphor of choice for explaining the mechanics at work behind the visible world. The shift from natural time, based on seasonal rhythms and the Sun, to mechanical time, divided into equal hours and minutes, was hailed as an enormous technological accomplishment . . . But this shift, from natural to man-made time, unwittingly gave the clock *machine* control over our thinking about and our experience of time. Nevertheless, it was seen as an example of man's ingenuity and his ability to understand and harness nature.
>
> (Sanders 1998: 44–45)

The natural world was considered as something that had to be controlled and manipulated in order to extract knowledge and information about how it functioned. This view encouraged and accepted a widespread disregard for the natural environment in which we lived. This disregard led to the creation of many of the factors which have contributed to environmental degradation on a global scale.

Order and disorder

Order was welcomed as the 'natural' or intended scheme of things, whereas disorder was not intended and had to be avoided or controlled. Violent storms, earthquakes, plagues, social upheaval and other violent and threatening events were all seen as aberrations from the natural order. This view accorded well with Christian religious beliefs at the time. The world and the inherent natural order had been designed and created by God out of the dark and chaotic elements that existed in the universe. This divine order, if seriously disturbed, risked plunging the world into outlying darkness and chaos. Unfortunately, many of the manifestations of human behaviours were considered disruptive and disorderly. Thus the need for 'command and control' to maintain the natural order.

Stability and instability – equilibrium and disequilibrium

So the universe was considered to be essentially a stable place, unless there was some kind of disturbance or breakdown in the workings of the universal machine. Instability was therefore a very unwelcome aspect of life and anything that could disturb the equilibrium or the natural order of things was to be avoided at all costs. Thus the importance of controlling things so that stability could be maintained. Understanding how the universal laws of science operated appeared to make this a real possibility. We could now understand the workings of the universe, which meant that we could now control it. Given that most people longed to live in a world full of certainties and limited disruptions, this was a welcome notion in European societies that had experienced bouts of political and religious instabilities for centuries.

Humans as machines

Human beings were now seen as machine-like entities with the human heart acting as the central pump within the machine. All other living forms too, including plants, were seen as mechanical creatures, but humans had special capacities for speech and reasoning which other creatures were without. Humans, like machines were made up of a host of constituent parts which worked together to create the mechanistic whole. If one part malfunctioned or was diseased, then some kind of intervention was needed to fix the 'machine'. Even today the science of medicine is primarily based on the notion of the body as a machine with illness as a consequence of some fault or breakdown and with the doctor's role as one of fault finding and repair.

The mind was viewed as being separate from the body and the two had to be treated as separate entities or parts of the body. Further, the mind with its rational, intellectual capacities was considered to be far superior to the sensory experiences of the body. This led to a focus on the pre-eminence of the intellectual and cognitive faculties as it was considered that they emanated solely from brain function. Even very recently this separation of the head from the body and the superior role of the intellect are reflected in the separation of blue-collar (manual/body) workers from white-collar (mind) workers and the significance often accorded to high-level planning and analysis over operational or shop floor activity.

Rationality, logic and the powers of reasoning

Cartesian dualism, whereby the workings of the body (senses) were seen as being separated from the workings of the brain (mind/intellect), encouraged scientists and then others to discount, undervalue and even downgrade the role of intuition, imagination and the sensory experiences in interpreting and understanding our world. This in turn encouraged a materialistic approach to the world. This way of thinking underpins the importance attached to detailed analysis and quantitative measurement over holistic approaches and qualitative measurements.

Reality and scientific truth

From classical science developed the view that there existed an objective reality that we could study and carry out experiments on. By using our logical, reasoning faculties we could objectively and therefore accurately explore our universe. This proved to be a valuable working hypothesis when studying simple physical systems, such as the way planets move, but it has proved less useful when considering biological and social systems. This approach assumed that those carrying out the experiments were in no way influencing the experiment itself. We now know that this cannot be the case. There is no such thing as a pure objective reality. Everything is influenced by everything else that exists around it, including our thoughts and observations. However, the notion of an objective reality that could be reliably researched and studied held sway for many centuries. In the meantime, experiments supposedly carried out in a rational way formed the solid foundations of our knowledge of how the world worked. It was a persuasive and powerful approach. The knowledge that arose from applying it to major physical systems encouraged many to believe that these explanations could confidently be applied also to human systems.

Hand in hand with this belief was the idea of scientific truth or the notion that there is one right and verifiable answer to every scientific question. This right answer could be found through the application of rigorous scientific methods of investigation. Thus arose a way of thinking dominated by the need to search for the 'one' right answer. It is a very black and white view of the world, where the answer to a question is essentially either wrong or right. By extension human behaviour could be viewed as good or bad, as right or wrong. It is not a many coloured world with complex shades of meaning and possibility. Further, science no longer saw the acquisition of wisdom as its primary goal but considered the acquisition of knowledge and scientific truth as necessary for the future benefit of mankind.

Reductionism, analysis, measurement and the quantitative approach

An important feature of the Newtonian–Cartesian paradigm was the develop-ment of the empirical approach to science and scientific discovery. This approach required that experiments were carefully carried out with the collec-tion of as many facts as possible and with further experiments to test any general conclusions. The emphasis was on the collection of objective data which was quantitative.

One aspect of this approach was reductionism. This decreed that the best way to understand something was to break it down into its smallest consti-tuent parts and examine them closely. The assumption being made was that all aspects of complex phenomena can be understood by breaking down and studying their constituent parts in detail. For example, to understand the workings of the brain one would break its structure down into different sections and then study each brain cell carefully and analytically. This, it was believed, would enable one to build up an accurate picture of how the whole brain worked. Yet breaking everything down in this way does not explain the workings of the whole phenomenon under study. It also led to a focus on entities and parts rather than on processes and flows of activity or behaviours. This method has proved highly successful in expanding our knowledge of the world and how it works. But it was found to have limitations when studying complex dynamical systems, especially human systems, as recent develop-ments in scientific method have shown.

Cause and effect, linear thinking and linear equations

The view of the universe as a giant machine gave rise to the idea that it was completely causal and deterministic. Everything that happened in the world had a definite cause and this led to a definite effect. Theoretically, therefore, in seeking an explanation for something one would seek for the cause. Con-versely, if one wanted to achieve a certain effect then, in theory, this should be possible by creating the appropriate 'cause'. This, of course, assumes that cause and effect are closely related in time and space and therefore it is possible to trace and understand the relationship between the two. The reality is, how-ever, quite different when dealing with complex systems, particularly over long time periods. Furthermore, this way of thinking often led to an oversimplifi-cation of complex phenomena and an undervaluing of small aberrations or flaws in a system or experiment. Simple linear equations underpinned the cause and effect model and encouraged a linear model of thinking which ignored or devalued the non-linear complexity of dynamical systems such as human societies, weather systems or fluctuations in wildlife populations. Cause and effect thinking also encouraged a tendency to assume that there are only one or two main causes underlying a phenomenon, when in fact there may be multiple causes.

Early organizations and the birth of the clockwork manager

The human species existed for many tens of thousands of years as hunters and gatherers. We lived by using animals and understanding their patterns of existence; by our abilities to make and use simple tools, and by our ability to identify and gather plants that were edible and beneficial. We survived by continuing to build on existing knowledge and by constantly adapting to the natural environment in which we lived. People lived in small family or tribal groups with significant distances between different groups. It was a very simple way of existence that was essentially nomadic. Then there evolved a major shift in our pattern of existence. People began to grow crops. Then instead of relying on hunting down animals to provide meat, they farmed them for meat and useful animal products instead. This was a major transformation and involved huge changes and adaptations in lifestyle. Families settled down to farm and small settlements and then villages and towns sprang up. Trade flourished and for some 6,000 years we existed as primarily a farming species. Then came the Industrial Revolution, the creation of vast manufacturing organizations and the emergence of a much more complex and complicated society. This is the world we were born into and is the world in which today's organizations have their roots. So how did these organizations form themselves? Why did the early industrial enterprises form themselves in the way they did?

At the beginning of the eighteenth century no one would have described the United Kingdom as an industrial country, although it was a busy trading and manufacturing nation. But this was to dramatically change over the next decades as entrepreneurs made use of improvements in technology, low interest rates and favourable trading conditions to rapidly expand manufacturing. For example, in the early 1700s blast furnaces produced some 25,000 tons of iron a year but by the end of the century this had increased to some 250,000 tons per annum. This rise in manufacturing continued to be fuelled by the availability of coal as an essential energy source and the development of the turnpikes and the canal system and later the railways. Until the birth of the Industrial Revolution in the eighteenth century most people were occupied in some kind of agricultural activity and most were self-employed. Apart from the church, the state and the army, large organizations did not exist. Thus when early entrepreneurs first set up their enterprises they copied these organizations and set up hierarchical, command and control structures. They required their employees to work together in large buildings in order to centralize production and ensure that improvements in production methods could be easily made. Division of labour was also introduced as a way of breaking down the overall process and controlling production activity. In 1776 Adam Smith, the Scottish economist, in his book *The Wealth of Nations* described the techniques of pin manufacturing and the inherent efficiencies in this way of organizing production. This way of organizing was supported by the reductionist method of scientific inquiry. Manufacturers were imitating science in order to improve their production processes.

It seems entirely logical and sensible that the early entrepreneurs who created the new industries and manufacturing bases of the Industrial Revolution should turn to Newtonian science (the Newtonian–Cartesian paradigm) for their ideas and inspiration. Their outlook on life and their way of thinking would already have been influenced and shaped by the great scientific discoveries of the sixteenth and seventeenth centuries. These had unlocked the secrets to so many of the mysteries of the universe. Many must have thought that understanding and applying these universal laws would help with the success of their enterprises. The application of intellect, logic and reason and an analytical, empirical, reductionist approach to business was based on the new and highly successful scientific methods. The prevailing scientific paradigm encouraged the development of linear structures and organizations designed on reductionist principles. Thus organizations as they expanded were broken down into functions and distinct compartments or 'silos', with complementary social and authoritarian structures also based on linear models. This way of thinking was encapsulated in the bleak linear architecture of the early manufacturing mills and plants.

The development of new technologies and new machinery for production also influenced the design of these early organizations and the way they were expected to operate. The new scientific philosophy claimed that non-material structures were of little value and so the machines became all important. The welfare and needs of the workers, even the children, were considered less important than keeping the machines in constant use. Many of these early workers were unused to factory life, having previously been agricultural workers. They found the disciplines of factory life very different from those of an agrarian existence which followed the seasons and time-honoured agricultural rituals. Rules and disciplinary procedures, including harsh punishments, were put in place to control these people and to ensure they conformed to the requirements of the production process.

Many of the early industrialists considered that science offered not only explanations for how the world worked but also a set of laws which could equally well apply to other processes, including the production process. So the new factory system emphasized not only the importance of the machines, but the need for a strictly controlled hierarchy of workers to maintain them. As businesses grew and expanded, it became the norm for production activities to develop along these lines. New, larger, organizational structures emerged which were patrimonial and hierarchical in nature and skilled jobs were broken down into new separate tasks or jobs. It was the beginning of the production line process. As the size of a business grew, so the number of administrative employees rose and this has been linked to the emergence and growth of bureaucracy.

Bureaucracy

In the early years of the twentieth century, Max Weber, a German sociologist became interested in bureaucracy as an organizational form. He saw it as offering many virtues over earlier forms of authority which had been based on the power of traditional groups, such as local landowners and the aristocracy. He considered the bureaucratic form of organization and management to be preferable to these older forms of authority, as it was both objective and impersonal and offered control that was based on rules and procedures under-pinned by rationality. Weber's work led to the formation of a comprehensive theory of organization and management, especially the theory of bureaucracy. He noted the similarities between the use of machines in industry and the widespread use of bureaucratic types of organization and in his work we find the first full definition of bureaucracy. Weber was interested in those forms of organization which had stood the test of time and studied the organization and structure of the church, government, the military and other long-standing organizations. His analysis of these led him to believe that hierarchy, authority and bureaucracy are at the roots of all social organizations.

Weber's theory was primarily a theory of organization structure, and he saw clearly defined roles, a stable hierarchy and written procedures as the ideal. In his view, efficiency was achieved through hierarchical supervision, the fixed allocation of tasks, a system of rules and regulations, and military-style dis-cipline. He considered that the rational use of authority and control was highly desirable for an organization. The bureaucracy was the most efficient form of organization possible as it worked like a modern machine. Here are strong echoes of early organizational forms and the long shadow of classical science and its continuing influence. This influence is also seen in Weber's belief that rules and procedures could be devised to cover and deal with every eventuality.

After the Second World War huge public bureaucracies were created in the UK with the nationalization of the public utilities and the creation of the NHS (National Health Service) in 1948.

> Tall structures were created with as many as 20 plus levels between the chief executive and the shopfloor operative. Managerial control of employees at all the multiple levels was based on a mixture of direct com-mand and budgetary responsibility. Hierarchy, command and control were the governing principles of employee management.
>
> (Mabey, Salaman and Storey 2001: 157)

Although many of the public utilities have been privatized large bureaucra-cies still abound today in both the public and private sectors and on a global basis. Bureaucracy, in spite of strident criticism about its failings, chief of which is probably its cumbersome and slow-moving response to events, is still a much-favoured form of social organization. The NHS is a good example of how the giant bureaucracies which did so well in the relatively stable conditions of the 1950s and 1960s have failed to adapt effectively to the massive technological and sociological changes of the 1990s and the 2000s.

Classical management and scientific management

Henri Fayol, writing at the beginning of the twentieth century is credited by many as being the founder of modern management theory and practice. Fayol was a French engineer and manager in the mining industry. He successfully turned around an ailing company and on retirement set up a centre to study and disseminate his successful practices. In 1919 his book, *General and Industrial Management* set out his universal principles for sound and rational management. Fayol advocated an organization structure that was centralized, functionally specialized and hierarchical, in which everything had its specific place. As far as he was concerned the specialization of tasks reflected the natural world where the higher the species the more specialized it was. He considered planning, organizing, forecasting, coordinating and controlling as essential management activities. Sanctions and close supervision were considered necessary to control the workers and to ensure that work was properly carried out. Human emotions or passions were seen as weaknesses and had to be subdued because they could hinder the work of the organization.

Fayol's work laid the basis for the development of classical management. His thinking suggests a blend of military and engineering principles, underpinned by classical science. Fayol's work has been built upon by subsequent writers and researchers and together they created the foundation of management theory in the first half of the last century. There is significant evidence to show that some key aspects of this theory are still in use up to the present day, particularly in traditional industries and in government funded institutions such as universities and the civil service.

Also in the early twentieth century, the American Frederick W. Taylor, drawing on his understanding of traditional science and scientific method, devised a theory of management which he called 'scientific management'. Taylor believed that work could be studied scientifically and through the application of scientific method, it was possible to increase productivity. He believed in the importance of objective measurement and the development of laws to govern efficiency at work. For him scientific method meant the use of systematic observation and measurement and his approach extended to all tasks however menial or small. At no time did he allow for the use of guess work or intuition. His development of the piece-rate incentive system allowed managers not only to define the tasks the workers had to carry out but also to determine how they approached their tasks. This shifted control of working tasks from the craft workers to management. This offered yet more control of the production process.

Taylor's ideas have been extensively criticized for the way in which they undermined the skills of the craftsmen and for ignoring the trust and co-operation between management and workers which helped organizations to function effectively. But his scientific management methods resulted in great increases in productivity, albeit at the expense of reducing many workers to little more than automatons. Taylor's approach to work design fitted very well with the development of the mass production assembly line most famously embraced by the US car maker, Henry Ford.

Taylor's scientific management continued a trend begun in the eighteenth century of treating men and woman as mechanical objects or parts of some larger machine. Another significant result of Taylor's thinking was the division of workers into those who thought and those who acted, which again shows the influence of the Newtonian–Cartesian paradigm.

Taylor's ideas were taken up and developed by other practitioners and researchers, most notably Henry Gantt and Frank and Lilian Gilbreth who developed Work Study or Industrial Engineering. It has been argued that Gantt carried the notion of the world as a machine to extremes in his proposal for an organization called 'The New Machine'. He advocated that organizations should be managed by engineers, who would design and run them with machine-like efficiency. Gantt's planning charts are still used widely today.

Management – 1950s to 1980s

In the first half of the twentieth century other theorists and practitioners also contributed their ideas on organization and management as well as major figures such as Taylor, Fayol and Weber. The Hawthorne Studies carried out during the 1920s and 1930s showed that organizations were not just about the use of machinery and working practices but also about human social systems. The notion of the organization as an organism and a natural system and not a formal mechanism was suggested by the behaviourists and the social and organizational psychologists. They envisaged a more 'organic' organization, which was less rigidly controlled, more adaptive and less rule bound. This was a very different kind of organization to the one recommended by the traditional theorists. During the 1950s and 1960s organizational psychologists such as Argyris, Herzberg and McGregor showed how it was possible to integrate the needs of individuals and organizations and, as a result of their influence, new models of organization began to appear.

Yet, the work of many of the behaviourists shows the influence of the classical scientific paradigm. For example, it is interesting to note the influence of the notion of a linear hierarchy in Maslow's 'Hierarchy of Needs' theory. This envisages human needs on an ascending scale, rising from the fulfilment of basic physiological needs to the final need for self-actualization. This five-stage model puts human needs into separate categories and assumes that we must satisfy each need in turn before moving on up to the next need. This model I find deeply flawed in that it categorizes and separates out human needs as if they are not interdependent and all necessary parts of the human whole. Maslow's approach was modified and followed by Herzberg and his

'Two Factor' theory, which explored notions of motivation and job satisfaction. Their ideas resonate in several aspects with a cause and effect approach and linear thinking which oversimplifies and attempts to rationalize the complexity of human behaviour.

Biology and psychology were important scientific influences on the behavioural theorists, both disciplines having strong roots in the Newtonian–Cartesian paradigm. Another significant influence on organizational and management thinking was the development of General Systems Theory which was put forward by Ludwig von Bertalanffy, a German biophysiologist, in the 1950s. Von Bertalanffy saw the interconnectedness between all phenomena from the smallest atoms to individuals, groups and societies and his theory sought to integrate and clarify the essential laws that affected all these systems. This proposed that while all parts of a system may be broken down in order to study them analytically their essential essence can only be understood by studying the whole. This made a break with the reductionist tradition. The systems approach to organizations took a more holistic stance and built on the notion that organizations, like organisms, are open to their environments. Resources like food, are taken in, worked on and then pushed out again. This thinking reflected a growing awareness of the organization's relationship with its environment.

During the 1960s the importance of an organization and its environment, both inside and outside was recognized. The importance of organizational form and how appropriate it was to its purpose and its environment was also coming into consideration. Two British sociologists, Tom Burns and George Stalker, based on their research in the 1950s, proposed two important types of organization, each at the edge of a continuum along which most organizations could be placed. One type which was particularly suited to a stable environment was the 'mechanistic' organization. This type of organization had a clear and defined structure, which was hierarchical in nature. All tasks were broken down precisely and strictly allocated within a command and control framework. The other organization, the 'organic' or 'organismic' one, was more flexible in structure and attitude and better able to adapt to changes in its environment. There was no command and control structure. Instead, management relied on the use of information and advice to achieve results. The rigid and precise definitions of roles and responsibilities were also missing. Many organizations, however, combined both organic and mechanistic features. For example, the administrative and financial areas of a large organization might be primarily mechanistic whereas the research and development and PR areas might be primarily organic.

During the 1980s the importance of the relationship between an organization and its environment was further developed by resource dependence theory and population ecology theory. Both considered that an organization depended upon its environment for the resources it needed to function. This movement in thinking now recognized that an organization did not exist alone, in some way unattached to the world around it, but that it depended on its environment for all its resources and further that it was in competition with others for these. Burns and Stalker together with the findings of Joan Woodward, who researched the relationship between technology and organization structure, laid the foundations for contingency theory which was further developed by Paul Lawrence and Jay Lorsch.

During this period the organization theorist, Henry Mintzberg's research challenged the notion that managers worked to the neat, functional model prescribed by Fayol. He constructed a model which broke the manager's role down into ten roles in three categories: interpersonal, informational and decisional. Mintzberg sought to recognize the human behavioural factor but in doing so his model still promoted notions of authority, control and the chain of command.

'Management by Objectives', devised in the 1950s by Peter Drucker, was seen during the 1960s and even in many textbooks today, as an ideal way to plan and control activities in an organization. This approach has been seen by a number of writers as a reinterpretation of classical management theories as are other management systems like Management Information Systems (MIS) and Planning, Programming, Budgeting Systems (PPBS).

Strategy and strategic studies emerged as a field of study in its own right during the 1970s and the 1980s. It was viewed as essentially a rational decision-making process and much of the research carried out was in accordance with the norms of classical management theory. It sought to provide managers with guidelines to direct them in devising strategies for a given number of situations. Michael Porter, for example, devised three generic strategies for achieving 'sustainable competitive advantage' and the notion of 'strategic fit'. Managers were encouraged to continue thinking in a cause and effect way and to assume that if they carried out a detailed analysis of their situation and their activities and did the right thing, that is, pursue the 'right' strategy, then they would achieve their desired outcomes. The importance of planning strategy and strategic activities was emphasized and separated from implementation and action, which was essentially viewed as of less importance. Here are strong echoes of Cartesian dualism. The development of strategy and its relationship with classical science is discussed in more detail in Chapter 3.

During the 1980s the concept of total quality management was seen by many organizations as the way to manage effectively. Employees were encouraged to think for themselves, to work in teams, to develop themselves and to seek for continuous improvements. Yet many aspects of this approach were Taylorist as groups broke tasks down into small parts in order to identify and solve problems. Further, most organizations in the western world did not combine strategic planning with operational activity, whereas in Japan thinking and doing were successfully combined.

What of the relationship between managers and 'workers' during the second half of the twentieth century? Much of this period was dominated by conflict and power struggles. Some of these arose through trade union activity, others from tensions created via dominant cultural relationships, perceptions of hierarchy and a managerial belief in the necessity of control.

> Despite the major efforts of senior executives to legitimise the activities, structures and inequalities of the organisation and to design and install 'foolproof' and reliable systems of surveillance and direction, there is always some dissension, some dissatisfaction, some efforts to achieve a degree of freedom from hierarchical control – some resistance to the organisation's domination and direction. Frequently this struggle is muted, mainly defensive and reactive, often individualised, spasmodic, intermittent. Frequently it is defined and presented as the result of trouble-stirrers, laziness, bloody-mindedness, inflexibility, or stupidity, as the result of the psychological pathology or inadequacy of the members. But in fact it is the systematic response to a form of organisation which is designed to achieve hierarchical control and domination of members' activities for the pursuit of objectives and interests which are not theirs, and with which they may be in conflict.
>
> (Salaman 2001: 124)

In some respects it would appear that very little has changed since the early years of the twentieth century and in some regards since the eighteenth century and the view that workers had to be firmly managed if they were to work properly and in the interests of the factory and its machines. Figure 2.1 summarizes and shows the key influences of the classical scientific world view (Newtonian–Cartesian paradigm) on organizations and management.

Management – the end of the twentieth century and the new millennium

The last decades of the twentieth century saw massive social, technological, ecological and economic changes on a global scale. These have continued at a

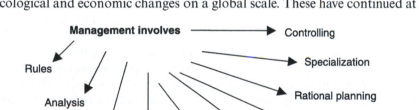

Figure 2.1 The influence of classical science on organizations and management.

relentless pace in the first decade of the new millennium as the world has shifted from an industry-based age to an information-based age. These changes have reverberated through all aspects of human society and nowhere has there been a more significant impact than in our approaches to organizations and management. Toby Tetenbaum, in her paper 'Shifting Paradigms: From Newton to Chaos' (1998), lists six characteristics which the modern organization now has to deal with. These are as follows:

1   *Technology*. The transforming spread of computer technology, electronic communications, multimedia and consumer electronics.
2   *Globalization*. The development of an interconnected world with global flows of information, money, people and goods.
3   *Competition*. An increase in competition as companies compete globally.
4   *Change*. Change happening faster than at any other time within our experience, such that organizations need to be able to respond rapidly and with agility.
5   *Speed*. An incredible increase in technological speed. For example, in 1946 the first computer was capable of calculating 5,000 basic calculations per second. In 1998 the Pentium chip was capable of processing 54 million calculations per second. Product life-cycles are now measured in months and not years.
6   *Complexity and paradox*. These are increasing as a result of all these changes and making more and more difficult demands on managers who are used to seeking certainties and 'either/or'-type solutions to issues.

A significant number of organizations have failed to survive these changes and have disappeared either through merger or failure. These dramatic shifts have led to the rise of a range of management concerns associated with uncertainty, globalization and the management of change. Many organizations responded to these unprecedented changes by experimenting with organization structures. Giant conglomerates were broken up and large bureaucracies slimmed down as they sought to become more effective and flexible. Companies merged and demerged, made acquisitions or sold them off. During this period organizations also experimented with a range of approaches designed to make them more effective and responsive to a rapidly changing world.

Some organizations tackled their problems by 'down-sizing', which they perceived as a way of adjusting their structures in order to be fitter and more effective. Kodak, IBM, General Motors and a number of other large organizations restructured in this way. This approach, while solving some problems, also created other unexpected ones. Many of those managers who survived the slimming-down process found themselves overloaded with work and increased work stress. The process was all too often accompanied by lack of vision, poor decision making and corporate in-fighting. Thus many of those organizations who had dramatically responded to the challenges of a rapidly changing world found themselves facing a new set of problems.

Further, this approach proved to be an unsatisfactory one because although the structure had changed it had not improved the overall effectiveness and long-term sustainability of the organization. This was because of the loss of many experienced and highly skilled employees and also because many organizations failed to capitalize on the restructuring and implement effective new support systems.

Business process re-engineering was energetically adopted by many organizations in the early 1990s as a way of improving efficiency and profits. This was to be achieved by streamlining or removing bureaucratic systems. Sadly, however, many organizations, dazzled by the opportunity to save costs and so improve competitiveness, did not reorganize effectively and in such a way as to improve organizational processes. Many organizations saw re-engineering as a form of downsizing and as an exercise in cost reduction primarily via staffing cuts. Some chief executives used the process to rid themselves of long bureaucratic chains of command but still held on to the controls. Teams, set up to re-engineer business operations, would begin their task by collecting significant amounts of data which provided information on the smallest of tasks. This would then be used to redesign a new process. Individual teams may have improved individual and specific processes but very often they failed to effectively connect to other parts of the organization and even to strategic priorities. This tight focus on detail meant that the bigger picture was often lost and operational gains would be short lived as the organization was unable to function as a coherent and strategically responsive whole. There were many critics of the concept and by the end of the century it was being described as a management fad that had failed to deliver because it had been misunderstood.

Decentralizing was a key trend for many large organizations during the last decades of the century as many organizations set up divisionalized structures and strategic business units. Corporate roles and responsibilities were devolved out to these new units. They had more autonomy and less centralized features than the original divisional structures. Many of the new structures, however, failed to build in strong links across units in order to maintain core competencies and corporate cohesion. Decentralization appears to be a continuing process but paradoxically some commentators have observed that it is a process which appears to be made possible by increased centralization.

The end of the twentieth and the beginning of the twenty-first century saw a wide range of new organizational forms emerge. These include: knowledge creating companies, networks, empowered teams, *ad hoc* organizations, boundaryless, and process-based organizations. There is a strong similarity about these organizations in that they have sought to break free from the traditional bureaucratic form.

> the new watchwords are teams (preferably cross-functional), lateral communications, the minimization (if not outright removal) of hierarchy, and the sparse use of rules. Informality and the exploitation of expertise,

wherever it may lie in the corporation, are the essential idea. With some variance in emphasis, the same basic tenets can be found underpinning the so-called 'high performance work systems' and the 'knowledge creating companies'.

(Mabey, Salaman and Storey 2001: 164)

Organizations as networks and as virtual organizations have arisen in response to the need for suitability for purpose and operation. There is widespread recognition that organizations have to be more flexible and suited to their own particular role, environment, situation in the market place and so on. The majority of managers have come to recognize that old models no longer work as well as they did because the conditions they were created for no longer exist. The challenge remains, however, what do you put in their place?

One of the most notable of the new ideas is the concept of the 'learning organization'. This had its origins in the 1950s when there was a major rethink about the nature of organizations and their role in a democracy. At the same time the disciplines of psychology, sociology, cybernetics, economics and ecology came together with existing notions of finance and production and combined to create the roots of management education. This prepared the way for today's learning organization.

A learning organization is continually developing its abilities in order to flourish and survive. There is a belief in learning at all levels, the development of an evolving shared vision and the use of systems thinking. Learning organizations facilitate the learning of all their employees and seek to continuously adapt and transform themselves. Here are ideas drawn from cell biology, evolutionary biology and new understandings about brain functioning and living systems. Some learning organizations still have many hierarchical features, mechanistic structures and processes, others are more organic, flexible and democratic.

Where are we now?

Classical management theory viewed the organization as a goal-seeking collective based on the notion of the organization as a rational instrument or a tool. It was an approach which formed the basis of modern organizational analysis and was underpinned by the assumption that if managers develop suitable means then they achieved desired ends. This is recognizably Newtonian–Cartesian thinking and in many organizations today it has become intertwined with notions of efficiency. Efficiency is obtained by careful and precise planning and an adherence to rationally designed structures and processes. This is frequently linked to notions of 'alignment'. An organization seeks success and sustainability by aligning all its structures and procedures with environmental circumstances in order to enhance efficiency. How realistic a notion is this, given the complexity of human systems and the dynamical nature of the many environments both internal and external, that managers have to contend with – and about which they cannot possibly know everything?

Mainstream management theory is still strongly influenced by the notion of the organization as needing to exist in a state of equilibrium and many management texts encourage the notion that stability and order are the desired state of affairs. This is viewed as especially relevant when the environment outside an organization is seen as turbulent and uncertain. In later chapters we shall show how this notion is supported by long-standing ideas about the nature of change in organizations and how new scientific interpretations seriously undermine such an approach.

During the last century there was a massive amount of research in the fields of management and organizational studies which practising managers turned to for guidance and inspiration. Yet in spite of this tide of research and new theory, many of the traditional ideas still seem to underpin developing thinking. Outwardly things may appear to be different but the traditional scientific paradigm often operates, albeit frequently at a subconscious level. Classical scientific thinking is manifest in organizations in the use of sets of rules, and planning and prediction activities. Many managers collect huge amounts of numerical data to inform planning and operational activities which proceed on the basis that the future is in some way predictable if planned properly. Decisions are made using sophisticated mathematical models and more and more advanced forms of business analysis and forecasting formulae are produced and used with confidence.

I know of several large organizations where many senior managers see themselves as progressive and enlightened, yet they continue to behave in the 'old' way. They devise complex and complicated plans or visions for some future venture with the minimum of consultation and then expect fervent support for their ideas from others in the company. They are perplexed when the employees who are supposed to deliver on these ideas are less than enthusiastic. The employees concerned, who are usually only involved at the implementation stage, are left wondering what it's all about and how it will affect them. All too often their local knowledge and experience tells them that some aspects of the plan simply will not work out and they are left with the problem of how they say to their managers: 'It's a great idea but . . .'

Managers are often required to behave like machines in respect of the long hours they may be required to work regardless of any possible implications for their long-term mental and physical health. The huge, impersonal, factory is perceived as an old model of how to establish and run a productive enterprise. But today's large paper-processing offices, set up to deal with insurance, tax or banking returns, are designed to operate like machines and the staff are in many ways expected to behave as if they were part of a machine. Modern call centres, too, operate on a similar model. In many of them employees are closely monitored and supervised all day and in some centres even have to request permission to leave their desk. How much has really changed?

Cartesian dualism still continues. As Fowler wrote: 'Distinctions between manual and non-manual employees are ingrained in the UK's employment culture. They have historic roots in the different patterns of factory and office work that evolved during the industrial revolution, and in related perceptions that link occupations with social status' (Fowler 1997: 21).

A new science of management

In many respects the influence of traditional management theory is so pervasive that even as organizations attempt to update their ideas and approaches to organizational life many are hampered by a subconscious mindset. All too often many of the ideas of classical management are reinforced under the guise of modern management and those attempting to devise new systems for organizations are only able to think mechanistically.

I would contend that a major shift in thinking is needed before we shall fully be able to develop organizations that are not rooted in the Newtonian–Cartesian paradigm and therefore are more appropriate to working life in the twenty-first century. In other words, a new science of management is needed.

We need a new science of management to help organizations cope with the complex problems, rapid change and uncertainties of the new century. The challenges today's organizations face are far too important to be neglected. Modern civilization is based on highly developed, information rich, globally spanning, technological societies and these in turn are underpinned by human social-organizing systems. Thus how we manage these systems and how well they resonate with the world in which they exist is of vital importance. The development of a new science of management is a real and emerging possibility. It should be a science that combines the best of the old scientific paradigm blended with the best of current management practice and the radical thinking offered by the new paradigm of complexity science.

In Chapter 4 we begin this journey of development by taking stock of managers' attitudes to change and the dynamics of change and how this affects the way managers approach organizational transformation. But before we can move forward to this it is necessary to understand the important concepts and approaches offered by this new scientific paradigm known as complexity science. This is covered in Chapter 3.

Part Two of this chapter investigates further the main tenets of classical science or the Newtonian–Cartesian paradigm, its origins, the key players, their contributions and the challenges made as scientific discovery has unfolded over the centuries.

Key questions

- What are the main features of the Newtonian–Cartesian paradigm?
- Why did the early industrial enterprises form themselves in the way they did?

- Is there any evidence to support the notion that organizations have been influenced by ideas derived from a Newtonian–Cartesian view of the world?
- Is there any evidence to show that this influence still exists?
- What challenges did organizations face at the end of the millennium and still face today?
- How did managers respond to these challenges and how effective were their responses?

PART TWO: CLASSICAL SCIENCE: A PRESTIGIOUS PARADIGM

Key points

- The founders of the classical scientific (Newtonian–Cartesian) paradigm
- Dramatic discoveries and technological developments
- Experimentation and new scientific methods
- Challenges to classical science
- Science and society

Significant scientific discoveries and events in Europe in the sixteenth, seventeenth and early eighteenth centuries led to the emergence of a powerful and prestigious paradigm: the Newtonian–Cartesian or classical science paradigm. This replaced the existing medieval world view which was built upon Aristotle's notion that a natural order existed which was maintained in a system of subtle and complex hierarchies. During this period improvements in scientific instruments such as microscopes, telescopes and barometers and new methods of experimentation, combined with major scientific work, weakened the spiritual view, so that notions of a spiritual universe declined and gradually faded away. This was replaced by the notion of a machine-like or clockwork universe operated by a set of universal laws and the development of a new empirical, systematic and mathematical approach to science. This world view has dominated science as practised in the western world for over 300 years and its influence has extended far beyond the thoughts of the scientific community. How did this paradigm come about and who were some of the key players in its creation?

The Scientific Revolution and the founders of classical science

Galileo is often referred to as the 'father of modern science' but he was preceded by others whose work he built upon, including the Polish priest Nicholaus Copernicus, who was born in 1473.

Copernicus

After many years of observation and study, Copernicus developed the theory that the earth revolved around the sun. Furthermore, planet earth not only moved around the sun but also moved on its own axis and was not stationary as had been thought at the time. This was a serious challenge to the existing religious and scientific orthodoxy of the day. His work was published in 1543, the year he died, but it did not receive much attention until it was built upon by Kepler and Galileo.

Brahe and Kepler

Johannes Kepler, a German mathematician and astronomer, further developed Copernicus' theory. He was able to work with extensive data on the stars and the planets which had been carefully compiled by the Danish astronomer Tycho Brahe. His book *Astronomia Nova*, published in 1609, described how the planets moved in elliptical orbits and the speed at which they travelled in their orbits. His work did not have a great impact at the time as many of his contemporaries still did not accept the idea that the earth travelled around the sun. His book *Harmony of the World*, published in 1619, contains his third law which relates to the time it takes a planet to orbit the sun in relation to its distance to the sun.

Galileo

Galileo Galilei was born in Pisa in 1564, the same year as William Shakespeare's birth. His parents had a medical career mapped out for him but he failed to complete his medical studies and went on to become one of the most famous scientific figures of all time. From the beginning he was highly inventive and productive with ideas emerging on pendulums and mechanics. He also developed the first thermometer and a calculator that helped gunners to work out the elevations needed to fire their guns accurately over different distances. This instrument was soon developed into a useful calculator with a number of practical applications including calculating exchange rates. A significant aspect of his work was that he always carried out experiments to test his hypotheses and he would modify or abandon his theories if his experiments did not support them. This approach to his work whereby he was prepared to test out his ideas and stand by the results set him apart from his contemporaries and he is considered by many to be the first modern scientist.

Early in 1610 using an exceptionally powerful telescope which he had designed Galileo discovered Jupiter's four largest moons. He went on to find that the Milky Way was not some large cloud but rather was a huge cluster composed of a vast numbers of stars. His telescope also found that, contrary to the beliefs of the time, the surface of the moon was not perfectly smooth but was rough and uneven. Its surface was scarred by craters and it had mountains whose heights he was able to estimate by measuring the length of the shadows they cast. These significant astronomical findings were described in his book, *The Starry Messenger*, published that same year. His discoveries provided significant evidence to support the Copernican model of the universe. This was to bring him into conflict with the more orthodox sections of the Roman Catholic Church which eventually led to his trial on charges of heresy, his 'confession' that he had made errors (while under threat of torture) and a sentence of life imprisonment. This was later softened to house arrest. In 1638 four years before his death at the age of seventy-seven, Galileo published his final book, *Two New Sciences*. This

> summed up his life's work on mechanics, inertia and pendulums (the science of moving things), and the strength of bodies (the science of non-moving things), as well as spelling out the scientific method. By analysing mathematically subjects which had previously been the prerogative of philosophers, *Two New Sciences* was the first modern scientific textbook, spelling out that the Universe is governed by laws which can be understood by the human mind and is driven by forces whose effects can be calculated using mathematics ... this book was an enormous influence on the development of science in Europe in the following decades.
>
> (Gribbin 2002: 101)

Galileo considered that the key to understanding the natural world lay with mathematics and quantitative precise systems of measurement. With this approach he made stunning discoveries. Thus he prepared the way for the domination of the language of mathematics and science as the prime language with which to explain our world.

It was a view which entailed the rejection of the Aristotelian view of nature and the importance of qualitative differences and distinctions. Furthermore, the world of the senses was considered unimportant or even irrelevant, as demonstrated by the following extract from Galileo's book *The Assayer*, published in 1623.

> Therefore I hold that these tastes, odors, colors, etc. of the object in which they seem to reside, are nothing more than pure names, and exist only in the sensitive being; so that if the latter were removed these qualities would themselves vanish ... I hold that there exists nothing in external bodies for exciting in us tastes, odous and sounds but size, shape, quantity and slow or swift motion. And I conclude that if the ears, tongue and nose were removed, shape, quantity and motion would remain but there would be no odors, tastes or sounds, which apart from living creatures I believe to be mere words.
>
> (Hampshire 1956: 33)

Thus the stage was set for the dominance of the intellect and the emotional detachment of the logical, rational scientific tradition.

Bacon

The Englishman, Francis Bacon, born three years before Galileo was also to make a significant contribution to the emergence and development of scientific method. In a nutshell, Bacon advocated the empirical, inductive approach to experimentation and disregarded the use of imagination and intuition. Experimentation should begin with the collection of as many facts as possible, these then should be tested by experiments and any conclusion drawn from these should then be further tested before any final conclusions are reached. Bacon passionately put forward his views and the notion of scientific progress as the key to the onward and upward ascent of man. Nature was viewed as existing chiefly for human benefit and should be exploited and used to this end. Bacon's ideas had a powerful effect on generations of scientists, yet he himself had carried out few experiments.

Descartes

René Descartes, who is regarded by some as the founder of modern philosophy and a key contributor to the Scientific Revolution, was born in Brittany, France in 1596. Descartes' first contribution to mathematics and science was the creation of what are now known as the Cartesian co-ordinates. This 'transformed mathematics by making geometry susceptible to analysis using algebra, with repercussions that echo right down to the twentieth century' (Gribbin 2002: 111). Descartes went on to publish ideas on meteorology, on the working of weather systems, on optics and on improving telescopes.

In 1637 his book *Discourse on Method* was published. The purpose of the book was to introduce its readers to science and it had a profound effect on learned thinking and on society as a whole. In it Descartes set out to construct a new method of thinking which was based on breaking problems down into small parts and using reason and logic as the tools of analysis. This analytical method of reasoning became one of the foundation stones of modern science.

Descartes was inspired by mathematics and the discoveries of his day and claimed that the human body could be explained by the same laws that ruled the planets. The universe to Descartes was nothing more than a giant machine that had no purpose and no spiritual or organic aspects. It functioned in accordance with mechanical laws and everything about it could be explained by examination of its parts and their mechanical movements. He considered plants and animals to exist like machines, though human beings had special capacities for speech and reasoning. The biological attributes of the human body he considered to be nothing more than mechanical operations and concluded that living organisms were merely automatons. This view of the living world has had profound implications for the way that science has pursued the acquisition of knowledge and its treatment of living entities. In medicine, for example, an inherent belief in the body as a machine has prevented the proper understanding of many complex major illnesses and a disregard for the patient's emotional and spiritual well-being. Furthermore, Descartes saw a huge gap between the mind and matter (the body) and argued that they should be treated as separate entities. The mind was considered superior to matter (the body).

Hooke

Robert Hooke, born in 1635 on the Isle of Wight, England, was a man of huge talent. He is believed by many to have made a contribution to the Scientific Revolution that is equal to the better known Sir Isaac Newton. While at Oxford University he worked with the Irish chemist Robert Boyle on developing his air pump. He also worked on improving telescopes and the accuracy of astronomical clocks.

Hooke was only twenty-nine years old when his major work, *Micrographia*, was published in 1665. The book was beautifully illustrated by Hooke and provided a stunning introduction to the minute world that was observable through the newly enhanced microscope that he had designed. It introduced its readers to, amongst other things, the compound design of a fly's eye, the structure of a bird's feathers, the wings of a butterfly, the body of a flea and even a detailed drawing of a louse holding onto a human hair. The book was remarkable too, not only for the new worlds that it opened up, but also in that it contained his theory of light based on wave theory and details of important experiments on combustion.

A year later, after the Great Fire of London, Hooke was involved with Sir Christopher Wren in surveying and designing many of the new buildings that were recreating the city's built landscape. Some years later he wrote a series of papers which described his own theories of gravity and the movement of the planets. Hooke was also much ahead of his time in recognizing that fossils were the remains of long-dead animals and plants. Then in 1678 he devised Hooke's Law of Elasticity which showed that a stretched spring resists with a force in proportion to how far it is extended.

Newton

The other great founding father of classical science and for many the greatest contributor to the Scientific Revolution is Isaac Newton. He was a great scientist and a great mathematician and also a lawyer, historian and a theologian. Newton, who was born in Lincolnshire, England in 1642, was a man of incredible genius. His work was to influence profoundly the development of science and the scientific tradition. As a young man Newton was sent to Cambridge University to study and soon he began his work on optics and light. He was fascinated by the refraction of light by a glass prism and over several years carried out a number of important experiments which culminated in his theory of light. In the summer of 1665 he was sent home because of an outbreak of plague and it was in Lincolnshire that he spent most of his time, until 1667 when the disease had run its course. It was during this period that he made some of his most important discoveries. The story goes that Newton was sitting in the orchard at home when an apple falling from a tree gave him a major insight into the properties of gravity.

One of his first significant pieces of work was the invention of calculus. Calculus provided scientists with a new mathematical tool that facilitated major developments in the physical sciences. For example, it made it possible for astronomers and physicists to accurately work out such things as the position of a planet in its orbit.

Before he was thirty years old Newton had completed his work on light and on calculus and was continuing his studies on gravity. In 1687 he published his amazing three-volume work, *Principia Mathematica*. This has been described as:

> the greatest scientific book of all time, a jewel in the crown of scientific literature. Built on the sturdy foundations laid by Galileo, it has been likened to a great edifice soaring about the ramshackle and temporary constructions around it ... This magnificent work was rooted in a distant past, but even today is used to calculate the trajectory of various objects lofted into the heavens, from space shuttles to missiles. Its influence will undoubtedly extend far into the future.
>
> (Coveney and Highfield 1995: 22)

The *Principia* contained his three laws of motion and the implications of his inverse square law of gravity. But more than that it laid down the base on which the modern science of physics is rooted, making it clear that the laws of physics were universal laws that applied to everything. Furthermore, it presented an indisputable view of the world as a giant machine. No longer was the universe a great spiritual mystery but a complex mechanical world which could be understood and explained by a series of universal, all encompassing laws. Newton's explanation of gravity, for example, demonstrated that the principles which led to an apple falling to the ground were the same as those which held the planets in their heavenly orbit. Thus by the use of mathematics and proper scientific study the secrets of the universe could not only be discovered but there existed the potential that mankind could even control things.

Newton's law of gravity together with Kepler's work concluded all arguments about the orbit of the earth. It was now indisputable: the earth revolved around the sun and in an elliptical orbit. Further, the planets moved in an elliptical orbit because of gravitational pull.

Newton not only made stunning contributions to science and mathematics but also to the development of scientific method. Newton combined Bacon's empirical, inductive method and Descartes' rational deductive method.

> Newton, in his *Principia*, introduced the proper mixture of both methods, emphasizing that neither experiments without systematic interpretation nor deduction from first principles without experimental evidence will lead to a reliable theory. Going beyond Bacon in his systematic experimentation and beyond Descartes in his mathematical analysis, Newton unified the two trends and developed the methodology upon which natural science has been based ever since.
>
> (Capra 1983: 64)

Although Newton is most remembered for his theory of gravitation and his three laws of motion, he also founded tidal theory, created hydrodynamics and developed the theory of equations. His contribution to science and learning is considered by many to be the most outstanding achievement of seventeenth-century science.

The Age of Reason

The Scientific Revolution radically changed the way we thought of our world and it reached its apogee during the seventeenth century through the interconnections of a host of ideas, influences and individuals. This century is often called the Age of Reason and the 'century of genius'. It was a time when the foundations of modern science and philosophy were being constructed and laid down for future generations to follow. During this century the Royal Society was founded and its membership included such distinguished names as the architect, Christopher Wren, Robert Boyle, the founder of modern chemistry, Samuel Pepys, the diarist, John Dryden the poet, John Locke the philosopher, Robert Hooke, Isaac Newton and the astronomer Edmond Halley. During this period there was an increased emphasis on the new scientific methods which heralded the decline of medieval notions of knowledge based upon Aristotelian methods. There was also a gradual shift from Latin as the language of learned publication to the use of English and French as the languages of learning. This meant that philosophical and scientific writings became more widely accessible and the exchange of ideas was more easily facilitated. This exchange was further facilitated by the setting up of a number of learned societies across the continent of Europe.

At the time a powerful partnership existed between physics, mathematics and philosophy and they exerted a strong effect on each other. For example, philosophers, like Descartes and the German, Gottfried von Leibniz, were both distinguished mathematicians and scientists. There was no clear distinction between philosophy and the physical sciences. The seventeenth century is referred to as the Age of Reason because almost all the great philosophers of the time were trying to introduce rationality, or the light of reason, and the rigour of mathematics into all areas of knowledge.

During this period developments and improvements in technology made possible significant and exciting advances on both the planetary and universal levels and on the microscopic and the cellular levels. For example, Robert Hooke did much to improve the telescopes, microscopes and barometers of the day and the Dutchman, Antoni van Leeuwenhoek, developed a microscope that made it possible to study blood cells and bacteria for the first time.

In this part I have tried to describe some of the great scientists and philosophers and their contributions which, woven together, came to create the foundations of what is now called classical science or the Newtonian–Cartesian paradigm. There was such an explosion of learning and discovery during the late sixteenth, seventeenth and early eighteenth centuries that I have only been able to refer to some of the most significant figures of that period. (See Table 2.1.) Many of them, like Galileo, Hooke and Newton, were so accomplished that it has only been possible to mention a few of their many contributions to science and technology.

Supporters and challengers

During the eighteenth century the Swedish botanist and zoologist, Carolus Linnaeus (1707–78) devised his taxonomy. This system classified all living organisms into clear hierarchies, starting with three major groups or 'kingdoms'. These were divided into 'classes', which were then divided into orders and so on. Linnaeus' system followed a linear, hierarchical pattern of classification that resonates very strongly with classical scientific thinking.

During the late eighteenth and early nineteenth centuries there was strong opposition to the classical scientific paradigm when it was challenged by the Romantic movement in the arts and philosophy. The Romantics rejected the rationalistic, materialistic view of things. They viewed the earth as a living, spiritual being and emphasized the importance of the imaginative and spiritual dimensions. The renowned German naturalist, geologist and explorer, Alexander von Humboldt (1769–1859) saw the earth as a living, organic entity with global climate providing the evidence for this hypothesis. Humboldt's influence was limited, however, and by the mid-nineteenth century the classical, mechanistic view of the world once again dominated philosophical and scientific thinking.

In 1859 the great English naturalist Charles Darwin published his masterpiece, *The Origin of Species*. This described his theory of evolution which had an astonishing impact on the scientific thinking of the day. This new theory of evolution challenged the traditional Newtonian view of the world as a machine fully developed and created by God, and showed that the world is an evolving, ever changing place. Furthermore, Darwin's ideas completely upset the biologists of the day by demonstrating that species are not fixed by the

Table 2.1 Significant contributors to the development of the Scientific Revolution and the birth of classical science

Name and nationality	Lifespan	Contribution to science
Nicholaus Copernicus, Polish astronomer	1473–1543	Posited that the sun does not rotate around the earth, nor is the earth the centre of the universe.
Tycho Brahe, Danish astronomer	1546–1601	Extensively catalogued the planets and the stars. His observations were used by Kepler to develop his own theories.
Francis Bacon, English experimenter	1561–1626	Developed empirical, deduction method of scientific study.
Galileo Galilei, Italian astronomer, mathematician and inventor	1564–1642	Confirmed Copernicus' hypothesis. Discovered four moons of Jupiter, showed true nature of moon's surface and composition of the Milky Way. Developed laws for falling bodies.
Johannes Kepler, German mathematician and astronomer	1571–1630	Devised three fundamental laws of planetary motion, most importantly, that the earth and planets travel in elliptical orbits.
René Descartes, French mathematician and philosopher	1596–1655	Devised the Cartesian co-ordinates. Developed the rational, deductive method of scientific enquiry and the notion of man as a machine.
Robert Boyle, Irish chemist and experimenter	1627–1691	Experimented on sounds and acids. Developed Boyle's Law on the relationship between gas and pressure. Founder of chemistry.
Robert Hooke, English inventor, architect and physicist	1635–1703	Work on combustion, developed theories on light and gravity. Published major work on microscopy showing detailed drawings of objects and creatures viewed microscopically.
Isaac Newton, English mathematician, alchemist and physicist	1642–1727	Built on the work of Kepler and Galileo and provided three laws of motion and a law of universal gravity. Devised calculus enabling mathematical methods to be applied to science. Laid foundations of modern scientific method and physics.

squares of the Linnean chart but rather evolve from one another. In spite of the impact of Darwin's ideas the scientific community did not abandon their reductionist approaches, instead they focused on fitting Darwin's theories into their traditional frameworks.

Gregor Mendel (1822–84), an Austrian abbot, founded the modern science of genetics with his work on hereditary mechanisms. His work has been considered by some scientists as reinforcing the classical scientific approach by concentrating on fundamental building blocks and ignoring the properties of the whole entity.

By the end of the nineteenth century the work of the Scottish physicist James Maxwell and Darwin's theory of evolution had severely challenged the accepted Newtonian machine model of the universe. Then in the twentieth century came further challenges with discoveries in the world of atomic and subatomic particles. Quantum theory or quantum mechanics, developed in the early years of the twentieth century by a group of scientists including Einstein, Planck, Bohr, Schrödinger, Heisenberg and others, was one of the most significant and successful scientific theories ever put forward. It made valid and important predictions about a wide range of atomic, molecular, optical, and solid state phenomena which in turn made possible a huge number of technological advances. These led to the development of lasers, nuclear power and computer chip technology. Albert Einstein's work on relativity and his progress on quantum theory not only advanced the structure of physics, but his radical new views on the concepts of space and time severely undermined Newtonian notions.

In the mid-twentieth century the new field of cybernetics explored the importance of negative and positive feedback loops in living organisms, machines and organizations. Cybernetics recognized the ubiquitous existence and many properties of both types of feedback everywhere at all levels in living systems, thus preparing the way for many of the discoveries in complexity science.

Advances in physics and chemistry in the 1960s and 1970s and work on systems in far from equilibrium situations acknowledged the amazing properties of self-organizing systems. Scientists were beginning to make significant discoveries in a world that was not at all like the ordered, predictable, machine-like world of classical science. Advances in mathematics and the arrival of high-speed computers further accelerated these discoveries. All these things and the ebb and flow of ideas and debate contributed to the emergence of the new science of complexity.

By the 1980s a significant number of scientists had recognized that traditional, analytical, reductionist approaches did not work for modern science and many were now looking for a newer and more holistic view of the world. The scientific author James Gleick wrote that the most passionate advocates of the new sciences believe that the twentieth century will be remembered 'for just three things: relativity, quantum mechanics, and chaos' (Gleick 1993: 6).

Science and society

Charlie Chaplin, in a famous scene in his tragi-comic film *Modern Times*, encapsulated the plight of the twentieth-century worker trapped in the wheels and cogs of a giant factory machine. For many employees the classical scientific vision of a machine-like universe had become a reality – even a mechanistic nightmare.

Many aspects of this mechanistic nightmare have thankfully disappeared as other influences have come to bear, but this does not mean that the powerful relationship between science and society has lost its sway. In the world of organizations concepts from classical science and scientific notions still exert an important influence. They may be observed guiding many of our business operating principles and activities such as planning, measurement, motivation theory, business management and organization design. Many modern managers still subscribe to the notion that organizations should be run in a highly structured, routine and regular way that is reminiscent of Newtonian–Cartesian thinking.

Classical science encouraged people to see the world as normally an ordered, stable, uniform and predictable place. This persuasive view of the world has become so deeply embedded and mainstreamed in our social, political, judicial, educational and cultural systems as to be inseparable from the way we think about and view the world. The Linnean classification system with its classical scientific resonances provides a good example of how reductionist, linear, thinking affects our view of the world. The system categorizes all living things into different classifications and today we continue to classify people according to race, nationality, profession, social group and so on. The influence of classical science has meant too that human beings have set themselves apart from other living species, when in reality we are all part of one closely connected and interdependent web of life.

Descartes' view that the mind and the body should be separated has had far-reaching consequences, affecting all aspects of society. His ideas have been used to justify and reinforce the class structure and the different systems in schooling and education.

The classical scientific paradigm, combined with cultural and religious influences, encouraged a western work ethic whereby industry on earth implied salvation and spiritual riches in the afterlife. Thus the technology of the Industrial Revolution, combined with the popular scientific paradigm, enabled the successful manifestation of the Protestant work ethic. This continues to affect western society even today where in many countries, including the UK, people often work exceptionally long hours, often at the expense of relationships, family life and their mental and physical health. Furthermore,

> The scientific notion of the world as a machine encouraged a disregard of the natural environment which resulted in the creation of vast industrial waste lands, the eradication of age old landscapes, polluted waterways and atmospheric degradation. This thoughtless destruction is only now being addressed by the ecological sciences. This disregard for the natural world was encouraged and reinforced by the traditional approach to scientific enquiry which set aside human and moral sensitivities in the pursuit of rational explanation.

> (McMillan 2004: 42)

The relationship between science and society is such that it exerts a powerful influence on society's collective unconsciousness. Many of the ideas and ways of thinking that are the epitome of classical science are so deeply imprinted on us that they have moulded the way we think. In my discussions with managers I have found that the majority concentrate on using their logical, reasoning, analytical faculties, often referred to as 'left brain' attributes, over and above their imaginative, intuitive, sensitive, or 'right brain', faculties.

Science and the scientific viewpoint, whether emanating from classical science or more recent and challenging world views, continue to exert a powerful influence on society. One reason for this is that the rational, empirical scientific tradition has been immensely successful for centuries. It has enabled us, for example, to discover new stars and planets in distance galaxies, to send men and women into space, to make motor cars and aeroplanes commonplace, to build steel ships and to make huge strides in medical interventions and disease control. Traditional science has made possible all the physical creature comforts of the twenty-first century and so has demonstrated its effectiveness in many domains, particularly in the hard sciences. But most importantly, 'The rationalistic orientation . . . is also regarded, perhaps because of the prestige and success that modern science enjoys, as the very paradigm of what it means to think and be intelligent' (Winograd and Flores 1991: 16).

Key questions

- How did the notion of the world as a giant clockwork machine come about?
- Why was the seventeenth century called the Age of Reason and the century of genius?
- What are the main features of the classical scientific method?
- What discoveries challenged the classical scientific world view?
- In what ways has the Newtonian–Cartesian or classical scientific paradigm influenced western society?

3 Complexity science: understanding the science

This chapter is designed to offer those new to complexity science or the science of complex systems, as it is sometimes known, an understanding of the basic scientific tenets. It also includes chaos theory, which was a forerunner of complexity science and which is an integral component of complexity science. The descriptions and definitions are not given in scientific terms and I have omitted equations and formulae. These explanations are not exhaustive, nor are they meant to be, as their purpose is not a scientific one. They are provided on the basis that without an all-round and proper understanding of the scientific background, it is not possible to properly consider the application of complexity science in organizational and management contexts.

Part One of this chapter describes the main concepts of complexity and briefly how they are currently being applied in a range of domains both scientific and non scientific. As the purpose of this chapter is to familiarize you with the theories underpinning the science, discussions of how these concepts are being interpreted and used in management and organizations are provided elsewhere, in Chapter 5. Chapter 5 includes examples and case studies of complexity science at work. Part Two of this chapter provides more background to the science. It briefly describes when the first ideas emerged and some of the key figures involved.

PART ONE: THE ESSENTIAL BASICS

Key points
- Introducing a new paradigm: complexity science
- Chaos theory: a non-scientific introduction
- The birth of chaos: the butterfly effect, strange attractors, fractals and other phenomena
- Complexity science: a non-scientific introduction
- Self-organization, complex adaptive systems, emergence, evolution and complexity.

The *Compact Oxford English Dictionary* defines 'chaos' as a noun with two separate meanings. The first one refers to 'complete disorder and confusion' and the second to 'the formless matter supposed to have existed before the creation of the universe'. The first definition in the dictionary neatly describes how the term 'chaos' is used in common parlance. People tend to use it to refer to a kind of madness that happens when things spiral out of control and the natural order of things appears to break down and disintegrate. In western Christian societies 'chaos' has strong biblical associations with darkness and disorder. This links to the second definition. The development of chaos theory or chaos science, however, gave the term 'chaos' a new scientific meaning.

Chaos theory

Chaos theory, or chaos science, as it is sometimes referred to, is a new science. It is new because most of its significant explanations and theories were first put forward in the last forty or so years, whereas classical Newtonian–Cartesian science has existed for over 300 years. So how and when did chaos science first arise?

During the late 1960s and 1970s a number of scientists, from different disciplines, became uneasy with existing scientific explanations and fascinated by the many unpredictable and highly dynamical aspects of our world. A number were dissatisfied with a mainstream scientific tradition that often ignored minor aspects in order to uphold an important theory or law. These scientists, often scientific mavericks, sought to understand and explain things in a radically different way. Chaos theory scientists worked in a wide range of disciplines including physics, biology, mathematics, meteorology, chemistry and computer science. They made a series of significant and unexpected discoveries and by the 1980s chaos theory had arrived and was challenging the conventional scientific wisdom in a number of ways.

Chaos theory concerns the study of the chaotic, often unintelligible aspects of our world and the apparent disorder that exists in the universe. It has redefined the meaning of the term 'chaos'.

> In the scientific sense chaos is not about darkness, breakdown, confusion and disorder. The scientific use of the term describes processes that appear to be random or chaotic but in fact are not. Paradoxically, this apparent 'chaos' is not an aberration in the planned scheme of things but reflects deeper more complex patterns and swirls of order than had previously been expected and understood. They are processes that have their own kind of internal order and their own kind of process principles.
>
> (McMillan 2004: 14)

Many of the early chaos researchers were fascinated by the behaviour of complex dynamical systems, such as weather systems and wildlife populations, and by the effects of small aberrations, such as dust or damp, affecting a physical process. These systems were considered too complex, too unpredictable and too dynamical to be effectively researched. It was the arrival of computers and the use of computer technology that made the study of these non-linear systems possible. Thus a combination of computer technology and scientific curiosity led to the development of chaos science.

The machine-like view of the world held by classical scientists had encouraged scientists to think in a cause and effect manner and to focus their researches on systems perceived to be linear in nature. This led to the development of linear equations and other linear methods of exploration and explanation. Chaos scientists and then complexity scientists effectively challenged this essentially linear view of things and disturbed many long held assumptions about the nature of our world. The simple linear equation $a + b = c$ will work if a and b are closely related in time and space and unchanging. In the non-living world within laboratory conditions it is possible to use such equations very usefully, but within the living world of dynamical systems a and b could be affected by many factors, including factors unknown to the observer. This makes the simple equation no longer simple and no longer linear.

Another significant feature of chaos theory is that its researchers questioned the traditional reductionist methods. As the English scientist James Lovelock writes: 'No one doubts that it was plain, honest reductionist science that allowed us to unlock so many of the secrets of the Universe ... But clear, strong, and powerful though it may be, it is not enough by itself to explain the facts of life' (Lovelock 1989: 214).

Chaos scientists took a holistic rather than a reductionist approach to their work. That is not to say, however, that they did not consider the fine details of the phenomena they were studying, but rather that they sought for explanations and patterns that connected things rather than separated them. They looked for connectivity, patterning and flow. They experimented with new ways of viewing our complex universe and developed a multidisciplinary approach that broke with the predominant scientific tradition.

The work of chaos scientists demonstrated that much of the world is made up of nonlinear dynamical systems and that although these systems may appear to be unpredictable and seemingly erratic in behaviour, they have their own kind of internal order. This order is not a still, quiet, unmoving kind of order. Rather, it is a complex, sometimes complicated, internal scheme of behaviours which weaves a coherent and integrated pattern out of which emerges a unique kind of order. It was the discovery of chaos theory which stimulated further explorations into the behaviour of complex systems and non-linear dynamics which are the essence of complexity.

A number of specific concepts are generally accepted as falling under the umbrella of chaos theory. These include: strange attractors; the butterfly effect (or sensitive dependence on initial conditions); the edge of chaos; fractals; and notions of order and disorder. Table 3.1 shows the major concepts of chaos science and some of the key researchers associated with them.

Table 3.1 Developments in chaos

Time period	Theory/concept	Key researcher	Discipline	Country of birth/experience
1854–1912	Topology (Strange Attractors)	Henri Poincare	Mathematics	France
1970s	Sensitive dependence on initial conditions	Edward Lorenz	Meteorology	USA
	Strange Attractors	David Ruelle	Mathematics and physics	Belgium and France
		Floris Takens	Mathematics	Holland
		Edward Lorenz	Meteorology	USA
1980s	Chaotic properties of dynamical systems	Stephen Smale	Mathematics	USA
	Notions of order and disorder	James Yorke	Mathematics	USA
	Order within chaos	Robert May	Biology and physics	Australia and UK
	Edge of Chaos	Chris Langton	Anthropology and computing	USA
	Fractals	Benoit Mandelbrot	Mathematics	France and USA
	Universality	Mitchell Feigenbaum	Physics	USA
	Flow	Albert Libchaber	Physics	France

Source: Adapted from McMillan (2004: 16).

The butterfly effect – sensitive dependence on initial conditions

The butterfly effect or sensitive dependence on initial conditions is a phenomenon whereby a small local change in a complex system can lead to unpredictable and major effects some time later. The classic example of this is that a small vibration in the air caused by the movement of a butterfly's wings can cause a change in the air currents that eventually, along with other perturbations in the air, could lead to the atmospheric conditions that produce a storm.

The butterfly effect tells us that:

• all complex dynamical systems are exceptionally sensitive to their initial or starting conditions;

- small variations over time can lead to major changes in a non-linear system;
- complex dynamical systems are highly responsive and interconnected webs of feedback loops.

Prior to the discovery of the butterfly effect it was generally believed that small differences averaged out and were of no real significance. The butterfly effect showed that small things do matter. This has major implications for our notions of predictability, as over time these small differences can lead to quite unpredictable outcomes. For example, first of all, can we be sure that we are aware of all the small things that affect any given system or situation? Second, how do we know how these will affect the long-term outcome of the system or situation under study? The butterfly effect demonstrates the near impossibility of determining with any real degree of accuracy the long term outcomes of a series of events. This is a real challenge for Newtonian–Cartesian certainties.

It also highlights the implausibility of simple cause and effect linear thinking when dealing with complex, dynamical systems, especially living systems. As a result of the discovery of the butterfly effect a number of long-held scientific notions have had to be reviewed. For managers and others working in organizations the butterfly effect has major implications for the efficacy of such activities as long-term planning, logistics and supply chain management and the wisdom of commitment to long-term strategies. How can a manager know all the possible starting conditions for any given organizational operation? How can he or she even know what it is they do not know? The UK science writer, John Gribbin writes:

> The classic example of chaos at work is in the weather. If you could measure the positions and motions of all the atoms in the air at once, you could predict the weather perfectly. But computer simulations show that tiny differences in starting conditions build up over about a week to give wildly different forecasts. So weather predicting will never be any good for forecasts more than a few days ahead, no matter how big (in terms of memory) and fast computers get to be in the future. The only computer that can simulate the weather is the weather; and the only computer that can simulate the Universe is the Universe.
>
> (Gribbin 1999: 9)

It is worth bearing in mind John Gribbin's comments when studying computer simulations (have they included all the starting conditions?); highly detailed business forecasts (is everything that could affect the forecast included – and if so how do they know how each small thing will behave?); and other possible predictions (e.g. sales predictions). How accurate can these things be when they are dealing with many different factors with in-built differences, however small or subtle.

The butterfly effect demonstrates that complex dynamical systems are highly responsive and interconnected webs of feedback loops. It reminds us that we live in a highly interconnected world. Thus our actions within an organization can lead to a range of unpredicted responses and unexpected outcomes. This seriously calls into doubt the wisdom of believing that a major organizational change intervention will necessarily achieve its pre-planned and highly desired outcomes. Small changes in the social, technological, political, ecological or economic conditions can have major implications over time for organizations, communities, societies and even nations.

It is important to realize, however, that just because a system is not predictable in the long term, it does not mean that it is impossible to understand or even to explain its behaviours. It means that these systems have to be studied in new ways. Researchers look for generic properties, patterns and flows of similarity in behaviours and from these they are able to build theories that offer explanations for the generic properties of the system without necessarily knowing the small details.

Paradoxically, complex dynamical systems, like weather systems, although they appear to be unstable are not unstable. At first glance the system may appear to be erratic and unpredictable but observation over time or on a larger scale will show unexpected patterns emerging. These patterns may be very diverse but there will be some unifying theme or themes that enable them to weave together into an unexpected and perhaps unusual but orderly whole. This paradox of order within disorder occurs again and again as one explores different aspects of chaos theory and it links with notions such as strange attractors, and concepts of patterning and universality which are discussed later in this chapter.

Strange attractors

The term attractor is used to describe the different behaviours or patterns of behaviour of dynamical systems. Classical science focused on attractors with repetitive behaviours, such as pendulums. A pendulum in a ticking clock exhibits a side-to-side motion; this is called a periodic attractor. When the clock is run down and the pendulum is unmoving then it is referred to as a point attractor. Scientists in order to visualize these systems draw graphs of the trajectories or patterns of the system as it moves through space. In this way they are able to describe in geometric form the behaviour of a dynamical system over a period of time. The range of behaviours within which the system operates is known as its 'basin of attraction'. In other words, the system is constantly attracted back to the same pattern of behaviours. Its behaviours seem to be magnetically drawn or pulled together within the 'basin'. These 'basins' and the patterns formed by the different trajectories or paths taken by the system within the 'basin' are represented by using computer generated graphics.

Attractors were important aspects of Newtonian physics and it was assumed that because the behaviours of an attractor were always repetitive and within the same range that their behaviours were essentially predictable. Then in the 1960s another attractor was discovered, the strange attractor. This concerned a 'basin' of attraction within which a range of similar but non-repeating and therefore unpredictable behaviours took place. The discovery of the strange attractor enabled scientists to consider how dynamical systems behave in more ways than had previously been thought possible.

A strange attractor has three distinct features as follows:

- it shows great sensitivity to initial conditions;
- its behaviours although unpredictable and unrepeated are bounded by its 'basin of attraction';
- it has fractal properties.

Fractals and their properties are discussed in the next section.

Since a strange attractor is sensitive to initial or starting conditions, it is impossible to accurately predict its precise behaviours. One of the best ways to understand strange attractors is to visualize the way a marble dropped into a large bowl or basin behaves. The ball will roll around up and down the walls of the bowl time and time again. It moves upwards and downwards around the bowl's interior until all its energy is spent and it finally comes to rest. The trajectories taken by the ball when plotted by a computer and produced on a computer screen show the patterns of behaviour made by the ball. These patterns of movement are all very similar in shape although each one is uniquely different and follows its own individual pathway. The trajectories may cross each other or even touch each other at some point, but they are always different. The ball is sensitive to initial conditions, so that should you decide to repeat the same exercise again, then the trajectories taken by the ball although similar in pattern would be different. They are different because the ball responds to a range of tiny differences that exist in the environment of the bowl's surface. For example, there could be small specks of dusts or tiny smears of moisture or grease. The bowl's surface may be slightly irregular. All these things affect the way the ball rolls within the bowl. You too will drop the ball in a slightly different way. Experience tells you what kind of behaviour to expect when you drop a small ball into a large basin. It will follow a recognizable pattern of behaviour. It behaves as a small ball usually behaves when treated in such a way. What you are observing and comprehending is the phenomenon of the strange attractor.

A dynamical system may appear to be unpredictable and even chaotic but it does have a shape and it does not move outside the bounds of its strange attractor. The British weather, for example, behaves like a strange attractor. It is a highly dynamical system which varies considerably from day to day and is famous for being unpredictable. But it always behaves like the British weather. There are no periods of Asian style monsoon or prolonged drought. It always behaves within certain bounds.

Although the potential for chaos resides within every system, chaos when it emerges never moves outside the bounds of its strange attractor. No point or pattern of points is ever repeated, and one might think that this shows a totally messy system with no order. But the chaotic behaviour exhibited is not random and unrestrained, it has its own kind of patterning and its own form of determinism. In other words, it has its own kind of internal order. The strange attractor may weave a range of complex, exotic patterns, each one different, yet the whole is creating and exhibiting a new kind of order. It is order within apparent chaos.

(McMillan 2004: 20)

I shall refer to the intriguing idea that there is order within chaos in a later section.

It should be noted, however, that a strange attractor has the capacity to change. It can grow or shrink and it can even exhibit a broader or a narrower range of behaviours. A strange attractor may even convert to a dramatically different attractor or even fade away depending on the conditions in which it finds itself. For example:

Like mathematical attractors, social behaviour drifts across time: Fads come and go, mores change, our relationships to institutions alters, our definition of family evolves. Social attractors occasionally experience radical change – witness what happened to the USSR in the late 1980s, for example. Systems like attractors, even fade away: An Incan empire once flourished in South America, the Romans once dominated the Western world, and the Turkish empire was the supreme authority in the Middle East, and all have dissolved back into the social ambiance that created them.

(Marion 1999: 22)

Russ Marion points out that the strange attractor is a useful metaphor for understanding social phenomena. This does not mean that such phenomena are strange attractors, nor indeed that they are not such attractors. But social phenomena exhibit so many of the behaviours of strange attractors that it can be indisputable that they provide us with a useful way of learning more about them.

Strange attractors have been used in medicine to study variations in the beat of the human heart, in cell growth and regulation, the effects of drugs on patients, respiratory disease, epilepsy and outbreaks of measles. They have also been used in astronomy and in economics to study the patterns of recessions.

Fractals

Fractals are everywhere in the natural world. It is the design trick that nature uses to create our world and she does so using a few simple principles. These principles we now refer to as fractals or fractal geometry. The use of fractal geometry enables us to describe and to capture the essential nature of these natural forms. When we were at school we were taught traditional Euclidian geometry. With this geometry we can measure and describe circles, triangles, squares and so on. In other words, we are able to use it to measure accurately and quantitatively all the smooth and regular shapes of the man-made world. But what of the natural world? How do you measure a cloud, for example? How do you describe the essence of its geometric attributes? How do you measure and describe the irregular crags and crevices of a mountain's slope?

Using fractals nature has created a world of astonishing diversity and richness – and she has done so by using simple repeating principles. The main features of fractals are as follows:

- they are irregular patterns or shapes repeating themselves up and down a scale of size;
- this scaling is about the relationships between things – colour, shape, texture, and dimension;
- they are ubiquitous in nature;
- they provide the basic design principles of many natural structures;
- fractal geometry is concerned with qualitative not quantitative measurement.

Probably one of the best examples of fractals at work is exemplified in the way a fern is built up from a few basic rules. If you look closely at a branch of a fern you will see that it is made up of a basic shape. If you look even more closely you will see that this shape is repeated in the tiny leaves that form the main branch. Look more closely again and you will see this pattern repeated on the tiny leaflets that form the leaf. What we recognize as a fern is created by constantly repeating this pattern on a series of different size scales. How is it that a small object like an acorn can produce a mighty oak? The answer is it uses fractal design principles and like many other trees these are based on a simple branching pattern. These patterns form the underlying design of their leaves, their twigs, their branches and their subsidiary trunks. Another example of a fractal branching structure is the blood circulatory system in the body. It has an extensive web of intertwining veins and arteries all branching out in fractal patterns. If you look carefully at the shape of the edge of a clover leaf you will discover that the edge itself contains still smaller clover type shapes. Fractal objects repeat themselves on different size scales. This property is known as self-similarity.

Fractal geometry is concerned with quality and qualitative things. It is a geometry about relationships including the juxtaposition of one thing to another. It is about patterning and design themes. It is about colour and textures. Using fractals we are now able to describe all the many different and complicated aspects of nature ranging from hard rocky landscapes, coastlines, and mountain tops to cloud formations and living things such as plants, corals, vegetables, trees and nervous and cardiovascular systems. Once we begin to understand fractals we begin to appreciate fully the complex relationship between the design of plants and animals and their natural environments. For example, consider the design of a daisy. The centre of the flower is designed to attract insects and to make it easy to pick up pollen and assist the plant's reproductive process. It is also designed to capture as much sunlight as possible to help it grow and flourish. The overall design of the plant resonates totally with its own needs and those of its co-dependents and its natural environment.

Once we begin to understand fractals then we begin to perceive the world differently. We are able to visualize things existing on different scales. These scales are essentially spatial but they also involve scales of time.

Fractal geometry takes a holistic approach to measurement and description and so breaks away from the traditional, reductionist approach to measurement. Fractal geometry is a geometry of the whole.

Scientists use fractals to describe the appearance and properties of a wide range of objects, materials, processes and behaviours. These include metals, polymers, the human heart, plant properties, predator–prey relationships, archaeology, and even art analysis. Geologists use fractal principles when looking for different mineral deposits. Business analysts too use fractals to study the patterns in behaviour of the stock market.

Order within chaos

The notion that order exists even within apparent chaos emerged from the work of a number of chaos scientists. As they researched into the apparently random behaviour of dynamical systems they discovered that even within the most seemingly disorderly of systems there are elements of order and thus a kind of unexpected stability. The phenomenon of the strange attractor demonstrates one way in which a unique form of order can emerge from apparently random and disconnected behaviours.

Many large-scale ecosystems appear to be full of instabilities, such as those caused by major population fluctuations or unexpected turbulent weather conditions. Yet taken as a whole these systems exhibit their own unique brand of order. It has been argued that the stability of all large-scale ecosystems depends on the existence of such internal chaos. Thus the existence of order within chaos is to be found everywhere in the natural world.

The edge of chaos

Complex living systems, from amoebas to ants to human beings, seek to exist in a balance between order and disorder, regularity and irregularity, stability and instability, equilibrium and non-equilibrium. By existing in this way they have sufficient stimulation and freedom to experiment and adapt but also sufficient frameworks and structure to ensure they avoid complete breakdown and disintegration. This ability to balance between stability and chaos is a vital survival process and this place of balance is known as 'the edge of chaos'. The edge of chaos is where the parts of a system never quite lock into place and yet never quite break up either.

Human beings tend to recognize the dangers inherent in living life in the chaotic zone, or 'fast lane'. Here, so much is happening that people become totally stressed out and nervous breakdowns and heart attacks are all too frequently the body's response. At the other extreme many old people lead isolated and very lonely lives with little happening. They are in danger of mental and bodily breakdown too. The trick is to balance between each extreme, dipping into either if needed. Spending some time in the chaotic area can help when extra stimulus and input is needed. Chilling out and doing very little by spending time in the stability zone can prove beneficial when calm and quiet are required. Sadly the machine metaphor is such that the notion of the body as a machine prevails and we continue to expect managers in some fast-moving industries to successfully operate continuously in the chaotic zone. A good example of this is the burn-out rate of young city professionals working in the financial markets.

As Figure 3.1 illustrates, the edge of chaos has been compared analogously to water. The biologist Stuart Kauffman reminds us that water can exist as solid ice, as a liquid and as gaseous steam. Kauffman's hypothesis is that if any biological life form becomes too embedded or too deeply involved in the highly ordered, stable area (ice), then it becomes too rigid to undertake the necessary activities to sustain and develop life. If the system becomes too embedded in the highly disordered, chaotic zone (steam) then it would suffer from a complete lack of order. Again it would be unable to carry out all the necessary activities to survive. Thus the best place for a living system to exist is in the fluid, flexible area (water) which lies between the other two areas.

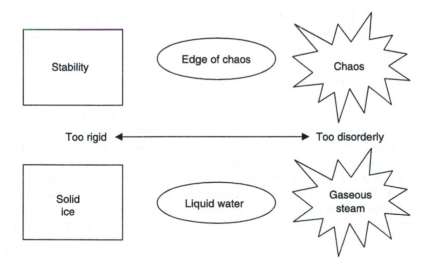

Figure 3.1 The edge of chaos.

This is referred to as 'the edge of chaos'. Here a complex living system may dip into and even blend, if needed, attributes from either of the other two zones without experiencing the disadvantages. Although this area of existence is called the edge of chaos, it could possibly be called the edge of stability or the edge of order depending how you look at the system. This makes the term not a completely satisfactory one but a better term has not yet been coined for non-scientific use.

Universality and patterning

The concept of universality is a feature of chaos theory and complexity and is applicable to many living systems. An American physicist, Mitchell Feigenbaum, discovered that different systems behaved in a similar way when they moved from an orderly state into a chaotic one. In other words, that they behaved in a universal fashion.

For example, Feigenbaum discovered that if a tap was dripping then a small turn of the tap to increase the flow would lead to a change in the sounds and the rhythm of the falling drops. The sound would change perhaps from a two-drop rhythmic pattern to a four-drop pattern. A further small turn of the tap would then increase the pattern to an eight-drop one and so on with each small turn of the tap. The length of the pattern keeps on doubling until it reaches a point, known as the Feigenbaum point. Then the pattern sequence disappears and the system has entered chaos. What is interesting is that it takes smaller and smaller increases in the water flow to introduce greater and greater changes. But, of course, each minute turn of the tap builds upon previous turns of the tap. Further similar patterns emerge in experiments on liquid helium, water, electronic circuits, pendulums, magnets and vibrating train wheels.

The natural world is full of universal patterning, rhythms and rhythmic cycles. Plants and animals respond to the rhythms of our planet: the seasons, night and day, tidal ebbs and flows. Ian Stewart, the UK mathematician, points out that there are a number of different kinds of patterning. There are numerical patterns, patterns of form, patterns of movement, as well as fractal patterning. Complex rhythmic patterns of movement are to be found in the way that mammals, fish, birds, insects, snakes, and even bacteria move and change position. Numerical patterns include the lunar cycle of twenty-eight days; animals that have two or four legs; insects with six legs and spiders with eight. Exotic patterns are created by flower petals. Almost all flowers have a number of petals which conforms to a number taken from the sequence 3, 5, 8, 13, 21, 34, 55, 89. The lily, for example, has three petals, the buttercup has five, delphiniums have eight, marigolds have thirteen, asters have twenty-one and daisies can have thirty-four, fifty-five or even eighty-nine petals. What is interesting about this pattern is that the numerical sequence is created by adding the previous two numbers together. For example, three plus five equals eight, and five plus eight equals thirteen and so on.

Patterns of form include the wave patterns that are universally found in desert sands, in the movements of the sea, the sands of the seashore, in the atmosphere and in some ancient rock formations. Then there are the stripe patterns and spot patterns that are found throughout the animal kingdom.

Complexity science

As I have already pointed out chaos theory emerged onto the scientific scene some years before complexity science and the two are inextricably woven together. It is simply not possible to fully understand complexity without a good knowledge of chaos.

Complexity science, or the study of complex systems, complex adaptive systems or complex dynamical systems as it is sometimes referred to, is new, very wide ranging and involves all scientific disciplines. The use of the term 'complexity' derives from the nature of the systems which are the chief focus of study. These dynamical systems are made up of many interacting agents who respond and react to each other in a constant interplay. This over time leads to the creation of ever more complex, complicated and multilayered patterns of behaviour and existence. For example, the activities of many agents (people) interacting in a common sphere of interest leads to the determining of prices and the creation of financial markets. The human brain, too, is made up of millions and millions of neurons or individual agents. These all operate within their own sub systems, such as the cerebellum, amygdala or the hypothalamus. But they all work together, co-operating and co-ordinating and in so doing create the amazing living system that is the human brain. Complexity scientists seek to understand these complex, dynamical, highly unpredictable features of our world in order to discover their underlying principles and to understand how they respond, react and create the natural order that binds our universe together.

Complexity science takes a holistic attitude to things. This gives it a fresh perspective and new insights into difficult concepts such as the nature of consciousness, intelligence and life itself. It has been found very useful in advancing understanding in a wide number of applications including biological, ecological, physical, social and economic systems. More recently it has been applied to legal studies, politics, psychology and psychological theory, philosophy, medicine and health care and, of course, management and organizational studies.

Complexity science (including chaos), challenges much of the established, classical, scientific view. For example, it considers that small details and changes do matter and are of considerable significance. It is concerned with understanding paradoxes and contradictions and with the exploration of irregularities. As regards scientific method it uses, and often prefers, holism to reductionism and uses qualitative analysis alongside quantitative analysis. It also makes great use of computer technology, using simulations to test theories (as indeed, does modern classical science) and to uncover new patterns of being. Its search for patterns and flows of activities makes it very different to classical science with its focus on the behaviour of entities and the need to categorize. Complexity science does not seek for, nor expect to find, predictable outcomes and universal stability. It considers the universe to be a turbulent, erratic and unpredictable place, but a place nevertheless imbued with a complex universal dance of order. In the view of many distinguished researchers and others complexity science is creating a scientific revolution and a new scientific paradigm: the complexity science paradigm.

The key concepts of complexity science are: self-organization/self-organizing systems; complex adaptive systems; emergence; and co-evolution/new interpretations of evolution. Table 3.2 shows the major concepts and some of the key researchers associated with them.

Self-organization/self-organizing systems

One of the most important areas of research carried out by complexity researchers has been in the area of self-organization. Self-organization is the ability that complex systems have to self-organize spontaneously into even

Table 3.2 Developments in complexity science

Time period	Theory/concept	Key researcher	Discipline	Country of birth/experience
1960s–1970s	Dissipative structures (Self-organization)	Ilya Prigogine	Chemistry	Russia and Belgium
	Self-organization/self-organizing systems	Herman Haken	Physics	Germany
	Self-organization, evolution, complexity, edge of chaos	Stuart Kauffman Brian Goodwin	Biology Biology	USA Canada and UK
	Patterns and patterning	Ian Stewart	Mathematics	UK
	Self-organization/autopoiesis	Humberto Maturana		Chile
1980s		Francisco Varela		Chile
1990s	Complex adaptive systems	John Holland Murray Gell-Mann	Mathematics Physics	USA USA
	Emergence	Chris Langton	Anthropology and computing	USA

Source: Adapted from McMillan (2004: 27).

greater states of complexity. Self-organizing systems are sometimes known as self-renewing systems because they dissipate their energy in order to renew or recreate themselves. This capacity to create new structures and new ways of behaving marks a significant difference between the early concept of self-organizing systems first devised by the cyberneticists.

Self-organizing systems are to be found everywhere in the living world. Self-organization is the principle which underlies the emergence of the wide variety of complex systems and complex forms that exist whether physical, biological, ecological, social or economic. It appears to be an evolutionary survival response in many species such as fishes, birds, and even humans, that has improved their survival chances.

The key attributes of self-organizing systems are as follows:

- they need energy in order to renew themselves;
- they are open to their environments in order to exchange energy and matter;
- they are spontaneous, exhibiting spontaneous behaviours which lead to the emergence of new structures and new forms of behaviour;
- they are non-linear systems with internal feedback loops;
- they have no centralized control.

Self-organizing systems need energy to enable self-organization to take place and to do this they need to be open to their environments. By being open they can exchange matter and energy and so stay alive and far from equilibrium. That is, they are able to operate on the edge of chaos as much as is possible. A simple living cell, for example, is a self-organizing system deriving its energy from food and excreting energy as heat and waste within its living environment. People need food and warmth from their environment which provides them with life-giving energy, but matter and energy may also consist of information and knowledge flows which are exchanged for physical and mental activity.

The ability to spontaneously self-organize is found everywhere in complex living systems. People, insects, animals, bacteria and cells are able to respond and adapt to the actions of those nearby and unconsciously organize themselves to their advantage. Many fish varieties, for example, shoal to protect themselves from predators. Many species of small birds self-organize spontaneously into huge flocks which rise into the air rapidly in times of danger. They are able to self-organize for foraging or for protection. In a small group of perhaps only a dozen garden birds there will be twelve pairs of eyes keeping a watch for domestic cats and other urban predators. Twelve pairs of eyes will also have a better chance of spotting some new food source for the group. Social insects such as ants and termites self-organize in order to build and maintain their nests or mounds, to protect themselves and to feed the next generation and so ensure the future of their colony. People too have self-organized over the centuries as they have sought to improve their chances of survival. By self-organizing spontaneously in response to a need or a threat they have created new structures in the form of small trading communities, market towns, and national and international economies.

There is no central controlling mechanism instructing these self-organizing systems. For instance, there is no bird in charge of the flock shouting out the order to take flight and telling them to fly higher, faster or slower. The birds all respond according to a set of underlying principles or instincts by which they know how to respond in different situations.

It is important to note that self-organizing systems include non-living complex systems which exhibit many, and sometimes all, of the attributes described above. A weather system, for instance, is a self-organizing system, but it is not a living one. Ocean currents, hurricanes, river systems, volcanoes, piles of sand, laser beams are all non-living, self-organizing systems that respond and change to differences in their environment. What differentiates them from living self-organizing systems is their inability to learn. This is because they are not complex adaptive systems.

Complex adaptive systems

Complex adaptive systems are complex dynamical systems which are able to learn and adapt to changes in their circumstances and their internal and external environments. They are able to modify their behaviours and to reconfigure their internal structures. These complex systems are living systems because they have this capacity to learn and to adapt. If a complex, dynamical system, even a self-organizing one (such as a laser or a weather system), is unable to learn and adapt then it is a complicated complex system but not a complex *adaptive* one. It is a non-living system. The term 'complex evolving system' is sometimes used to refer to human complex adaptive systems in order to distinguish them from other complex systems. Complex adaptive systems include systems as diverse as social systems, biological systems and organisms, human and insect organizations, the human brain and immune system, economies, stock markets and ecosystems.

The main attributes of complex adaptive systems are as follows:

- they consist of large numbers of agents interacting in a non-linear way creating higher and higher levels of complexity;
- there is no central controlling mechanism;
- they are constantly learning;
- they learn to adapt to changing circumstances;
- they actively try to turn events to own advantage;
- they constantly revise and change their structures as they learn about the world;
- they anticipate the future;
- they are self-organizing;

- they seek to exist on the edge of chaos;
- they have emergent properties.

So complex adaptive systems are composed of large numbers of agents or individuals interacting in a non-linear way. They are responding to changes in their environment and their circumstances, both collectively and as individuals, and responding and reacting to each other constantly in a spontaneous and unplanned way. Try to visualize your brain composed as it is of billions of neurons reacting and responding to all that is happening outside your head in the world in which you move and exist. It is continuously organizing and reorganizing its billions of neural connections as it responds to these changes – and as it learns from your experiences. It is operating as a complex adaptive system.

Complex adaptive systems create higher and higher levels of complexity with many levels. Agents at one level act as building blocks for agents at other levels. Individual species collectively form ecosystems; humans co-operate and compete and form social groups, cultures and national societies; trillions of living cells interact and respond on upwards and downwards scales of being and so create living wholes that may emerge as mammals, or other complex life forms. In an organization individual agents or employees interact with each other and form teams or small groups and networks. These in turn are part of larger groups or departments and groups of departments make up a division or branch of the organization and so on.

There is no central controlling mechanism that directs a complex adaptive system. (Organizations introduce and try to impose centralizing controls – but that is a man-made system based on perceptions of organization.) As in a self-organizing system, competition and collaboration creates order and the emergence of coherent behaviours.

On the global scale national economies are also complex adaptive systems. They are made up of millions of individuals, and thousands of groups and organizations, and they respond to events and changes in trading patterns and lifestyle choices.

Learning and adaptation are key properties of complex adaptive systems. They do not respond passively to events but as they learn they modify and revise their structures and behaviours. Think of flu viruses and bacteria. As we have developed drugs and healthcare technologies that threaten their survival so they have responded by changing their structure and behaviours. Some have been successful, others less so.

Recently there was a wonderful example in the news of how complex adaptive systems learn to their advantage. Two seabirds regularly 'catch' the Falmouth ferry at 8.15 am. This takes them across to their feeding grounds. Then at 4.30 pm they land on the deck and enjoy the return trip to their roosting place. The clever birds have learnt how to save both time and energy by using the boat. Will their offspring learn to do the same thing?

As they gain experience so complex adaptive systems reconsider their structures and reorganize themselves on an ongoing basis. The science writer, Mitchell Waldrop, notes:

> Succeeding generations of organisms will modify and rearrange their tissues throughout the process of evolution. The brain will continually strengthen or weaken myriad connections between its neurons as an individual learns from his or her encounters with the world . . . At some deep fundamental level . . . all these processes of learning, evolution, and adaption are the same. And one of the fundamental mechanisms of adaption in any given system is this revision and re combination of building blocks.
>
> (Waldrop 1994: 146)

Complex adaptive systems also actively try to turn events to their own advantage. This may be of advantage to others sometimes, at other times it may not. When societies break down in times of warfare or civil commotion there will be many human beings who will turn these calamitous events to their own advantage creating black market economies and other exploitative practices.

Another property of complex adaptive systems is that they try to anticipate the future. They have the ability to recognize patterns, shifting patterns and emerging patterns. They learn to use this to recognize and anticipate changes and modifications in patterns of process or structure. This enables them to speculate about possible futures. All complex adaptive systems, whether they are simple bacteria or sophisticated animals, have the ability to make predictions about the future as part of their genetic make-up. These are dependent on their own interpretations of how their world and the world around them works. These assumptions whether they are implicit or explicit are then tested in the real world and as they learn from their experiences so their assumptions are refined, re-organized and retested. It is part of their genetic survival kit.

Complex adaptive systems are self-organizing with all the attributes of these systems. But not all self-organizing systems are complex adaptive ones. The significant difference, as I have pointed out, is that complex adaptive systems learn and adapt to changes in circumstances. A laser beam is a self-organizing system, it has changed as a result of changing circumstances, but learning is not part of, nor a by-product of, its adaption process. As systems with self-organizing attributes, complex adaptive systems need energy to exist – without energy they will wind down over time and die.

Complex adaptive systems have evolved so that they seek to operate at the edge of chaos. They have done so because it is here that they are able to operate flexibly and creatively. Here they can exist at maximum dynamical activity which is necessary for their survival. In order to do this they experiment and test out their assumptions and ideas, try out new processes and structures, and to do this they need to constantly explore the world around them. Another feature of these systems is that they have emergent properties.

Emergence

The concept of emergence is an important theme that flows through studies of complexity. It is a phenomenon of the process of adapting and transforming spontaneously to changes in circumstances. This process leads to the development of something else, something more complex, usually much richer, than the original. It may also be something unexpected that takes shape. Emergence is a property of all complex adaptive systems including ecosystems, food chains, animal groups, insect swarms and human societies. The interaction and responses of the individual agents leads to the emergence of a much larger system. (See Figure 3.2.) In this way the myriad interactions of billions of individual brain cells result in a collective intelligence and an emergent phenomenon: consciousness. This too is true of human collectives whether they be tribal societies, regional clusters or national groups. They are able to share and exchange memories and experiences, pass around knowledge and skills and in so doing superbly advance their collective abilities such that their own specific cultural identity emerges.

Evolution is probably responsible for the emergent phenomenon. Ants and humans discovered that by working together rather than operating

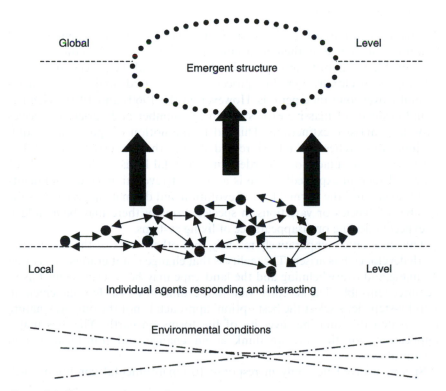

Figure 3.2 Emergence in complex systems.

individually they improve their survival chances. For both species obtaining food, defending territories and building and maintaining homes are all more easily achieved by working collectively. Individual ants may not be highly intelligent, but by working together they create a super intelligence. As a group their intelligence is far greater than the sum of their individual parts, or individual ants.

In Chapter 2 I was critical of the linear, categorizing nature of Maslow's famous Hierarchy of Needs Model. On reflection, I consider that his final need at the top of his pyramid which is 'self-actualization', could well be an emergent property. That is to say, that if a person's biological, physiological, emotional and esteem needs are all fulfilled, then 'self-actualization' emerges from the interaction of all the attributes needed to create the whole, that is a totally fulfilled being.

Thus a significant aspect of emergence is that study of the individual components or agents of an emergent phenomenon does not enable you to understand the whole. In other words, intense study of an individual brain cell will yield up few clues to explain consciousness. Listening to a full orchestra playing a Beethoven symphony could not be imagined or understood by careful study of each individual musician and their instrument. This has important implications for reductionist approaches to scientific inquiry.

Evolution and complexity

The naturalist Charles Darwin observed that species or living systems evolved as a result of changes in their environments – changes that sometimes species were unable to adapt to or cope with. He also viewed the process of natural selection as essentially a gradual process that produced small changes incrementally over long time periods. However, in the 1960s and 1970s scientists found evidence of massive explosions in the number and variety of species as well as massive extinctions. This led to the notion of 'punctuated equilibrium'. Researches of the fossil record showed that the evolution of different species takes places on an orderly incremental basis for long periods of time and then unexpectedly there is a burst of revolutionary developments that 'punctuates' the normal flow of evolution and dramatically increases the number of species or variations in species. Equally there may be a sudden unexpected decline or disappearance of living systems.

Thus it is only comparatively recently that other views of the way life on earth developed has arisen. The reality is that change is not gradual, it is often dramatic and overwhelming and the landscape may be so transformed as to be unrecognizable. The accepted view that evolution was a slow, incremental, step-by-step, 'let's select the best option' approach is not the only way nature has created the amazing diversity of life forms on earth. This has major implications for the way we think about change and transformation in organizations.

Species evolved not only in response to environmental conditions such as climate changes but also as a result of spontaneous co-evolution. This happens when species interact with each other in such a way as to create local selective pressures and this over time leads to a symbiotic relationship. A good example of this is the way that insects and birds have co-evolved with different plant species such that both have developed features that support the relationship. Some plants, like foxgloves, have developed trumpet or tube shaped flowers. Insects crawl inside to collect nectar (food) and pick up lots of pollen on their way. This ensures that the plant's reproductive processes are helped as the insects fly off and pollinate other flowers. Some birds have developed special bills in order to collect nectar from plants. Some small fishes eat the parasites that cling to the sides of large, often, predatory fishes. These species have co-evolved in a very special and mutually interdependent way. Other species, of course, are not dependent upon each other even though they have co-evolved. Parasites feed off other creatures and they and not their hosts are usually the beneficiaries of this co-evolution.

Co-operation and self-organization were as essential for evolution as natural selection. Both led to the creation of more complex structures and forms and their ability to self-organize in response to local conditions and environmental changes determined which of these would survive.

The notion of the 'survival of the fittest', which is falsely attributed to Darwin, is now considered erroneous. Perhaps the term 'survival of the most adaptive' might be more appropriate. The idea of the natural world as being fiercely competitive and 'red in tooth and claw' has been challenged by modern biologists and complexity scientists. There is intense and often brutal competition between species on many levels, but there is in fact more co-operation than competition. If one thinks about it, then it is clear that competition can waste or destroy precious resources whereas co-operation enables collaborative and often life enhancing co-existence. Thus the evolutionary *raison d'être* for some of the worst excesses of early industrialism and capitalism no longer holds good.

Complexity scientists have contributed to more recent interpretations of natural selection. Many consider that natural selection does not explain the origins of different life forms or species but that these caused themselves. In other words, they are the emergent properties of self-organizing and developmental processes which co-evolve over time.

The notion of a 'fitness landscape' is used by biologists to study different species and their survival history or their future chances. The high peaks on this theoretical landscape represent the best places to be, lower peaks less so, and the valleys are places where a species may be trapped or stuck and become vulnerable to predators. This landscape, however, is always changing as different species move across it seeking the best possible positions for their evolutionary success. The landscape itself too is constantly changing as each species moves and evolves across it. How a species survives depends on how it moves across this landscape. If it is too timid it could get caught in the foothills or if it is too bold it may get trapped on a peak. Successful species strike a balance somewhere between the two and flow along the ridges towards new regions of fitness.

The US biologist Stuart Kauffman considers that all organisms and organizations are evolving structures moving across a fitness landscape. Each is searching for the best possible pathway that will ensure its survival and all too aware that the ground is constantly shifting around them. Use of this model enables managers to consider realistically their strategic options and reminds them of the shifting organizational landscape and its moving populations of competing or collaborating organizations.

Finally, connectedness is a vital part of any living system. Connectivity within a system enables responses and reactions to take place within a non-linear dynamical system as it responds via internal feedback loops. This excites and disturbs the system leading to the creation of new life forms and also the precipitation of declines and extinctions. Thus connectedness has a key role in evolution.

> Connectedness, is a theme that links with concepts of patterning and concepts of organization. It implies more than spatial relationships. One senses a mysterious, unifying rhythm at work between all the entities within a system and again this resonates with aspects of chaos theory.
>
> (McMillan 2004: 34)

Key questions

- How does a complexity science view of the world differ from the Newtonian–Cartesian or classical science world view?
- What distinguishes a complex adaptive system from a system that is merely complex?
- What are the key differences between self-organizing systems and complex adaptive systems?
- What universal themes keep recurring in complexity science (and chaos theory)?
- What do the newer interpretations of evolution suggest for management practice?

PART TWO: THE BASICS PLUS

Key points

- Edward Lorenz, the butterfly effect and strange attractors
- Benoit Mandelbrot and fractals
- John Holland and Chris Langton – complex adaptive systems and emergence
- Biologists Robert May, Stuart Kauffman, Brian Goodwin

- Mitchell Feigenbaum, universality and patterning
- Ilya Prigogine, Herman Haken and self-organizing systems

Chaos

The work of the early chaos pioneers brought together many scientific disciplines that had been heading down their own exclusive paths. Some of the discoveries of the chaos scientists were completely new, but others consisted of fresh ways of looking at old ideas, building on the work of great scientific pioneers such as Einstein, Poincaré and Maxwell.

Edward Lorenz and the butterfly effect or sensitive dependence on initial conditions

A major landmark in the emergence of chaos theory was the discovery of the 'butterfly effect' or sensitive dependence on initial conditions. This phrase was coined by Edward Lorenz, a meteorologist working at the Massachusetts Institute of Technology in the 1960s.

As part of his research Lorenz, was using a simple computer programme to simulate weather patterns. One day he decided to take a shortcut and instead of keying in the full sequence that started the weather cycle, he chose instead to start it up using only half the sequence. He went off for a coffee break and returned to his programme assuming that the change was inconsequential and would have no major impact on the overall pattern of the weather. But as the programme unfolded the weather patterns that emerged started to become increasingly different from the previous ones, until all further resemblance disappeared. The small change in the keying in sequence had, over time, produced significant differences. Lorenz realized that small perturbations in the behaviour of the weather were what made weather systems so changeable, unpredictable and complex. His discovery later became known as the 'butterfly effect' as a result of his paper: 'Predictability: Does the Flap of a Butterfly's Wings in Brazil Set Off a Tornado in Texas?', given at the annual meeting of the American Association for the Advancement of Science in December 1979.

Strange attractors

Edward Lorenz is also renowned for the strange attractor known as the 'Lorenz attractor', or the 'butterfly attractor'. It was called the 'butterfly attractor' because when the different trajectories of the system were mapped out by a computer, the image that unfolded on the computer screen formed an exotic figure of eight, not unlike that of a butterfly's wings.

The term 'strange attractor', however, was first coined by David Ruelle, a Belgian-born mathematical physicist. He devised the term in order to describe and explain the patterns of behaviour of turbulence in fluids.

Like so many of those who began studying chaos, David Ruelle suspected that the visible patterns in turbulent flow – self-entangled stream lines, spiral vortices, whorls that rise before the eye and vanish again – must reflect patterns explained by laws not yet discovered.

(Gleick 1993: 138)

Ruelle worked with the Dutch mathematician, Floris Takens, on the idea of a strange attractor. Their findings were published in 1971 but it was a number of years before their work was fully recognized.

Benoit Mandelbrot and fractals

Benoit Mandelbrot, is a mathematician who was born in Poland but moved to France as a young boy. He was unconventional and questioning and became fascinated by coastlines and the question of how one measured them accurately. If you try to measure a piece of coastline using conventional methods, then the results vary considerably according to the scale of the measurement used. If, for example, you used a metre as your unit of measurement you would produce one result. If you used half a metre as your unit of measurement you would produce another result. The metre unit of measurement would not include all the tiny indents and cracks in the coastline that were under a metre in length. Whereas the shorter unit of measurement would include everything but the tiny indents that were less than half a metre. This latter would find the coastline to be longer than the first which had skated across the small indentations. It was in pondering this problem that Mandelbrot realized that at whatever scale you measured the coastline certain features remained the same. Thus you may not be able to accurately measure it in terms of its length but you could measure its repeating characteristics. Mandelbrot found that the patterns and irregularities formed by the coastline were the same at whatever scale you looked at them. Coastlines have self-similarity properties.

Mandelbrot realized that fractals are everywhere around us in nature but until he devised his new geometry there was no qualitative means of measuring the amazing variety of shapes in the natural world. He coined the term 'fractal' to describe this new type of geometry, one that is concerned with irregular shapes that repeat themselves up and down the scales of length. His work was to significantly influence the new generation of mathematicians who were working on chaos theory.

Order within chaos

The Australian born biologist Robert May made a significant contribution to our understanding of how order exists even within apparent chaos. May was interested in understanding the behaviour of wild life populations and how they survived their boom and bust cycles.

He developed a computer programme designed to simulate the different changes in fish population sizes. He investigated hundreds of different values, setting feedback loops in motion and watching to see where and whether the numbers would settle to a fixed point. His programme showed how dramatically the fish population in his 'pond' would fluctuate, sometimes coming close to extinction and at other times rising rapidly and erratically. May observed, however, that these cycles of boom and bust were not totally disorderly. For example, the pattern of changing population might repeat itself on a three- or a seven-year cycle. These appeared on the computer like windows of order within the chaotic or disorderly sector. Also when portions of these parts of the graph were magnified they turn out to resemble the whole diagram – a fractal pattern.

May's work on fish populations demonstrated that whatever changes took place, there emerged an underlying pattern of order as population changes repeated themselves over different yearly cycles. May argued that the standard scientific view had misled scientists about the overwhelming nonlinearity of the world. His work showed how a complex systems could be responsive to small differences in starting values and reaffirmed the importance of 'sensitive dependence on initial conditions' discovered by Lorenz.

Edge of chaos

Much of the evidence for the edge of chaos has emerged from biology and studies on living species, although further evidence has arisen from ecology, microbiology, and palaeontology. The US biologist, Stuart Kauffman, is credited by many for advancing this notion and pointing out its relevance not only to evolution but to economics and management.

Research on ant colonies including computer simulations has provided evidence for the existence of the edge of chaos. Individual ants appear to behave in a chaotic fashion. They rush about, have a rest, then rush about again. Thus they are constantly moving from an active pattern to a stable or inactive one. But their individual behaviours reflect the overall pattern of the colony which as a whole has an orderly rhythmic pattern to it. Research has shown that the pattern of their behaviour is affected by population density.

> Evidently ants have a sense of density in the colony, since they regulate it at a fairly constant value. As ants come and go from the nest, changing the density, rhythmic activity patterns appear and disappear, replaced by disordered activity. This suggests that the colonies are regulating their densities so that they live at the edge of chaos.
>
> (Brian Goodwin 1997a: 176)

Universality and patterning

The US physicist, Mitchell Feigenbaum developed the concept of 'universality'. He showed that completely different dynamical systems all behaved in a similar way when they started to become chaotic. Feigenbaum's work demonstrated that it was possible to use the same universal numbers to work out the transition points of a system as it moved into chaos. His findings and the 'Feigenbaum numbers' as they are called, have enabled scientists to study the behaviours of a wide range of systems including optical and medical systems, electrical circuits and business systems.

Universal laws concerning scaling have been recognized for some time. Consider the relationship between the body mass of a species and its metabolic rate. Metabolic rate is proportional to mass to the power of three quarters and this scaling relationship affects species from the smallest micro-organism to huge mammals such as whales. It is also known that there is a relationship between heartbeats and life span. Within a specific group of species, mammals, for instance, the total of number of heartbeats per lifetime is the same. An elephant's heart beats more slowly than that of a mouse and it has a much longer life span – but they share the same number of heartbeats. Yet another example of nature's universal patterning at work.

A recent study has demonstrated that vegetation self-organizes itself into specific patterns when growing in semi-arid conditions. The most common pattern was a stripe which was found growing in parallel with the contours of the ground. It would appear that the plants are able to self-organize themselves into patterns according to local or initial conditions and rainfall. The interesting question this study raises is this: do the plants self-organize into specific patterns in order to increase their survival chances?

Complexity

The development and recognition of complexity science received a considerable boost with the establishment in the mid 1980s of the Santa Fe Institute in New Mexico, USA. Santa Fe brought together a number of renowned researchers from a range of disciplines, including physics, zoology, botany, archaeology, economics and computer science. This led to the creation of a broadly based scientific community which sought to explain and apply concepts from this new science. In the UK in 2002 Peter Allen and I led the way in forming the Complexity Society (www.complexity-society.com), designed to encourage interest in complexity science and the dissemination of complexity principles and ideals within all aspects of British and European society.

*Ilya Prigogine, Herman Haken and self-organization and
self-organizing systems*

The concept of self-organization first appeared in the 1940s and 1950s when cybernetic scientists started to explore neural networks and by the late 1950s Heinz von Foerster a physicist and cybernetics had developed a model of self-organization in living systems. This model was built upon and refined by other researchers including Ilya Prigogine, Hermann Haken, Manfred Eigen, James Lovelock and Lynn Margulis.

Ilya Prigogine's work on dissipative structures is considered key to the development of our understanding of self-organizing systems. Prigogine was a Russian-born physical chemist who was fascinated by the way that living organisms are able to survive in highly unstable conditions. In order to understand this better he decided to study a non-living situation called the Benard instability, which is a phenomenon of heat convection. This is now considered a classical case of a self-organizing phenomenon.

Prigogine's work showed that systems existing in highly unstable conditions can induce changes in themselves that can lead to the emergence of new patterns of order and stability. His work was considered of such groundbreaking importance that in 1978 he was awarded a Nobel Prize. This acknowledged that he had fundamentally transformed and revised the science of thermodynamics. Prigogine's research demonstrated that we live in a world in which systems are essentially non-linear, dynamic and able to transform themselves into new states of being and not a world where systems ran down and were subject to an ongoing deterioration. Thus the concept of dissipative structures offered an alternative view to that implied by Newton's Second Law of Thermodynamics. It suggested that Newton's law may still apply, but only in situations where a system is in equilibrium, that is to say, in a very stable and unchanging state. Dissipative structures or self-organizing systems are the basic structures of all living systems, including human beings.

The German physicist, Hermann Haken, studied lasers and found that the transition from normal light to laser light involved a self-organizing process typical of systems operating far from equilibrium. In 1970 he published his non-linear laser theory which makes it clear that although the laser needs external actions on it to keep it in its disordered state, the co-ordination of the light emissions are carried out by the laser itself, and thus it is a self-organizing system.

Complex adaptive systems

John Holland, the US computer scientist and a professor of psychology and electrical engineering is well known for his contribution to our knowledge of complex adaptive systems. During the 1980s his work with computer modelling led to the serious study of complex, adaptive systems at the Santa Fe Institute. Murray Gell-Mann the distinguished US physicist and Nobel Prize winner is another renowned scientist who, during his years at the Santa Fe Institute, made a major contribution to complexity science and understanding of complex adaptive systems.

John Holland, Chris Langton and emergence

John Holland played an important role in the development of the concept of emergence during the 1970s and 1980s, as did Chris Langton, a former student of Holland's.

Holland and Langton were both influenced and inspired by a computer simulation designed by Craig Reynolds. This attempted to show the essential nature of flocking behaviour in birds and the schooling behaviour of fishes. It simulated an environment full of obstacles and programmed each 'boid' or bird-like agent to follow three simple rules of behaviour. These were as follows: to try to maintain a minimum distance from other objects, including other boids; to try to fly/move at the same speed as other boids in the vicinity; to try to move towards the perceived centre of the mass of boids. Significantly, there was no rule that instructed them to form a flock. The rules, referred only to what an individual boid could see and do. Every time the simulation was run the boids formed into flocks. No matter how the boids were scattered they still formed up into flocks that were able to navigate in a fluid and natural way. The simulation gave important insights into how self-organization can take place. It demonstrated how the phenomenon of emergence arises from the use of simple local rules that allow the boids to react to each other and to the changing conditions in a spontaneous way.

Stuart Kauffman and Brian Goodwin

The US biologist, Stuart Kauffman and the Canadian-born biologist Brian Goodwin have both played an important role in the development of complexity science. Both have contributed through their research and their writing to our understanding of self-organizing systems, notions of the edge of chaos, and evolution and complexity. Brian Goodwin has written that organisms have to be understood as dynamical systems and cannot be reduced to the properties of their genes and ponders whether or not complexity science research is leading to the development of a new science of qualities.

Key questions

- How did Ilya Prigogine's research challenge established science and earn him a Nobel Prize?
- What contributions have biologists made to the development of complexity science?

- Patterning is a significant, recurring theme in complexity. In what ways does it enhance our understanding of the natural world?
- Can you think of other examples of 'flocking'-type behaviour and emergence as illustrated by Craig Reynolds' simulation?

4   Change and the dynamics of change: thinking differently

Key points

* Perceptions of change
* Traditional views and approaches to change
* Three well-known change models
* Comparing old and new approaches to change
* Strategy and strategic change

As discussed in Chapter 2 and as you will be all too aware, the world has moved on very rapidly in the last decades. The twentieth century saw unprecedented upheavals in all aspects of human life as we have manipulated and changed our world bringing about massive technological, sociological, ecological and economic changes on a global stage. In some ways this has prepared the way for the acceptance of complexity science in the wider community. It was all too easy to argue that this new science with its talk of paradoxical, turbulent and unpredictable events was unrealistic and even fanciful when the world about you seemed to move at a steady pace. But this was before the crumbling of traditional manufacturing industries, the advent of the Internet, the development of fast-moving global economies, media frenzies, designer mores, terrorism and climate change. Faced with such dizzying changes is it any wonder that many managers struggle to keep up and all too often cling to old ideas like comfort blankets? Unfortunately, as I hope was demonstrated in Chapter 2, too many managers and writers on management are still influenced by old ways of thinking. These ways of thinking are essentially laboratory based and while very useful for the hard sciences and the creation of new technologies, they are extremely unhelpful for dealing with the real, very volatile world of people and organizations that exists 'outside the lab'.

In my experience most thinking managers are all too aware of the shortcomings of many of the approaches offered by mainstream management literature and some of the business schools on how to introduce effective organizational change. The prescriptions offered usually amount to 'adding another lane to the motorway' to solve traffic congestion – and as we all know this offers only temporary relief. In other words, they are merely doing more of the same thing. They continue to do the 'things' that they have always done. It is a way of thinking that does not help us to deal with modern realities and hinders the development of intelligent and sustainable management practice.

I would argue that if we are to learn to cope much better with our changing world then we need to radically change our thinking and our perceptions of change and the dynamics of change. Understanding and using concepts from complexity science – and the real world – will enable us to do that. In fact, it should enable managers to dramatically shift their thinking. No longer will they see change as an item on their agenda or 'to do list', but rather adaptation learning and change will be the normal flow of organizational life and managerial practice. Organizational change will be like breathing in and out. It will be something we do all the time that is absolutely necessary for our existence and totally commonplace. But before I move on to specifically describing how we might do this I shall consider some of the popular notions and models of change, something on the nature of change and on the nature of change in organizations today as a necessary prelude. I shall also briefly refer to the work of Mintzberg and Waters, Quinn and Mintzberg, Ahlstrand and Lampel as they provide an invaluable framework within which to consider approaches to strategy and strategic change. Finally, in order to compare strategy from both a classical, Newtonian–Cartesian perspective and from a complexity paradigm perspective, I shall briefly refer to my own work with Dr Ysanne Carlisle.

Perceptions of change

As I pointed out in my 2004 book, there appears to be very little discussion of change as an abstract concept or a universal phenomenon in current UK and US management books. I believe that we need a much wider perspective on change and the nature of change if we are to enrich our understanding of how to live with it and how to ensure that we manage it better. When I use the term 'manage', I do not mean 'control' it. Here I differ very significantly from most management texts. Change cannot be controlled and to think that it can be is to think in a very unrealistic and outdated fashion. A manager who thinks this way is 300 plus years behind the times!

So how do we think about change? How do we engage with it? In management and organizations change is usually thought of as some kind of event or series of events which may be part of some designed internal strategy or something happening in the external environment. It comes along and disturbs an unchanging reality. But change and changes are not discrete events. They are part of an ever flowing, ever present reality that is constantly undergoing change. The 'event' or 'events' we have observed or recognized are the tip of an ongoing wave. Change is the underlying essence of life. Classical science's concentration on the parts of a system or an object may explain why individuals and organizations have this 'entity'-based view of change. The physicist David Bohm contended that the universe is a flowing whole that is in a continuous process of flux and change. It has an underlying process or reality which he calls the implicate order. This order flows on, unfurling endlessly and creates the hidden dynamics from which arise the explicate order, or manifest forms of activity or change which we observe. Thus sometimes we may think that the world is a stable place but that is because we are not observing the implicate order, only the explicate order. The planet is, in fact, in a state of permanent change.

Bohm's view of an endlessly changing universe is mirrored by an ancient Chinese view which saw change and transformation as a never ending flow and an essential feature of our universe.

> Change in this view, does not occur as a consequence of some force but is a natural tendency, innate in all things and situations. The universe is engaged in ceaseless motion and activity, in a continual cosmic process that the Chinese called Tao – the Way. The notion of absolute rest, or inactivity, was almost entirely absent from Chinese philosophy.
>
> (Capra 1983: 37)

The Taoist philosophy considers that the natural world is created by a cyclical pattern of comings and goings, of growth and decay. This arises from the interplay of the complementary opposites of yin and yang. The yin of night and the yang of day, earth and heaven, of dark and light, of winter and summer, cool and hot. This view in turn resonates with the beliefs of the ancient Greek philosopher Heraclitus, who lived *circa* 540–480 BC. He thought that change was an inherent characteristic that flowed through the natural world and wrote: 'Everything flows and nothing abides; everything gives way and nothing stays fixed . . . Cool things become warm, the warm grows cool; the moist dries, the parched becomes moist . . . It is in changing that things find repose' (quoted in Morgan 1986: 233).

Are heat and cold opposites? Are dry and wet opposites? Or are they just replacing each other as part of a universal transformation process? If we think like the Chinese and Greek philosophers then we appreciate that nothing is fixed, nothing exists forever in a permanent state of being. Paradoxically, the only permanent thing in the universe is change.

These are views echoed and supported by complexity scientists today. For example, within these ancient philosophies are echoes of Prigogine's dissipative structures.

> If one considers change from a complexity science perspective then one thinks of change as forming patterns and of flowing through time. Like a giant stream flowing forever, within the flow of change there will be flows, and flows within flows, and eddies and ripples within these, all interweaving to create an overall dynamic whole. These flows could well form repeating fractal like patterns over a long time period.
>
> (McMillan 2004: 60)

We should not forget too that this flow of change affects each of us. It has been observed that it might be more accurate to refer to us a human 'becomings' rather than human beings. We, in common with living creatures from the smallest virus to the greatest mammal, are living processes 'under the skin' and not static entities.

Types and degrees of change

So if we accept the view that the universe and our world is constantly transforming itself, how do we describe and better understand the many different eddies and effects within the explicate flow of change? The nature of observable change can vary and its effects can vary in impact, magnitude and time span. A number of writers have sought to describe these different types of change within an organizational context. They refer to:

- first-order or first-degree change (single-loop learning);
- second-order or second-degree change (double-loop learning);
- deep-level change, transformation, self-renewal and sea change;
- closed, contained and open-ended change – Ralph Stacey.

First-order change tends to change things superficially or in a limited way. A technician may learn to use a new process that makes his or her job easier. This may make an improvement to productivity but overall his or her way of thinking about the job may have changed very little. This is known as single-loop learning or simple learning. He or she has acquired a new skill but his or her thinking and behaviour has not really changed. A very common example of this type of change is found when companies decide to improve their service to customers and focus on their receptionists. They decide that they can improve their customer service by introducing a more friendly telephone greeting. A customer making an enquiry is thus answered in a new way. Often, the new mantra is something like: 'My name is . . . How may I help you?' The response to the customer may have changed, but how much has their attitude or their ability to help the customer changed? Do they feel better able to help the customer? Do they see their role in a new way? Do they have more information on the company and its services to back them up? How different are the back up services required to support them? If the answer to these questions is 'no', then in reality very little has changed. The receptionist has learnt a new telephone greeting but perhaps little else. This again is single-loop learning. Sometimes an organization changes from a manual system to an automated one. This is a more significant change than the customer service example, but it is a limited change unless it involves other major differences in procedures, behaviours and structures.

Second-order change, or second-degree change makes a much more significant impact on people and an organization. This is the kind of change that really makes a difference. Double loop learning takes place. This means that people have not only learnt to do things differently, they have also learnt to think and behave significantly differently. People have shifted their mental models and their internal perspectives in such a way that they have important new insights and these in turn lead to changed behaviours. Such changes may take place as part of some pre-planned event or process or they may happen during the normal flow of working life. A manager may stop and have a conversation with one of his or her team in order to discuss an irritating issue. As a result of this conversation he or she may discover some new and unexpected information. This and other observations by the employee may be such that the manager's whole perception of the problem is turned upside down. Perhaps they have realized that he or she is part of the problem! As a result they have not only taken on board some fresh facts (single-loop learning) but they have had to reassess their own role and their own behaviours and they now think and behave differently (double-loop learning).

Deep-level change or transformation describes the kind of change that radically transforms people and their organization. This is second-order change and double-loop learning at work throughout an organization. This transforming change is described by some writers as self-renewing change or self-renewal. This kind of change affects not only the thinking and the behaviour of everyone in the organization but it also affects the structure of the organization. This is Prigogine's dissipative structures, where an organization and its existing order is dissolved or disappears and a new one emerges.

This kind of change is sometimes referred to as a sea change. The term 'sea change' is derived from the verse in Shakespeare's *The Tempest*.

> Full fathom five thy father lies;
> Of his bones are coral made:
> Those are pearls that were his eyes:
> Nothing of him that doth fade,
> But doth suffer a sea change
> Into something rich and strange.
> (Shakespeare 1960: 7)

Shakespeare describes how a man's body has changed from a recognizable human shape into a sea creature made of pearls and coral. It is a total transformation. The man that once existed has vanished and been replaced by something exotic and unrecognizable.

Ralph Stacey in his book *Strategic Management and Organisational Dynamics* (1996) suggests that there are three major kinds of change: closed, contained and open-ended. Closed change is a change or changes that are easily recognized and understood and contain a measure of predictability. He cites, for example, changes in the number of customers a company has had over a given period, and how they might change in the future and how this will help the company to act in the future.

Contained change is more difficult to understand than closed change. Again there may be evidence from the past to help with a future change but it will be less helpful. For example, a particular product may have sold well in the past but why did it sell better than others, and how it will do in the future? Closed and contained change Stacey describes as developments that usually have short-term consequences. They are considered short-term because they are more or less repetitions of previous events or activities. It may, in fact, be possible to discern some cause and effect linkages with these kind of changes. They relate closely to notions of first-order change and single-loop learning.

Open-ended change is unique because it has never happened in that particular way before. Thus managers cannot relate it directly to past experiences nor discern any cause and effect linkages. It is very different to closed or contained change and it is extremely difficult to know what may be the possible outcomes of this kind of change. This is change that could involve double-loop learning and bring about transformation or renewal.

Stacey considers that managers need to consider all three forms of change if they want to ensure the survival of their organization. Closed and contained changes tend to be the kind of change that most managers recognize and understand. They relate to more traditional views of change.

This section has considered some of the different types of change that take place in organizations and the types of change that managers and writers discuss. I present them to you as they represent the language managers use today when they think and act with reference to change. These terms are useful as they enable us to ensure that when we think of change we know what kind of change it is we have in mind and the range of outcomes or possibilities we expect the change to bring about. I endorse Stacey's view that organizations if they are to survive need to embrace all kinds of change. In fact, they need all kinds of changes to be flowing through them as they respond to events and invent their own futures. Organizations need to be continuously adapting and creating new flows of relevant activities. They need to be constantly learning about their own world and connecting worlds, and they need to be adapting as they go. In other words, they need to engage in both single- and double-loop learning experiences and behave as complex adaptive systems.

Time to change – some traditional views and approaches

So why and when do managers decide that they need to introduce changes or remodel their company? One common situation is that of the new broom. A new chief executive takes over and decides to make his or her mark. All too often this means transforming the company into the kind of company that he or she has just left and is familiar with. This often means employing the same techniques. If the new chief executive has left a thriving organization then the raft of changes will sweep through embracing both single- and double-loop learning as appropriate. These changes may be needed, or it may be change for change's sake. Most employees are familiar with that. This can be as much about reputation building and boosting self-esteem as improving a company's viability.

Other internal factors which can stimulate an organization to want to make changes are the need to make improvements. These may be desired in order to bring about an increase in productivity, to improve the quality of goods and services, or to tackle staffing issues such as sickness absence rates or high employee turnover. These improvements may be important for the organization's competitiveness and future survival chances but all too often they are tackled in isolation. For example, productivity may be increased but this in turn may lead to work overload, workload stress and a haemorrhage of employees. Sometimes the effects of an improvement in one part of an organization are not considered fully in terms of its likely impact on other parts, other processes and other people. Much of this is due to the continued compartmentalization of companies and a lack of integrated thinking and action. Communication and connectivity is often poor or uneven. Much of this is down to the notion of the organization as a machine to be fixed, rather than a strong but highly sensitive living web of interaction and response.

Another reason why organizations decide to make changes is in order to 'fit'. Significant numbers of senior managers subscribe to the notion that an organization will not be truly successful unless it 'fits' with its external environment. Thus strategy and structure have to be designed and operated so that they match the external environment. This suggests: 'a semi-concealed Darwinian concept of gradual evolution and survival of the fittest' (Durcan *et al.* 1993: 6). You may recall that survival of the fittest does not mean survival of the toughest, most competitive or the one in the choicest niche. Evolutionary processes are not simply about 'fit', they are much richer and much more complex.

The literature on change management also suggests that many managers introduce major change in response to some challenge or significant change in the external environment. This is often perceived as a threat to the organization's current position. These threats may arise for a wide variety of reasons: changes in the market place; changes in customer preferences; shortage of raw materials; aggressive new competitors; exchange rate fluctuations; new technologies and so on. STEP or PEST is an often used acronym to help managers identify external pressures for change.

Political
Economic
Sociological
Technological

More recently have been added:

Legal, and
Ecological
These form: PESTLE.

To this list one should also add Chance or the Unexpected. This would lead to the inclusion of such thinks as storms, earthquakes, tornadoes (which do affect the UK), accidents, flu pandemics and so on. The value in the use of this acronym is in developing wide environmental awareness of these and other fluctuations in an organization's external environment. Unfortunately, external threats, whether real or perceived, often elicit a crisis reaction. Managers introduce a variety of rapid responses, often relying on past approaches. Their aim is to overcome the present difficulties or threats as rapidly as possible and to restore any loss of confidence. This may be useful in the immediate or short term but that is all and in some instances may be storing up more trouble for the future.

Another reason why organizations decide to introduce changes is due to outdated thinking on the nature of organizations and management – a Newtonian–Cartesian based mindset. This is the idea that control is essential for organizational success and good management is all about controlling and steering the 'ship'.

Change is all about control

As I pointed out in an earlier chapter many writers on management have mindsets strongly influenced by the classical scientific (Newtonian–Cartesian) view of the world. Considerable research has been carried out on organizations over the last fifty years and this has influenced the literature on management. It is worth bearing in mind that empirical research on organizations would have been carried out on many firms that were themselves highly influenced by the classical scientific world view. Many of these organizations would have been places where 'command and control' was the prevalent management ethos. The researchers themselves would be looking at the world and their data primarily through a classical scientific lens. Also they may have analysed their findings from a linear, reductionist perspective. This may help account for the continued stream of evidence supporting a machine or quasi-machine model of organization.

Control is seen by most managers and many writers on management (though this is changing) as necessary for stability. There is a widespread perception that it is only with stability that an organization (and economies) can progress. (Incidentally, you may recall that the notion of progress itself as the onward and upward ascent of mankind derives from the Scientific Revolution and some interpretations of evolution, and it replaced an earlier notion of life as an ongoing and eternal cycle.) As a result of this mindset some managers become worried if they feel that things are running out of control and not going to plan. Even in more modern thinking organizations where the old 'command and control' ethos was replaced years ago, there is often a tendency to believe that if an organization is to be successful it must function smoothly and harmoniously, and that managers must plan and predict for the longer term. Part of this approach is the need to control things and a belief that managers must be incompetent if they are not in charge of events. In the days before electronic messages I recollect several conscientious heads of departments who insisted that all letters and memos had to pass across their desk for their signature. This slowed everything up considerably and left them working exceptionally long hours. It was impossible to get them to change their behaviours as they truly believed that in order to do a good job they had to oversee and check everything leaving their department. Even today management is seen by many as being all about control, though nowadays this is much more likely to be an implicit rather than explicit assumption. In fact, many of today's young managers would probably recoil in horror at the thought of being an agent of control, nevertheless, this is very much the role that many of them fulfil.

Many senior managers were brought up at a time when science and the scientific method were held in high esteem. Thus they are convinced that a scientific approach will provide them with accurate tools and techniques for achieving results. Consequently they make great use of logical analysis of data and other sophisticated pseudo-scientific techniques in the belief that they will help determine future business outcomes and ensure that the right decisions are made at the right time. As a result of this desire to control events too many managers follow limited and repetitive strategies convinced that success may be arrived at via long-term planning, monitoring of progress, and tight control systems. While middle and junior management is busy enacting this controlling mindset and applying it to operational and related activities senior management continues to plan at the top level, setting strategic direction and directing (controlling) from above.

Many organizations attempt to inspire and introduce change by producing mission statements, strategic planning interventions and new (usually linear) organizational structures. All these changes are essentially top-down and support classical notions of authority and the role of hierarchy. Managers design and support change by producing elaborate plans, often neatly bound and printed, that include detailed graphs and charts and considerable statistical data. These may be supplemented by consultation sessions, a special edition of the in-house newsletter, a letter from the MD and the presence of external consultants. All these approaches are used not to create fresh organizational dynamics that will disturb the current equilibrium but rather to introduce new processes and procedures that will move the organization from one stable state to another. (New, unexpected and possibly disturbing, organizational dynamics will arise as a consequence of these approaches and will present further challenges to the controlling manager.) It is acknowledged that there may be difficulties and a short period of uncertainty as the change takes place, but handled properly things should go smoothly. It has been argued that this snapshot-style approach to change leads to the creation of static management approaches which hinder, and sometimes destroy, an organization's effectiveness by restricting its ability to adapt to turbulent and chaotic events. By comparison much less attention has been given to the notion that organizations themselves should constantly be seeking change in an active way, such that changing is an organizational way of living. But would that lead to a loss of management control?

Case study vignette

Geoff Walsham in a chapter written in 1993 provides an example of how the need to control can sometimes override common and business sense. A subsidiary of a large manufacturing company decided to introduce some changes. Informal systems were very much a part of the existing set up and it was planned to introduce new systems with increased regulations. These would reduce the need for such informal processes. Senior management saw the new system as a tool which they could use to increase their overall control of the business. The affected employees lost their responsibility for transport arrangements and the allocation of warehousing space. But once the changes were in place they adapted to them by finding ways of working around the new regulations. They became so adept at this that they were able to identify a number of cost-saving improvements. Some years later a new management team was brought in which had a different perspective. They came to recognize the value of these informal systems and practices.

As this example demonstrates informal processes based on informal human networks can offer a more adaptive approach than formal ones based on notions of control. The importance of recognizing and supporting informal systems is discussed in subsequent chapters.

Machine and other metaphors

As I have already pointed out in this chapter there is evidence that managers and the management literature still have a strong tendency to think of the organization as some kind of machine. Some writers and managers refer to the 'levers' of change and in so doing betray a mechanistic view of organizations. Others talk of the need to 'fine tune' an organization as if it were a sophisticated, possibly even delicate, instrument, or to 'fix' an organization as if it were a broken object. Many consultants and others involved with organizations and business life use a language derived from classical science or the military. They talk of 'quantifying', 'leveraging', 'intellectual capital ratios' and 'success factors as quantifiable ratios'. Organizations still refer to 'officers' such as project officers, chief executive officers and so on. Many new words have entered the language of business but still the old military and machine metaphors persist. The continuation of this mindset makes it more difficult for managers to understand the paradoxes, ambiguities and complexities of organizational life. In continuing to think in a machine metaphor they have false expectations about the efficacy of change tools and accompanying strategies and interventions. Further, they have little chance of understanding the reality of the living organization and creating one that is flexible, intelligent, constantly adapting – and long living.

Resistance to change

A significant amount of the literature on how to manage change is devoted to the topic of resistance. Thus there is a widespread perception amongst managers and teachers of management studies that any attempts to introduce major change in an organization will be met by resistance from some or all employees. This is viewed as essentially a psychological response to something new, something different in the pattern of an individual's working life. The change literature cites a variety of causes for this expected resistance. These include:

- loss of control
- loss of face
- too much uncertainty
- fear of failure or lack of competence
- job insecurity
- lack of consultation
- suspicion.

Accordingly, the literature on the management of change provides a list of possible strategies for overcoming or neutralising resistance. They cite such things as: participative discussion and consultation; training and education; facilitation support; negotiation and agreement. Some texts even suggest using manipulation and coercion.

The change equation is offered by some writers as a way of determining how to overcome resistance to change. It states that change will occur if A + B + C > D. A = dissatisfaction with the *status quo*. B = a shared vision. C = knowledge about knowing where to make a start on the proposed change. D = the cost of the change in both financial and psychological terms. The simplicity of the equation makes it an attractive tool for managers. Its simplicity is misleading, however, for it underestimates the many factors involved in introducing change and can create false expectations of outcomes. Introducing changes into an organization is not a simple linear equation, although the use of an equation suggests some kind of scientific veracity and reliability.

The problem with the emphasis on resistance to change in the literature is that it predisposes everyone to expect trouble in one form or another and this in turn leads to a range of behaviours and activities that can be unhelpful. But most importantly, it leads to a powerful misconception and misdirects everyone's thinking about change and the dynamics of change. Individuals in organizations, whether senior managers or junior employees, have it in their heads that there will be resistance to change. In other words, they have developed mental models based on this view. These mental models are often so deeply embedded that people are not even aware that they are simply ideas or points of view. They are often mistaken for the reality of organizational life. Research has shown, too, that inappropriate mental models can be a major factor in creating organizational dysfunction and in damaging performance and threatening organizational survival. A false view of things is likely to lead to false and inappropriate actions to handle them.

It is worth noting that research into employee resistance to change found few major instances of true resistance. If change means job losses then for some employees this is a threatening development and could lead to opposition and determined resistance. Others may well look forward to a good redundancy package and a new job elsewhere. True, there may be opposition from those who have a vested interest in the *status quo* or the preservation of their empires, but how representative are they of the majority? There might be a lack of an enthusiastic response to the proposed changes – but this is not resistance as it has come to be understood.

Eric Dent and Susan Galloway Goldberg have suggested that the notion of resistance to change has its origin in the work of Kurt Lewin in the 1950s. Lewin models, which we shall discuss in a later section, refer to forces for and against change and the need to overcome barriers and weaken opposition, in order to move from one state to another. These encouraged the notion of individual psychological resistance, whereas Lewin conceived of change and any forces for or against as part of an organization-wide system composed of roles, practices, processes and behaviours. Dent and Goldberg (1999: 37–38) list a number of ways of thinking derived from the management literature on resistance to change that hinder our current understanding of change and change dynamics. These are as follows:

- Resistance may be due to the way a supervisor or other implemented the change – which they did so in such a way that they met resistance from subordinates. The blame for the resistance, however, is put upon the subordinates, whose reaction is not considered normal. As a result resistance has become a pejorative term which is attached to subordinates. 'The implicit assumption is that subordinate resistance is always inappropriate.'
- Prescriptions for overcoming resistance to change assume that the supervisors will carry them out and not the subordinates. It is assumed that the real issue at stake is the failure to change – and not the change itself.

- Prescriptions are given for preventing resistance, not for overcoming it should it arise. 'In other words, they all are strategies for preventing resistance in the first place, not for overcoming resistance once it has occurred. This difference would be like having a paper on measles vaccinations titled, "Overcoming an Outbreak of Measles".'
- Resistance to change is normal and should be expected. The danger here is that a manager responsible for a change intervention will assume there will be resistance and will act accordingly. (For example they may scheme ways to minimise the change or disguise it so that the grapevine is on fire with rumour and innuendo.) The result may be that his or her actions actually create resistance and thus it becomes a self-fulfilling prophecy.

As Dent and Goldberg point out, expecting that there will be resistance to any change along with the recommended strategies for dealing with any resistance do not provide a useful framework for dealing with any problems that may arise from introducing changes.

So have managers influenced by the literature and the perceived wisdom on change management mistaken hostility and lack of engagement for opposition and resistance? Does criticism of a proposed change amount to resistance? A process may be introduced and be accompanied by grumbling and complaints – but is this resistance? I would argue that these responses are *responses*. They are a human interaction and a human response to an environmental change. They are responding as complex adaptive systems. If the change appears to be to their advantage they will support it. If they are not sure they will want to know more and suspend judgement. If the proposed change is not to their advantage then they will try to find ways of turning it to their advantage. This is how complex adaptive systems behave. Further, the huge complex and complicated web of everyday activity is composed, even in a small organization, of the multiple and varied actions of many individual agents (employees). Each employee has their own individual, interconnected webs of responses and interactions. There are webs within webs. Any vibration, especially one that is perceived to be major, will trigger a response. How the action is perceived will influence and determine the nature of individual and collective responses. However, these will be unfolding alongside other vibrations in different webs that will all influence each other.

For example, if an individual is existing too close to chaos, because of an overload of challenging and novel situations in their family or social life then another novel and challenging event may push them into chaos and a stressed out response. Another person may be drifting towards equilibrium and a major change and the possibility of doing new and demanding things may prove inspirational and highly motivating. Managers do not have the complete picture of any individual's position on the edge of chaos. It is simply not possible for them to know this of one person let alone a complete team, a whole department or a large company. So how can they possibly predict whether the collective response will be one of resistance or enthusiasm? This perhaps sounds as if there is no way forward – but this is not the case. It just requires a very different kind of thinking about change. This thinking will emerge as you proceed through this chapter and the rest of this book.

Change models

There are many models on how to introduce change into an organization but in this section I intend to focus on three models which in my experience have been very influential and are standard fare on most change management courses. They are: Kurt Lewin's Force Field Analysis; Lewin's Freezing and Unfreezing Model; the Seven-S Framework Model.

Kurt Lewin's Force Field Analysis

Kurt Lewin's models have dominated change management teaching for many years and his Force Field Analysis is a useful and well-used tool. (See Figure 4.1.)

Lewin was a physicist who then became a psychologist and so we can understand his use of images drawn from physical science. Lewin held that an organization was held in balance or equilibrium between the forces which supported the *status quo* and those that were driving for change. Some force field diagrams show the line of equilibrium as a straight line but I have shown it as curved so that it shows more clearly the forces pushing one against another. If the forces stay the same then so does the position in which the organization finds itself. The longer and thicker the arrows then the stronger

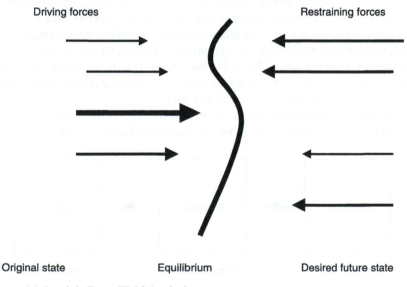

Driving forces   Restraining forces

Original state   Equilibrium   Desired future state

Figure 4.1 Lewin's Force Field Analysis.

the forces concerned. Managers can draw their own force field analysis and use it to determine the factors that are pushing for or against any proposed changes. They are then able to focus on how best to weaken the opposition and to improve the strength of their support. They may need to convince the finance team that a new move will make savings, or persuade the head of HR that proposed changes in working practices will benefit staff.

The model can be a useful tool as long as it is recognized that it is necessarily a simplification of any given situation. It is also a snapshot in time. Further, it inevitably only shows a simplified version of the complexity that is organizational dynamics. But it is for many managers a useful starting point. Finally, the notion that an organization should be kept at equilibrium is based on old ideas of the importance of stability. Equilibrium in complexity science terms is the equivalent of death. Managers would, in my view, be better advised to think of analysing those factors that will assist or hinder change developments in the context of achieving ongoing changes and not a static state. Also change is not pushed or pulled by 'forces', we are not talking of gravity here, but rather the complex, and sometimes volatile, dynamics of human interaction and response.

Lewin's Freezing and Unfreezing Model

Lewin's Freezing/Unfreezing Model is probably the best known model on change management in existence today. (See Figure 4.2.)

This model is very clearly based on a physical science analogy. A change process is here viewed as having three major stages. First of all, the organization needs to be 'unfrozen' from its stable state so that changes can be made. This is the first stage and it may involve training and preparing people for new roles. Some authors suggest using this time to identify and overcome resistance. Once stage one is complete then the unfreezing stage represents the implementation phase of the change process. During this stage all problems internal or external are addressed. Once stage two is complete then stage three comes into play. This is the freezing stage when the change is embedded in the organization and a new normality arises.

The main problem with this model is that it suggests that organizations or parts of them are static and can be moved neatly from one state to another

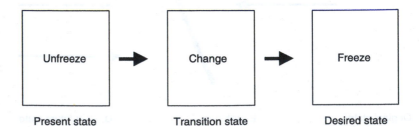

Present state   Transition state   Desired state

Figure 4.2 Kurt Lewin's Change Model.

with the right amount of planning and managerial skill. Again there is an assumption that equilibrium is a desirable state for an organization to be in. The freezing and unfreezing analogy is a powerful one. It captures the hard essence of the physical, non living world but not the complexity, unpredictability and volatility of living human beings interacting with each other. It reinforces mechanistic and top down approaches to change. Along with other models it also reinforces the notion popular amongst both managers and their staff that change has to be bedded down and everything returned to stability as soon as possible.

The Seven-S Framework Model

This model is used to analyse an organization and to suggest strategies for change. It was devised by Richard Pascale, Anthony Athos, Tom Peters and Robert Waterman as a tool that encouraged a holistic systems approach to strategy implementation. (See Figure 4.3.) It has subsequently been widely used by consultancy companies. The model is significantly different from Lewin's model for introducing change, particularly in its systemic approach, its recognition that there are 'soft' and 'hard' factors at play at any given time and that they are all interdependent.

The 'hard' factors are structure, strategy and systems. These can be identified and understood by studying mission statements, company plans, charts and other corporate documents. The 'soft' elements of the model are less easy to determine and are always changing. These include style, staff, skills and shared values.

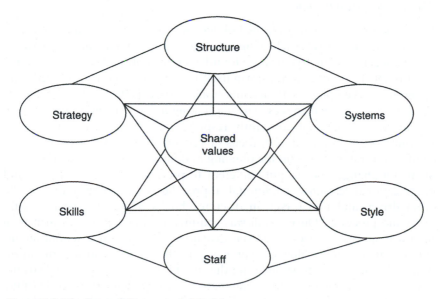

Figure 4.3 The Seven-S Framework Model.

The model has real value in ensuring that managers consider all these seven aspects of an organization in order to analyse and understand the need for change and to assist in its introduction. In my view it is less helpful when used with an emphasis on the accumulation of quantitative data and when the different elements are treated in a compartmentalized fashion.

The model itself shows each element of an organization that needs to be taken into account but it has a static feel to it. There are no arrows or shapes that would suggest flows or movements, or any hint or organizational dynamics. Further, in my view, it encourages and supports a top-down approach to strategic change.

There are many other models for change in the text books and the brochures of management consultants but most describe introducing change as some kind of linear process. The first stages will involve some kind of analysis or audit; then follows a vision or mission building stage which is then shared (in a top-down process); then the change is introduced; problems are dealt with; and the change monitored and embedded. If only it were that simple. What is also worrying about many models is the assumption that change may be stopped or started at will. If there is a problem, then the process will wait while it is fixed. This is the machine model again.

Old and new approaches to change – some comparisons

The management of change, in both theory and practice, has moved on in recent years, particularly with the emergence of the learning organization.

The learning organization

Interest has been growing over the last decade or so in the idea of the learning organization as a way of achieving ongoing organizational change. A learning organization is an organization founded on the notion that through learning it is able to adapt and transform itself in order to meet its own needs and the needs of its employees. Rich continuous learning is the key to this process. This approach to change sees learning linking individuals and groups in an organizational web that constantly responds, reacts and transforms itself. Learning organizations do not focus or rely on specific events to introduce changes but rather focus on the ongoing and underlying patterns and movements for change. This is quite different to previous notions of change and organizational learning. Traditional approaches to learning tended to be event driven and undertaken in discrete chunks related to specific skills, tasks and processes. Once a skill was acquired or a new process learnt then the learning was deemed to be over. Learning was not seen as a continuous, stimulating, enriching, flow of experience. In the modern learning organization attention is paid to stimulating the organization's capacity for learning and value is attached to the accumulated learning that arises. In learning organizations both single- and double-loop learning takes place. Employees are able to develop the skills of reflection and inquiry and are encouraged to develop new mental models and to become creative as well as adaptive.

Peter Senge played a leading role in developing the concept of the learning organization. In his view, traditional, controlling approaches were not adequate for dealing with the unpredictable nature of the modern world. He recommends lifelong learning for individuals; the creation of shared visions; learning in teams and systems thinking. Many organizations have been inspired by his model and have used it with varying degrees of success. There are obvious difficulties in trying to introduce new ideas into organizations, particularly if the existing frameworks are not supportive and if the under-pinning design principles are essentially hierarchical and linear.

Learning organizations tend to take an approach to strategic change that considers that the learning that takes place is as important as the achievement of strategic goals. Change is seen as a continuum with learning as a necessary and valuable part of the process. Thus change takes place as a result of the changes that arise in individuals and groups as they undergo different learning experiences. These in turn change the culture and behaviours of the organization. In this way an organization is changed from within, rather than as a response to external pressure or perceived threats from outside. Some writers contend that a learning organization learns most effectively and creatively when it is going through a period of major upheaval or drastic change. This fits well with the notion that creativity flourishes at the edge of chaos.

Traditional views of change versus modern views of change

Figure 4.4 illustrates the main characteristics which define and describe traditional and modern views of change and the nature of change in organizations. Traditionally change within an organizational context is seen as a linear, step by step, sequential process that has to be implemented in a careful and controlling fashion if certain objectives are to be achieved. Change is viewed as an event that is deliberately planned for in a cause and effect manner. If management decides to introduce changes then once they have taken place and have become embedded in organizational thinking and routines, then everything is expected to return to 'normal'. 'Normal' is considered the desired state for an organization to be in. Given that a primary goal of the organization is to create a stable environment in which the business can flourish, then any unexpected changes in the outside world, or any unplanned ones within, are viewed as disruptive and sometimes even abnormal. In some circumstances they may even be viewed as calamitous.

Newer, more modern views of change challenge traditional views which are rooted in classical science and its mechanistic notions of the world. These more recent views consider change as a normal occurrence that should happen continuously in organizations. Change whether part of the constant flow or a 'peak' in the flow offers opportunities for learning and creativity.

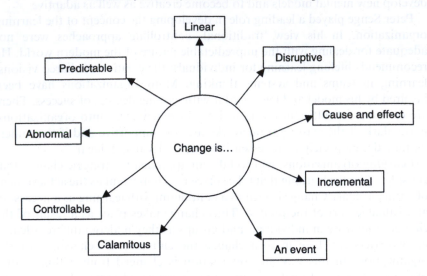

Traditional, classical, mechanistic views of change

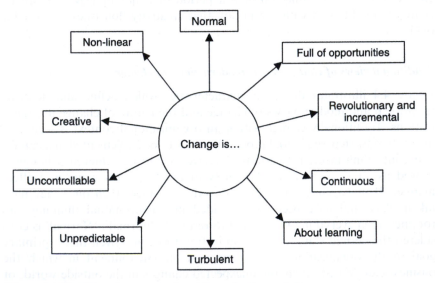

New, modern, dynamic views of change

Figure 4.4 Traditional versus modern dynamic views of change.

Source: Adapted from McMillan (2004: 67).

Managers have long abandoned any notions that change can be planned and controlled in a predictable way. Change is not about driving towards a specific business destination, it is about the way an organization exists. Managers, when they ponder specific initiatives or innovations, recognize that changes may be incremental or revolutionary and that both kinds are needed for the healthy development of the organization.

Most managers have views on change that are a blend of the traditional and the modern. The newer, more radical views on change reflect influences from more modern science, specifically quantum physics and complexity science.

Strategy and strategic change

The word 'strategy' is derived from the Greek word 'strategia', which means 'generalship', or the art of war. In its original sense, the term refers to the management of an army in such as way as to fight an enemy on preferred conditions to create and sustain an advantage. The contextual setting of management is different, but the battlefield analogy has powerful resonances in many organizations. Just like any general in ancient times the modern manager wants to hold onto his or her territory and the riches collected and maybe even find fresh fields to conquer. Generals and managers both need strategies and tactics to give them an edge over rivals in environments where information may be variable and incomplete and where there is great uncertainty as to outcomes. In management, strategy is concerned primarily with how organizations create and sustain competitive economic advantage over time. Strategic thinking has been refined to reflect specific challenges faced by organizations and for managers performance has replaced territorial gain as the desired return. A successful strategy is generally considered to be one that consistently delivers better returns than competitors in such a way as to assure the long-term survival of the organization. But how do managers set about making that objective a reality? How well do long term aims and strategic level plans unfold in reality?

Planned and deliberate strategy – Mintzberg and Waters

Henry Mintzberg and James Waters spent over ten years researching how strategy and the strategic process took place in organizations. They were particularly interested in the relationship between the planning process and strategic intentions and what actually happened when these were implemented. They defined strategy as 'a pattern in a stream of decisions' (Mintzberg and Waters 1989: 4) and identify these 'streams' in order to investigate and explore the relationship between top-level planning and intentions and what organizations actually did. The planning part of the process they referred to as the 'intended' part of the overall process and 'realized' referred to what actually happened when the strategy was put into place. They further described strategies as either 'deliberate' or 'emergent'. The 'deliberate' strategy was one that unfolded in the way it was planned or intended, whereas the 'emergent' strategy was one which arose in spite of, or in the absence of, prior intention. Thus they identified a range of approaches to strategic change each of which embodied different degrees of either deliberate or emergent aspects. Table 4.1 is taken from Eccles (1993) and shows the different types of strategies observed by Mintzberg and Waters and their tendencies towards 'emergent' or 'deliberate'.

Table 4.1 does not include the eighth form of strategy: imposed strategy. This is because in Eccles' view as it was a strategy imposed from outside the organization and therefore not the organization's own. Mintzberg and Waters found that deliberate strategies were more widespread than any other form, but truly deliberate strategies were rare because they relied on predictability and order. Most real world strategies, they contended, fell somewhere along a continuum between deliberate and emergent.

The planned strategy relies on authority, detailed planning and strong control mechanisms. This approach to strategic change show the influence of classical science and its acolyte, scientific management. An entrepreneurial approach exists where one person is in control and this approach is most commonly found in entrepreneurial organizations. The planned and the entrepreneurial strategies are created at the centre of the organization and everyone has to subscribe to their vision of the future. In an organization that has an ideological approach this vision is shared by everyone and is often rooted in past traditions. The umbrella strategy does not seek to so tightly control people and deliberately creates the conditions for strategies to emerge. Here managers realize that it is more effective to respond to events rather than to try to control and direct them. The process strategy is similar to the umbrella strategy in that top management directs the strategy making process while leaving the content to others. The disconnected or unconnected strategy is found where managers implement strategies in their own departments or divisions without reference to any central or unifying strategic plan.

The consensus strategy is not driven by top management but rather arises out of a host of individual actions. It is a strategy which has evolved from learning. This is a fundamental difference between emergent and deliberate strategies. Deliberate strategies are primarily about setting direction and controlling everything in order to achieve stated objectives and learning is not a

Table 4.1 Deliberate and emergent strategies

Strategy type	Deliberate or emergent
Planned	Highly deliberate
Entrepreneurial	Relatively deliberate but can emerge too
Ideological	Rather deliberate
Umbrella	Partly deliberate, partly emergent (deliberately emergent)
Process	Partly deliberate, partly emergent and (deliberately emergent)
Disconnected	Can be deliberate for those who make them
Consensus	Rather emergent

Source: Adapted from Eccles (1993).

stated objective or a recognized outcome. This approach can be so focused that important environmental changes are ignored or unappreciated and very little is done to adapt to a changing world. Emergent strategy, on the other hand, is receptive to environmental changes and the notion of learning is viewed as strategically important. As Mintzberg and Waters wrote: 'Emergent strategy itself implies that learning works' (1989: 17); and 'Openness to such emergent strategy enables management to act before everything is fully understood – to respond to an evolving reality rather than having to focus on a stable fantasy' (1989: 18).

The idea that managers and organizations can learn from their strategic actions resonates with learning organization concepts and our understanding of complex adaptive systems. The idea of strategy and strategic planning as a learning process is an important one. It signifies a move away from the more deliberate strategies with their focus on centralized, hierarchical, top-down approaches towards the more emergent strategies which recognize that organizations are not machines but living systems.

Mintzberg and Waters point out that strategic activity in most organizations has aspects of both' deliberateness' and 'emergentness' and they conclude that organizations need both. Employees need to know which direction they are going in so that they can begin their journey and at the same time they have to be able to respond and react to events as they unfold. There are echoes here of the edge of chaos and the need to 'dance' successfully between formal and informal systems.

Mintzberg and Waters use the term 'emergence' in the sense that something unplanned and unintended arises, but not in the sense that something greater than the sum of the parts arises.

Logical incrementalism – Quinn

James Quinn (1989) considers that change is introduced into organizations not by the use of standard changes prescribed by text books and long range planning techniques but in a step-by-step way, which he describes as 'logical incrementalism'. This notion of change being introduced on a step-by-step basis reflects the influence of the Darwinian concept of gradual evolution. It is now known, however, that changes also occurred in unexpected and massive shifts. The punctuated equilibrium model of organizational change accords with this more recent view. It considers the build up of inertia which over time leads to tension between the organization and its environment which then provokes a crisis and a rapid response. From a complexity perspective punctuated equilibrium is explained by the large and small changes that arise from the adaptive actions and interactions of complex adaptive systems or individuals who together create organizations.

Quinn believes that managers actively work to successfully bring about change in a number of ways. These include:

1   Creating awareness and commitment on a step-by-step basis. This is done through the development of informal networks; the testing of ideas; building awareness and support for change ideas; high-level tactical shifts; widening political support; and overcoming opposition. (This pattern of activity is very much a blend of traditional, top-down approaches with more participative ones.)

2   Any progress that is made is embedded or solidified. This is brought about by gaining commitment from different groups; focusing; managing alliances; supporting champions; integration of key processes; identifying, measuring and rewarding. (These approaches are highly resonant with political, even militaristic approaches to change. Note too the need to solidify any changes. This reminds us of Lewin's freezing and unfreezing model and his force field analysis tool.)

Quinn emphasizes the importance of logic and the use of control when introducing change which should be carried out via small, step-by-step activities. He suggests that managers wait until they have everything in place if they want to be successful in bringing about change. This assumes, of course, that the world will stand still and wait while they put things in place. This ignores the dynamic nature of organizations and their many environments.

Schools of strategy

Henry Mintzberg, Bruce Ahlstrand and Joseph Lampel chart the development of strategy and strategic activity over the last century in their extremely readable and helpful book, *The Strategy Safari* (1998). In it they succeed in pulling together the many different strands of strategic thinking into ten different schools of thought. (See Table 4.2.)

The ten schools which are listed can all be found in the literature on

Table 4.2 Schools of strategy

Nature of school	School	How strategy is formed
Prescriptive	Design	Via a process of conception
	Planning	Via a formal process
	Positioning	Via an analytical process
Descriptive	Entrepreneurial	Via a visioning process
	Cognitive	Via a mental process
	Learning	Via an emergent process
	Power	Via a process of negotiation
	Cultural	Via a collective process
	Environmental	Via a reactive process
Integrative	Configuration	Via a process of transformation

Source: Adapted from Mintzberg, Ahlstrand and Lampel (1998).

strategic management. Some of them have been extremely influential and have now declined and others are still developing. The schools fall into three main categories: prescriptive, descriptive and integrative. The prescriptive schools focus on the process of how strategy is formulated and the emphasis is on planning and then a separate implementation process. These schools approach strategy from a perspective that is strongly influenced by classical science and scientific management. The six descriptive schools are so called because they are not focused on prescribing how strategy should be formulated but rather in describing how strategy takes place. The configuration school is described as integrative in nature. Mintzberg *et al.* describe it as integrative because it seeks to bring together all the different aspects of the strategy making and delivery process.

Table 4.3 shows some of the key features of the different schools. *The Strategy Safari* provides an extremely comprehensive table of the many attributes of each school but I have selected those which I consider most pertinent to our considerations of strategic change. Note the difference between the intended messages and those that were in fact realized and relate it to the approach to change that was used. These then map onto the type of organization which uses this approach and the key individual or individuals associated with, or even driving, the strategic changes. It is clear from this that in the majority of schools/organization types strategic change is a top-down exercise. Note too, that six of the organizations identified are machine types or with strong machine aspects.

Carlisle and McMillan

In our paper 'Thinking differently about strategy: comparing paradigms' my colleague, Ysanne Carlisle, and I wrote that we considered that many existing theories on strategy did not adequately deal with the challenges managers face today. In our view, much of this is due to the influence of the Newtonian–Cartesian mindset and consequent views of reality. Three major content-based theories of strategy arose during that second half of the last century. Each sought to offer an effective approach for managers. The strategy–structure–performance model based on the work of Alfred Chandler was prominent during the 1960s and 1970s. This was followed in the 1980s by the market-product positioning theories of Michael Porter. In the mid 1980s, the resource-based view emerged and during the 1990s it overtook the market-product positioning perspective to become the dominant strategic theory. Each of these theories assumed economic rationality, linear causality, and stable conditions. It is clear that all were developed under the influence of classical, Newtonian science.

As we reflected on the development of strategy and strategic studies Dr Carlisle and I concluded that there had been in the past too detailed a focus on material systems and rational logical processes at the expense of human dynamics. The prescriptive schools, for example, with their focus on

Table 4.3 Schools of strategy – different aspects

School	Intended message	Realized message	Approach to change	Central actor/s	Organization type
Design	Fit	Think	Occasional, quantum	Chief executive	Machine (centralized, formalized)
Planning	Formalize	Program	Periodic, incremental	Planners	Large machine (centralized, formalized, divisionalized)
Positioning	Analyze	Calculate	Piecemeal, frequent	Analysts	Large machine (centralized, formalized, divisionalized) global
Entrepreneurial	Envision	Centralize (then hope)	Occasional, opportunistic, revolutionary	Leader	Entrepreneurial (simple, centralized)
Cognitive	Frame	Worry or imagine	Infrequent	Mind	Any
Learning	Learn	Play (rather than pursue)	Continual, incremental and occasional quantum insight	Learners (anyone who can)	Adhocracy, also professional (de-centralized)
Power	Grab	Hoard (rather than share)	Frequent, piecemeal	Anyone with power (micro) whole organization. (macro)	Any, especially adhocracy and professional (micro) closed machine or networked adhocracy (macro)
Cultural	Coalesce	Perpetuate (rather than change)	Infrequent	Collectively	Missionary, also stagnant machine
Environmental	Cope	Capitulate (rather than confront)	Rare and quantum	'Environment'	Machine (obedient)
Configuration	Integrate, transform	Lump, revolutionize (rather than nuance, adapt)	Occasional and revolutionary, sometimes incremental	Any to the left, in context (CEO especially in transformation)	Any to left, preferably adhocracy and missionary for transformation

Source: Adapted from Mintzberg, Ahlstrand and Lampel (1998).

formulation, planning and then a separate implementation process did not consider the human dynamics of an organization and did not seek to integrate them into strategic thinking in a coherent and thoughtful way. They did not properly recognize that the unfurling of strategic intent does not take place in an unresponsive vacuum. Thus they gave insufficient consideration to the role of feedback and reverberation across the human web of the organization and tended to neglect the importance of individual organizational members as contributors to the strategy making process. Strategy and strategic analysis is of necessity a multidisciplinary pursuit and prescriptions based too heavily upon economic and financial considerations overlook the salience of other potentially significant factors.

If we consider organizations as complex adaptive systems then there is the potential to think quite differently about how they change and adapt. From such a perspective we recognize that they have the potential to change and adapt by virtue of the ability of everyone within the organization, as individual complex adaptive systems, to explore and interpret their experiences. This learning, provided it is not impeded or unrecognized, can contribute to the collective knowledge and intelligence of an enterprise. Our understanding of complex systems suggests that organizations are in reality created by individual actors as they respond, react and learn from their on going experiences. It is these dynamical human learning systems which offer better strategic possibilities for long-term sustainability than short-term, rationalistic approaches.

If we think of strategy as a learning process and combine it with a complexity perspective then we create a new approach to strategy. This blends with aspects of learning organization theories and builds upon the current thinking of the learning school of strategy. It offers radical possibilities if one considers the human dynamics of complex adaptive systems as vehicles for shared learning and emergent strategy development.

Human beings are affected by internal biological and neuropsychological processes as well as external environmental and social factors (Cooksey and Gates 1995). This goes some way to explaining why it is not possible to predict how any one individual will behave over time and why efforts to control and manipulate human dynamics in an organization are not feasible. Thus, in our view, a focus on strategy as process, and as a complex, non-linear learning process reflects the reality of human dynamics and offers a more realistic and helpful way of thinking about change.

Key questions

- How does transforming change differ from other types of organizational change?
- What factors and attitudes lead to change initiatives within organizations?
- How widespread is resistance to change and how does it arise?
- What are the strengths and weaknesses of Lewin's models?

- What are the key differences between traditional notions of change and modern dynamic views of change?
- In what ways do managers create strategy?
- How well do strategic plans unfold in reality and how well do they consider the human dynamics of an organization?

5 Complexity in practice: doing things differently

Key points

- Applying complexity: some significant publications
- Doing things differently: definitions and the transformation of Japanese companies
- Managing without control: Semco and Oticon
- Using the butterfly effect, strange attractors, the edge of chaos: 3M, BPX and other companies
- SENCORP and fractal management
- Using self-organizing principles and self-organizing leadership
- Complex adaptive organizations: St Luke's, Sears, W.L. Gore and others

Applying complexity

Some years ago a large number of writers and scholars argued that there was very little firm evidence that concepts from complexity science could be usefully applied in organizations other than metaphorically. Furthermore, one study claimed that there was no properly validated evidence to support the notion that complexity ideas when used in organizations were as effective as claimed. It is difficult gathering evidence from large, complex organizations, but there was plenty of evidence from studies of small firms to dispute these assertions, and it was pointed out by Ted Fuller and Paul Moran (2000) that small businesses have many of the characteristics of complex adaptive systems.

Further evidence that ideas derived from complexity science could be usefully applied in organizations was also provided by Stewart *et al.* (2000), who carried out research on three different organizations, using a model derived from complexity which they called the 'Conditioned Emergence' model. The organizations they studied included a Scottish bakery, the Scottish Advisory Health Service and the Estates and Building Division of the University of Glasgow. As Stewart *et al.* wrote: 'In applying complexity theory within live organisational research, we feel our experience has demonstrated that such concepts are of critical value in helping those organisations involved in transformation efforts, to secure lasting business benefit' (2000: 474).

It takes time to carry out proper research studies on organizations, especially if they are large ones, but slowly the evidence has been building up and the last few years or so have seen a significant change in this situation. Research papers have appeared in growing numbers in prestigious academic journals, new books have appeared and increasing numbers of students are studying the application of complexity in business and management at graduate and postgraduate level. In this section I list just a few of the publications which have contributed to this gradual change. The list includes books and articles which are written primarily for practising managers, as well as those which are aimed at management students and an academic audience. (Full publication details are given in the Bibliography.)

Journal papers

Allen, P.M. (2001) 'A Complex Systems Approach to Learning in Adaptive Networks'.
Anderson, P. (1999) 'Complexity Theory and Organization Science'.
Berreby, D. (1996) 'Between Chaos and Order: What Complexity Theory Can Teach Business'.
Knowles, R.N. (2001) 'Self-Organizing Leadership: A Way of Seeing What Is Happening in Organizations and a Pathway to Coherence'.
Levy, D. (1994) 'Chaos Theory and Strategy: Theory, Application and Managerial Implications'.
Macintosh, R. and Maclean, D. (1999) 'Conditioned Emergence: A Dissipative Structures Approach to Transformation'.
McKelvey, B. (1999) 'Avoiding Complexity Catastrophe in Coevolutionary Pockets: Strategies for Rugged Landscapes'.
Nonaka, I. (1988) 'Creating Organizational Order out of Chaos: Self renewal in Japanese Firms'.
Pascale, R.T. (1999) 'Surfing the Edge of Chaos'.
Stacey, R.D. (1993) 'Strategy as Order Emerging from Chaos'.
Stacey, R.D. (1995) 'The Science of Complexity: An Alternative Perspective for Strategic Change Processes'.
Stacey, R.D. (2003) 'Learning as an Activity of Interdependent People'.
Styhre, A. (2002) 'Non-linear Change in Organizations: Organization Change Management Informed by Complexity Theory'.
Tetenbaum, T.J. (1998) 'Shifting Paradigms: from Newton to Chaos'.

Books

Brown, S.L. and Eisenhardt, K.M. (1998) *Competing on the Edge. Strategy as Structured Chaos.*
Clippinger, J.H. III (ed.) (1999) *The Biology of Business.*
Knowles, R.N. (2002) *The Leadership Dance: Pathways to Extraordinary Organizational Effectiveness.*
Lewin, R. and Regine, B. (1999) *The Soul at Work.*
McMillan, E. (2004) *Complexity, Organizations and Change.*
Pascale, R.T., Millemann, M. and Gioja, L. (2000) *Surfing the Edge of Chaos.*

Sanders, T.I. (1998) *Strategic Thinking and the New Science*.
Stacey, R.D. (1996) *Strategic Management and Organisational Dynamics*.
Stacey, R.D., Griffin, D. and Shaw, P. (2000) *Complexity and Management. Fad or Radical Challenge to Systems Thinking?*
Wheatley, M. (1994) *Leadership and the New Science*.

In the sections that follow in this chapter I shall refer to a number of these authors and their work in order to provide descriptive frameworks for activity and thinking, for real-life examples of application and for illustrative case studies.

Doing things differently

Chapter 4 was about change, the nature of change, attitudes and approaches to organizational change and exploration of the possibility of thinking differently about change. This chapter is about acting differently and introducing change using complexity-based principles. If management is to act differently then first it has to think differently about organizations and management, and complexity science offers this possibility. As I pointed out earlier the idea of the organization as some sort of machine or quasi-machine is still very prevalent amongst managers, who tend to act in accordance with their perceptions and beliefs. Complexity science tells us that organizations are created by the many and varied activities of the people within them. So if we remove the machine or quasi-machine model how do we describe and define organizations from a complexity science perspective? Here is a list of suggestions.

Organizations are:

- Dynamical living human systems and responsive and fluid structures as individuals come and go over different time scales.
- Interdependent complex webs of human interactions and responses.
- Repositories of collective memories and shared experiences all understood and perceived from unique individual perspectives.
- Created of ebbs and flows of complex patterns of thoughts, emotions and behaviours. These are influenced, encouraged and/or impeded by the interactions and responses of others within and without the organization.
- Situated in, and part of, a constantly evolving external 'landscape' that offers both opportunities and threats and is unpredictable over the long term. This 'landscape' is composed of many elements, e.g. economic, social, technological, political and ecological, at close/personal, local, national and global levels.
- Paradoxical in nature as they seek stability, security and familiar things, but also excitement, novelty and risk. This manifests itself in long established routines, deeply ingrained cultures and attachments to the past, and in challenges to the *status quo*, risky innovations and leaps into the unknown.

- At risk and their survival jeopardized when they are too stable, too inflexible, over-dependent on long-established routines, fail to reflect, share and acknowledge learning experiences and are too deeply attached to the past.
- At risk when they fail to value, acknowledge and make 'business/strategic' use of the individual and collective experiences of employees at all levels.
- At risk when their structures, processes, values and norms reduce the ability to learn and adapt, sometimes spontaneously, to changes in their landscape.
- Intelligent, able to reflect on the past and create visions of possible futures via their human co-creators.
- Unpredictable over the long term and their survival cannot be guaranteed.
- Not amenable to control which when employed leads to a range of disengaging and avoidance activities by those not wishing to be so manipulated.
- Complex adaptive systems which are able to exist on the 'edge of chaos' when not inhibited by mechanistic mindsets and the machine model of organization.

By thinking of organizations in this way managers can think and act differently and start to transform organizations by developing a better understanding of their real structure and their internal human dynamics. Further, a manager who views his or her organization from a complexity perspective acknowledges the shared nature of all human experience.

A complexity perspective on organizational change focuses on process and dynamics and acknowledges the uncertainty, unpredictability and the paradoxical nature of life in today's organizations. A manager considering change from a complexity standpoint will realize that it is pointless to attempt to control all the key variables in a given situation and will instead focus on what it is possible to know and understand. Critically, he or she will need to reflect at length on how they may best engage with the human dynamics of the organization and all their many intricacies and nuances.

In his 2002 paper 'Non-linear Change in Organizations: Organization Change Management Informed by Complexity Theory', Alexander Styhre considers the value of a complexity theory approach to change management and compares it with Lewin's freezing and unfreezing model and rational linear approaches.

Case study vignette

Styhre's case study is an organizational change programme in the Alpha factory of a Swedish telecoms company, TelCo. The company wanted to empower its workers in order to improve production and also to attract and recruit, on the basis of an enhanced reputation, young highly skilled staff. The process was planned in a rational way and the first steps in the programme took place more or less as anticipated. The working environment at the factory was greatly improved and free fruit was provided for everyone in the company cafeteria, as an egalitarian gesture. The workers were involved in training courses as part of their preparation for future changes (unfreezing). Some workers had been sceptical but they were soon impressed by the commitment shown by their senior management. A planned expansion of the workforce began and new workers started arriving.

But this progress was soon disrupted by external events which could not possibly have been predicted when the programme commenced. First of all, there were problems in firming up the technical specifications for a new product to be made at the Alpha factory. Second, the terrorist attack on the World Trade Center caused a minor recession in the telecoms market and an unexpected lack of interest in the company's products.

As a result of these unexpected happenings the company had to completely change its plans, newly recruited workers had to be laid off and production priorities changed.

Styre concludes that:

> an analysis of organization change activities based on a complexity theory framework recognizes the ruptures and breaks, points of bifurcation, flows of energy and information, and so forth, that constitute, enable, or inhibit organization change. In this view, organization change is never solely a one-dimensional series of succeeding activities, but it always taking place amidst the turmoil of transient states and interconnected flows of activities.
>
> (Styhre 2002: 349)

In many organizations the human resources management function will need to be involved in a supporting role in any organizational change endeavour as managers engage with the human dynamics. It has been noted however, by Ray Cooksey and G. Richard Gates (1995) in their paper, 'HRM: A Management Science in Need of Discipline', that some HRM departments are very reliant on formal processes and systems which are mechanistic in origin and non-linear in design. These do not map well onto the reality of human behaviours. These include, for example, theories and approaches to job descriptions, job evaluation, employee motivation and work performance. Thus they are not able to support effectively the human dimension of change. Another concern is that many HRM managers actively seek to fine tune and manage an employee's performance so that it attains a steady state. This is patently not possible but still many managers cling to this belief. In considering a complexity approach to organizational change managers may need to engage the support of the HRM team in putting into place supportive and dynamic learning processes. It is vital that there is a meeting of minds over this.

Nonaka and the transformation of Japanese companies

One of the first important studies on organizational transformation using concepts derived from complexity, or in this instance, chaos theory, was provided by Ikujiro Nonaka. Nonaka drew on his knowledge of Ilya Prigogine's work on dissipative structures and the emergence of order out of chaos and his observations on how Japanese companies had transformed themselves. In his 1988 paper, 'Creating Organizational Order out of Chaos: Self-renewal in Japanese Firms', he describes how an understanding of chaos theory could be used to create disorder and instability in order to bring about major changes. An organization using this approach would generate internal chaos that was linked to its external environment.

Nonaka proposes the following actions to encourage transforming change via the creation of chaos:

1　Strategic ambiguity and creativity. To do this management needs to develop a strategic vision of the future that is unclear and ambiguous. Such a vision would suggest a broad direction but offer lots of scope for varying interpretations. This would encourage creativity and a range of responses, and thus the opportunity for people to engage with the strategic vision in their own way. This should lead to enthusiasm and energy directed towards solving the ambiguities and creating a new future. Experimentation should also be encouraged.
2　New information and new technologies. New information should constantly be introduced into the organization as should new technologies. These would create fluctuations that would disturb the *status quo*.
3　Movement and dialogue. Managers should aim to encourage movement between areas and roles, involving all employees in discussions and dialogue throughout the organization regardless of status.
4　Amplification of fluctuation. This process would seek to stimulate the creative activities of employees by the creation of a crisis. This is a dangerous strategy: it could lead to the emergence of new ideas and approaches to solve the crisis, but in some cases it may lead to the organization's disappearance. Nonaka refers to a manager from Honda who likens such an approach to putting the people on the second floor and telling them to jump, or else. (This seems to be pushing the concept to an unacceptable extreme. Would it work successfully in other countries?)
5　Encouraging lively cooperation between employees. This should help in problem solving. It would do this by creating processes that encourage people to change their point of view and when this happens dynamic co-operation can emerge.

6   The use of self-organizing teams. This is the key to encouraging co-operation and the exchange and collection of information and a consequent accumulation of knowledge and relevant learning. These teams would need to be protected by senior management.

When you read the case study on the Open University in the next chapter you will find that several aspects of Nonaka's recommendations were introduced into the organization. These included the introduction of new information and information flows; discussions and dialogues between employees from different roles from all across the organization; and the setting up of self-organizing teams. Significantly the University did not create a crisis or push people towards the edge – but many perceived that substantial external changes were pushing the institution towards a crisis.

Managing without control

A world without control is a world in chaos – or is it? Chaos in the scientific sense is not as disorderly as one might expect. There is structure and order even within the chaos zone. This is created by non-linear structures and patterning. These may be irregular patterns of behaviour but they share recognizable similarities. This is not the neat tidy order of a linear process but it is order nevertheless. Further, when a phenomenon is undergoing a transition then it will appear to be chaotic and disorderly. The reality is, however, that it is undergoing a renewal process and apparent chaos is a vital part of that process. The natural living world was once thought to be disorderly primarily because of its non-linear and unpredictable nature, but it is now recognized that it is inherently ordered, though not in accordance with classical science's notions of order. These notions have major implications for the way we view change and our understanding of order and disorder. We can no longer look in horror at the natural world and its apparent chaos as a justification for our controlling activities.

The short example which follows concerns the Park Service in the USA and their management of Yellowstone National Park. It is a classic example of what can happen when we impose human notions of control and our need for a stable state of affairs upon the natural order of things.

Case study vignette

For more than a century, the Park Service had maintained equilibrium in the forest by quickly extinguishing fires, denying the natural rhythm of fire and re-growth whereby forests cleanse and renew themselves.

In theory, the Park Service allowed fires to burn if they did not threaten people at campsites or hotels. In fact, because fires can so

> easily get out of control (and always attract bad press), they were
> extinguished as quickly as possible.
>   As a result, a thicker-than-normal layer of deadfall and debris
> had built up on the forest floor. The 1988 lightning strikes created
> multiple fires. A prolonged drought during the preceding months
> and ill-timed winds then conspired to incinerate the forest with
> intensity and velocity that are rarely witnessed in North America.
> The conflagration destroyed large trees and charred the living com-
> ponents of topsoil that would otherwise have survived.
>
> (Pascale *et al.* 2000: 20)

As a consequence of their desire to control the forest, and its fires, the
Park Service's actions eradicated approximately 25 per cent of Yellowstone
National Park's forests. As Pascale and his co-authors point out, what applies
to the living world of the forests can also apply to the business world. The use
of control in order to achieve stability can unwittingly lead to disaster.

In her book *Leadership and the New Science* (1994), Margaret Wheatley
makes a very important distinction between our notions of order and our
notions of control in organizations. In her view we have confused control
with order. This is a very significant observation. Wheatley describes how
organizations have focused on controlling structures and processes in order
to create some kind of control over human activities. Also buildings and
other physical structures have been designed with control in mind. Organizations are designed and operated using detailed plans, complex organization
charts, job descriptions, complex procedures and so on. Managers and entrepreneurs have been encouraged to do this by a heavy emphasis in management literature and practice on the need to install controlling functions in
order to control people and be successful. In Wheatley's view management's
search for control has been as destructive as Lenin's controlling political
processes. If organizations were machines, then operating them and controlling them like machines would make sense, but they are not machines and
such a mindset is totally counterproductive. Wheatley suggests that managers
look around them and study the natural world closely then they would
see the inherent orderliness that exists all around them and discover new ways
of working.

One person who introduced a completely new way of working that
removed existing management controls and sought the creation of a new kind
of order was Ricardo Semler.

Case study vignette

When Ricardo Semler took over the family firm it was on the brink of
collapse. His radical, transforming approaches to business have made it

a hugely successful company. The title of his paper 'Managing With-out Managers' (1989) encapsulates the non-controlling nature of his approach. Semco is a Brazilian company and thus exists in an environ-ment where business paternalism and business fiefdoms flourish. It is not a world that would readily welcome a management style that created employee democracy or equality for women workers. In Semco, when Ricardo took over, employees where given considerable responsi-bilities, access to company information, including financial informa-tion, involved in major decision-making processes and treated with trust.

Semler writes in his book *Maverick!*

> When I took over Semco from my father 12 years ago, it was a tra-ditional company in every respect, with a pyramidal structure and a rule for every contingency. But today, our factory workers some-times set their own production quotas and even come in on their own time to meet them, without prodding from management or overtime pay. They help re-design the products they make and for-mulate the marketing plans. Their bosses, for their part, can run our business units with extraordinary freedom, determining business strategy without interference from the top brass. They even set their own salaries, with no strings. Then again everyone will know what they are, since all financial information at Semco is openly dis-cussed. Indeed, our workers have unlimited access to our books . . .
>
> For truly big decisions, such as buying another company, every-one at Semco gets a vote. A few years ago, when we wanted to relocate a factory, we closed down for a day and everyone piled into buses to inspect three possible new sites. Then the workers decided. Their choice hardly thrilled us . . . we moved in anyway.
>
> (Semler 1994: 1–2)

I shall refer again in this chapter to Ricardo Semler and his radical trans-formation of Semco for it maps onto a complexity approach to management and illustrates the many possibilities open to managers when they manage in this way.

The next case study which follows is about a European company which was privately owned. In this case a new CEO was brought in to make radical changes.

Case study vignette

The Danish company Oticon is one organization which was prepared to experiment with notions of order and control. The company which manufactures hearing aids and provides hearing care was founded in 1904. Today it is one of the market leaders in its field. In the late 1980s it was struggling to survive and a new chief executive, Lars Kolind, was brought in to make improvements and to put the company back on its feet. Kolind made a number of valuable changes but the company still faced fierce competition from larger companies like Siemens and Philips. Kolind decided that if Oticon was to prosper then he had to make some substantial changes. In 1990 Kolind 'disorganized' the company. He dismantled the strongly established, old formal organization which was composed of a complicated hierarchical structure with many controlling layers and separate functions. This was replaced by people working in self-managed project teams. The new structure was described as a 'spaghetti' organization. The term succinctly describes the complexity and informality of the new order.

A few years later Kolind decided to disorganize again. He had noticed that the company was returning to former behaviours and that departmental structures more reminiscent of the old order were emerging. This time he created disorder in the company by physically moving the project teams around the company's buildings and disturbing everyone. Kolind deliberately created 'chaos' and destroyed the old controlling structures and mechanisms so that the company would renew itself and survive.

For a detailed description, analysis and critique of the Oticon story I refer you to papers by Nicolai Foss (2000) 'Internal Disaggregation in Oticon: Interpreting and Learning from the Rise and Decline of the Spaghetti Organization' and Henrik Holt Larsen (2002) 'Career Management in Non-Hierarchically Structured Organizations'.

So if managers do not focus on control as necessary to achieve change and other important objectives, how are they to proceed?

- Managers should recognize that it is impossible to control the unexpected and disorderly and that to attempt to do so is to waste energy and resources.
- Managers should recognize that the future is unpredictable over the long term and therefore future outputs and outcomes cannot be controlled in the longer term.
- Managers should try to understand the unpredictable and the unexpected.
- To do this they should look for patterns, flows of similarities, fractals and seek for evidence of strange attractors.
- Order and disorder should be viewed as something that at times should be encouraged and created as out of the apparent turmoil a new order will emerge.
- Organizational disturbances, although uncomfortable, stressful and

sometimes painful may be part of a major transition process that the organization needs.

- Managers must learn to work with disorder and not against it. Like captains of a ship in a storm they must learn to ride the waves, to flow with the ocean currents and the winds that blow – and to use them to come safely into port. The ship's captain that tries to control the elements and resist their force would surely be deemed incapable or even mad – so why do managers try to sail their 'ships' in such a fashion?

Instability equals order. The new stability is instability. These strange and paradoxical notions of order and stability are further explained when one considers the webs of order created by strange attractors and looks for the calm of non-linear patterns rather than linear sequences.

(McMillan 2004: 86)

The butterfly effect

Small changes can make a real difference in our lives and have the potential over time to make massive differences. Small events can lead to the most unexpected outcomes. The case study which follows is a brilliant example of the principles of the butterfly effect at work in society.

Case study vignette

One evening in December 1955 in Montgomery, Alabama, Rosa Parks, a black woman, refused to give up her seat on a bus to a white man. The bus segregation laws strictly separated black and white citizens. Although black people made up the majority of those who rode on the buses they were severely restricted on where they could sit and in some circumstances were required to get off the bus and give their place to a white person. Mrs Parks was arrested, charged with breaking the law, fined and made to pay the court costs. She had been thrown off a bus previously but on this occasion she felt that she could no longer tolerate such an inhuman and degrading system.

Mrs Parks' action and her subsequent treatment by the authorities led to a boycott of the buses that lasted for over a year. Her courage and the stand she took made the national headlines and brought to the nation's attention the plight of black people in Alabama and elsewhere. Further, it gave national and international recognition to Martin Luther King, the young minister who led the Montgomery organization formed by black people to fight for their human rights. This led to the emergence of a national civil rights movement which campaigned for decades to achieve racial equality in the USA.

The story of Rosa Parks is one of many that illustrates the potential of the butterfly effect to make substantial changes in people's lives. It is also, of course, possible for such changes to be made in organizations. The actions of one employee can over time lead to real changes being made. In one example a manager introduced a small set of changes in her own department in order to improve things. These proved to be so successful that other areas of the organization copied them and they were later adopted throughout the whole company.

The butterfly effect is so powerful because societies and organizations are complex, highly interconnected dynamical webs such that one small vibration or change in the web will reverberate throughout it. Over time a vibration, even a very small one, in this highly responsive and interconnected system of feedback loops is amplified. It is in this way that small events grow larger and their effects are felt ever more widely. It is impossible to predict how events will unfold and what new behaviours may emerge because of our inability to know the extent of the web or how people will react and respond to events. Also, most times, it is impossible to trace the source of the original 'vibration' or fluctuation. This means that standard notions of cause and effect become irrelevant when trying to locate the origins of many changes.

The butterfly effect suggests that encouraging and empowering people to make small changes can be very effective in creating large-scale organizational changes. Form filling and paperwork, for example, can be tedious and time consuming. Small changes that streamline or simplify paper-driven procedures can produce benefits for all concerned and over time may reduce the overall paper burden. One small but powerful change that managers can make is the way they conduct meetings. Far too many meetings go on for too long and lose sight of their original objectives. Small changes that speed up the proceedings and keep everyone focused can make real differences to everyone's working day. All these things can have a knock on effect on people's morale and performance. Encouraging everyone to make small improvements to their own jobs and areas of responsibility wherever possible may, over time, lead to significant differences to the organization and its functions.

It is important to remember that the butterfly effect is also called sensitive dependence on initial conditions. This means that how events unfold is very dependent on the initial or starting conditions – and these are different for everyone and every set of circumstances. What will work well in one organization or in one industry cannot be precisely replicated in another organization or in another part of the same industry, as each will have different initial or starting conditions. Each organization is unique with its own history and culture. Every individual, every team, every department will respond in its own unique way. The differences may be slight or they may be substantial. So rolling out a standard, 'one-size-fits-all' change programme across an organization is no guarantee that it will be effective. In reality, the responses to the programme will vary from one individual to another and from one area to another and the results may prove to be quite unexpected. Such an approach could be courting disengagement and even disaster. Many traditional approaches to organizational change based on linear notions of predictability assume that the same methods and approaches will work effectively in most situations and produce similar results. Knowledge of the butterfly effect explains why this is not so and why so many well thought out, company wide, change programmes fail.

On the other hand, understanding how the butterfly effect phenomenon works can enable energetic new managers to create important changes in an organization. They are able to do this because their activities cause reverberations across the dynamic web of the organization. Thus it is perfectly possible for one person to affect the life of an organization. Further, that person does not have to be in a position of formal authority or leadership, but if they are, then they have the potential to make a huge impact over time.

Unfortunately many small changes go unremarked on and unrecorded. Given their potential to substantially change things recognition of these and a 'tuning' in to such actions should be a key part of everyday managerial life.

Strange attractors

The world of organizations can be thought of as a strange attractor, or rather as a series of strange attractors that form and reform, touching, colliding and influencing each other. Each organization is engaged in a dance between order and disorder. Each is sensitively dependent on its initial conditions. In other words, each is a strange attractor that through the actions of its people (or human agents) is constantly engaged in activities and actions that never exactly repeat themselves but form complex and recognizable patterns that are bounded or constrained by the organization, its culture, norms and values. For example, if two companies merge then two strange attractors become one larger, possibly more complex, strange attractor.

Cooksey and Gates (1995) provide an insightful illustration of how managers can use the notion of the strange attractor in the workplace. They examine the idea of work performance as a strange attractor. It is a strange attractor as over time it constantly changes. Cooksey and Gates point out that all employees are affected by sensitivity to initial conditions and they illustrate this by referring to the notion of a marble in a bowl, which was the example used in Chapter 3. In their example the marble equates with the individual employee and the bowl represents the interactive nexus of organizational, social, and work systems. The surrounds of both the marble and the bowl represent the surrounding environmental system. They then describe a number of trajectories which the marble might take after it has been dropped into the bowl. The marble (or employee) is highly sensitive to initial starting conditions, to its own changing conditions, to the bowl and environmental factors.

Cooksey and Gates describe four possible models of performance behaviour based on using the strange attractor analogy in their research.

Each model shows a range of responses which behave like strange attractors as they interact with the different conditions in and around the 'bowl'. They conclude that each is different as each individual responds to small changes in initial conditions.

Model A shows moderate level chaotic work performance over time around the performance strange attractor. Paths are never retraced and no fixed point arrived at, but overall it is constrained by boundaries. This they considered is analogous to the work performance of a fire officer, a police officer or a sales person. These are workers whose jobs make their 'paths' sensitive to the environmental systems they are surrounded by and by the social components of their roles.

Model B shows low-level chaotic work performance over time around the performance strange attractor. Performance does not retrace its paths nor does it arrive at a fixed and steady state. The work performance is thus relatively stable. They conclude that the performance trajectory space shown would map onto the work performance patterns of assembly-line workers or others with largely physical roles.

Model C shows high level chaotic work performance over time around the performance strange attractor. This shows considerable amounts of chaotic behaviour as the trajectory patterns move across large areas of space and display major shifts and changes. These shifts may be responses to changes in individual, internal and external systems because individuals are highly sensitive to these when compared with individuals in other professions. This may be due to the cognitive and highly social aspects of their work and would be considered representative of the work performance of a politician or an academic.

Model D shows low-level chaotic work performance over time which eventually stabilizes at a fixed point attractor. This pattern might be representative of a car assembly robot or a neural network based expert system.

The current approach to work performance:

> lulls management into a false sense of security and control with regard to expectations of HRM policy impacts and outcomes, and it contributes to the continuation of management 'fads' where dissatisfaction with one set of policies and practices (because the policies fail to meet predicted outcome expectations) leads to their displacement by another 'more modern' set of policies and practices ... However, replacing one equilibrium-orientated linear approach to management with another merely perpetuates the problems and unrealistically high expectations.
>
> (Cooksey and Gates 1995: 35)

Complexity has important implications for current mainstream notions of leadership including the idea of leadership as a strange attractor. Lars Kolind, when he was made chief executive of Oticon, created a butterfly effect as he arrived at the company and created a number of changes which radiated throughout the business. The old strange attractor, which was the long standing practices and values of Oticon, was replaced by a new strange attractor which arose from Kolind's leadership. Kolind's role is discussed further in the next section.

The edge of chaos

Organisms as complex adaptive systems that live on the edge of chaos are able to self-organize and adapt effectively to changes in their environment in such a way as to improve their survival chances. They are able to 'dance' between the extremes of stability and instability and dip into each of these in order to experiment and exploit their existing circumstances. Constantly exploring, constantly learning and adapting are key features of these complex adaptive systems. This means that an organization that wants to exist at the edge of chaos needs to provide a stimulating and challenging environment to encourage learning. An environment that is flexible and able to respond to advantageous learning and experimentation. An environment that is able to respond effectively to relevant changes in its external landscape. It must also provide strong frameworks to ensure that there is not too much novelty and surprise. These frameworks, for example, could include strongly shared organizational values, necessary legal or financial procedures, clear decision making and accountability processes, and sensible human resource systems.

Understanding of the edge of chaos has major implications for job design and how managers allocate work and roles to their people. Too often the prime focus on job design has been the completion of a task or set of tasks with little or no regard for the effect such a design would have on the employee carrying out the role. Too many people are in jobs where they work at a PC all day with very little chance to interact with colleagues, learn and develop new skills and make a unique and satisfying contribution to their organization. Managers need to think imaginatively about how the work in their area can be distributed. They should consider the setting of realistic but challenging deadlines and the creation of a working environment that encourages co-operation with colleagues, chances to show creativity and opportunities for learning and the exchange of learning experiences. In a later chapter I shall discuss the use of the notion of the edge of chaos in more detail with reference to the Edge of Chaos Assessment Model.

Rosabeth Moss Kanter, in her book *When Giants Learn to Dance* (1990), describes two organizations in the 1980s which needed to dramatically change if they were to survive. The two companies were Apple Computers and Kodak. Kodak was a very large, traditional, hierarchical and long-standing organization which was inflexible and unresponsive to changes in its environment and short on genuine innovation. Apple was a completely different kind of company. It was very new, confident and highly creative but it lacked a clear organizational structure and as a result its decision making was poor and accountability was very unclear. Thus Kodak was too stable whereas Apple was too chaotic. Both were in danger of going out of business. As Kanter points out, an approach was needed that brought together the best aspects of the two types of organization.

> The traditional large, hierarchical corporation is not innovative or responsive enough; it becomes set in its ways, riddled with pecking-order politics, and closed to new ideas or outside influences. But the entrepreneurial firm – the fast-growing start-up – is not the answer either; it is not always disciplined or co-operative enough to move from heady, spend-anything invention to cost-effective production, and it can become closed in its own way, too confident and too dependent on the magic of its individual stars. Something new is required, something that marries the entrepreneurial spirit to discipline and teamwork, something that helps loosely managed companies get a little tighter and tightly controlled companies loosen up.
>
> (Kanter 1990: 32)

In other words, both companies needed to move closer to the edge of chaos. Kodak needed to reduce bureaucracy and encourage creativity and innovation and Apple needed to put in place and use strong but flexible frameworks.

In the case study that follows I refer to 3M, a renowned innovator that has managed its affairs so that it has succeeded in primarily operating on the edge of chaos for many years.

Case study vignette

3M or the Minnesota Mining and Manufacturing company has survived for over a hundred years (founded in 1901) and it has done so by continually reinventing itself and by a strategy of operating on the edge of chaos.

> In a business world in which stagnant firms have been the norm, 3M managers have continuously reinvented the corporation through a parade of technologies that have allowed the corporation to remain the mainstay of the U.S. Fortune 500. These managers rarely make huge moves and rarely place risky bets; instead they relentlessly change the company year after year.
>
> (Brown and Eisenhardt 1998: 15)

The company is a paradoxical place: on the one hand it is orderly and very focused and on the other hand it is erratic and disorderly. Brown and Eisenhardt (1998) have analysed how the company manages to be

---

so successful by operating on the edge of chaos and list seven major characteristics. These are as follows:

1   It is chaotic. The company's scientists are allowed to spend 15 per cent of their time doing whatever they chose and individual business units are able to operate with considerable freedom and little planning. Senior scientists within the company can apply for start up grants to fuel projects which are outside the normal scope of the business.

2   The company has a sound framework or structure of financial controls and information systems. All divisions of the business are expected to make a specified profit every quarter and to hit growth and innovation objectives.

3   3M acknowledges and values the past. Many of its senior managers have been with the company for many years. The past is made use of in the present as scientists frequently consider past technologies and use them in order to create new ones.

4   The company has a very keen focus on the future which informs its research and project funding approach. This focus on the future is designed to ensure that the business does not stand still and that from time to time all parts of the business renew themselves.

5   Time pacing is used to set a rhythm for change that affects the whole company. This rhythm is established by the setting of corporate sales targets. Usually, this is a target that 25 per cent of sales must come from new products. When the company needs to increase the rate of change then it does so by raising the percentage figure of new sales.

6   Strategy and strategic direction are semi-coherent. Strategy is based on the imperative that new products are found and new markets too. From this strategic direction has emerged.

7   3M has achieved a constant flow of competitive advantages. 'The firm continuously reinvents itself, is perennially among the most-admired firms in the United States. And year after year is a strong global performer.'

(Brown and Eisenhardt 1998: 17)

For more information on 3M and other organizations and the edge of chaos consult with Brown and Eisenhardt's informative book, *Competing on the Edge of Chaos*.

When Ricardo Semler took over Semco, the family firm, he found a company that was operating close to equilibrium and in danger of going out of business. Semler completely reorganized the old traditional multilayered structure by reducing it to three levels of management and restricting the size of all operational units to less than 200 people. Further, he also changed the physical nature of the workplace by removing walls and using plants to separate different areas. Thus he changed the formal management structure, the physical lay-out of things and also the ethos and values of the company. This latter he did by founding the business on three core values by which all management activities were to be guided. These were democracy, profit sharing and information. In this way he pushed the company away from equilibrium and into operating on the edge of chaos. I strongly recommend that you read his book *Maverick!* for all the details on his remarkable achievement.

Living at the edge of chaos has many advantages for an organization, for it is able to experiment with different ways of doing things and so avoid getting trapped in one particular routine or way of thinking. If an organization becomes too formal, too rigid and too inflexible it will struggle to survive in our rapidly changing and uncertain world, as was the case with many of the large bureaucracies at the end of the last century. Likewise those organizations that are too disorderly with little or no structure or underpinning frameworks for accountability and action will also find it hard to survive as did many of the dot-coms.

Earlier in this chapter I provided a case study vignette of Oticon, a Danish hearing-care company, and how Lars Kolind revived its fortunes. Kolind not only introduced a new form of order to replace the controlling ethos, but he also pushed the company closer to the edge of chaos.

Case study vignette

Oticon was a long established hierarchical organization with a top management team that had been in control for thirty years. It was devoted to maintaining the *status quo* and to stifling disagreement and differences of opinion. There were three main functional areas in the company which had very limited contact and poor communications links. The dominant function of the three was the engineering function, so technology was of prime importance. The company was operating very close to equilibrium. As a result the company's research and development was too focused on traditional, external hearing aids, when the growing market was for internal hearing devices.

Kolind, first of all disturbed the equilibrium by introducing a range of traditional short term measures to improve things. These included cutting costs dramatically and taking power in his own hands. Then he announced that the company had to: 'Think the unthinkable'. This was a clear signal to everyone in the organization that things were going to be very different from now on. Kolind then dramatically restructured the company, introducing project team working and new electronic information systems. Not only did he restructure the organizational hierarchies he also altered the physical landscape of the company, relocating the company's headquarters and introducing open plan offices. Further, he empowered all the employees and gave them increased responsibilities. This radical restructuring severely disturbed the long-standing equilibrium of the company and pushed it away from stability and towards the edge of chaos which turned the business around.

> The spaghetti organization apparently delivered rather quickly what was expected of it. Thus, it demonstrated its innovative potential by re-vitalizing important, but 'forgotten' development projects that, when implemented in the production of new hearing aids, produced significant financial results, essentially saving the firm from bankruptcy, as well as by turning out a number of new strong products.
>
> (Foss 2000: 10)

Another example of a company that was propelled towards the edge of chaos in order to ensure its survival was the exploration unit (BPX) of British Petroleum (BP). This is described by Richard Pascale, Mark Millemann and Linda Gioja in their book *Surfing the Edge of Chaos* (2000).

Case study vignette

BPX's transformation was brought about by a new managing director, John Browne. When Browne arrived BPX was doing badly and had failed to find any major new oilfields in the last twenty years yet there were many opportunities for global oil exploration. Those oil companies with good business and technical expertise could prosper. Unfortunately for BPX it was over staffed and many of its people were unco-operative and did not work well together.

The first thing that Browne did was to call a meeting of the top hundred managers. At that meeting he announced that he intended to slim down the unit with some standard cost cutting. The next thing he then did at the meeting was to divide the managers into different groups and asked them to explore the current situation in which BPX found itself in relation to the Seven-S framework. People became more and more involved in the discussions as the day wore on and many had to rearrange journeys home, change appointments and so on. Browne's approach sent out an important message. It was that things were going to change and be different from now on. Browne was challenging the everyday norms of the business and moving it away from equilibrium.

Browne continued to put pressure on the organization. Next he brought together the top eight executives and with them continued to work on distilling the issues down to nine major challenges. He then arranged for some 120 staff to meet up to discuss how they would address these challenges. The meeting was to take place at a very busy time of year and Browne gave them six weeks' notice. This was a deliberate move to turn up the heat as the company worked to very long time scales. Browne's actions made it very clear that things were going to change even more.

Staff from all sections and all roles came to the meeting. They were given three days to explore and discuss the challenges and then to present their findings. Browne then told them to proceed with their ideas and to produce their recommendations within ninety days.

This instruction again disturbed the organization's equilibrium. BPX managers were not used to such pressure or such deadlines. Further, in order to meet Browne's demands they had to re-think their own roles and working practices. Many had to delegate work to junior colleagues who then became involved in the drive for change. The deadline was met and the papers were presented and discussed in detail. By heating up the temperature at BPX Browne was able to re-energize the unit and turn it around.

> Utilizing the simple devices of (1) overloading the organization beyond its business-as-usual carrying capacity, (2) using deadlines, public scrutiny and other action-forcing events to sustain disequilibrium, and (3) identifying adaptive challenge (but not stepping in to save the organization from it), Browne amplified disequilibrium and moved his organization out of its frozen state. Damping mechanisms such as milestones, resourcing, and deliverables brought closure at the end of the process.
>
> (Pascale *et al.* 2000: 101)

The case studies in this section with their focus on bringing an organization to the edge of chaos and/or maintaining them there are real life examples which illustrate a key aspect of the dynamics of organizational change. It is important to remember and recognize the impact of human interactions and responses on the life of an organization and its current 'state' when deliberately disrupted and disturbed.

Using fractals

Thinking in fractal terms can give managers fresh insights into how an organization is structured and how it operates and 'behaves' at every level. An organization where core values are strongly held throughout will provide evidence for this at every level. These values will be repeated and evident at every scale from strategic level negotiations with senior management to reception service and greetings on arrival. Such fractally discerned evidence would suggest that such an organization is well connected throughout and has a coherent structure that is 'fit for purpose'.

Thinking in fractal terms encourages managers to look not for tidy, linear, entity based evidence but instead to look for flows of patterning and repeating patterns that are not identical but have shared qualities or textures. For example, what is the quality of an organization's communications systems? Instead of looking at documents that describe and outline the company's approach to internal corporate communications, a fractal approach would suggest that one looks for emerging patterns of process. Do managers throughout talk informally to their staff on a regular basis? Is this a pattern that is repeated at all levels, albeit with different degrees of regularity? Are employees, when questioned, able to describe company communications policy? Descriptions of this may vary but overall a pattern should emerge that will suggest a coherent and rich approach to communications or conversely one that is confused and even incomprehensible, that is, no discernable repeating pattern emerges throughout the company.

Margaret Wheatley suggests that by using fractal principles it is not only possible to see an organization's communications' system afresh but also to re-energize its communications' flows. By way of example she describes the 'Future Search' conferences. These involved about fifty to seventy people from all different areas of an organization who were brought together with other people external to the organization. These people were, however, linked to the company in some way. At the conference everyone was put into groups and asked to create collective visions of the organization's past, present and future. To begin with lots of information was generated and many rich descriptions and scenarios arose as everyone swopped information on all aspects of their organization. As a result of this process new connections between people were made and new flows of information arose. After a few days everyone self-organized using all the information they had collected and used it to create vibrant future visions for the organization. As Wheatley (1994: 114) points out this process was rather like a fractal where information fed back upon itself creates 'elaborate levels of definition and scaling'. The people at the conference needed only lots of information to feedback and generate rich pictures of possible futures.

SENCORP – a fractal management model

SENCORP is a private USA company set up just after World War II. It has three main operating companies. One produces pneumatic fastening systems. Another which arose from collaboration with Johnson and Johnson in the late 1970s and 1980s develops products and services for the medical industry. The third which was created in the late 1980s offers financial services. Overall SENCORP was very successful but by the late 1970s it was facing a number of challenges due to uncertainties in the world's economy. Thus during the early 1980s the company began look for new ways to manage and to develop fresh and effective approaches to strategic change.

There were several years of discussion and reflection before some key principles emerged. These are as follows:

1   A model had to be developed that was applicable to the whole of the company and had to be based on analyses of the behaviour of individuals in the company.
2   The development of knowledge had to be integrated into daily operational activities. This would make it possible for employees to learn more and to build up their knowledge base while simultaneously working and improving upon day to day operational activities. This would be achieved via ongoing discussions and decision making which would take place at all levels throughout the company.
3   It was essential that all employees were able to participate in the discussion process. Thus adequate resources had to be provided to ensure that this took place. This was necessary so that everyone could bring their own knowledge and experiences to the process of creating better business practices.

Based on these three key principles a fractal model of management was created. (See Figure 5.1.) The model is based on three interacting areas or 'realms'. The A realm is dedicated to decision-making, the communication of these decisions and the equal allocation of resources. There are no controlling mechanisms. The B realm is focused on thinking, the development of new ideas, the creation of new knowledge and new possibilities using discussion, analysis and communication. The C realm is concerned with activity and is the 'doing' realm. This is the area where things happen and ideas are imple-

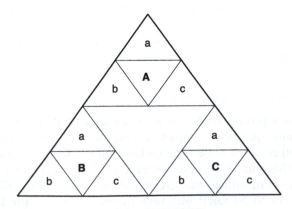

Figure 5.1 Fractal management model at SENCORP.

Source: Adapted from Slocum and Frondorf (2000: 239).

mented. Here the person responsible for the implementation of a new idea or a new option decides how best to make them a reality.

In most organizations employees are given clear cut targets and then monitored for effectiveness and progress by the use of quantitative performance measures. This is often carried out at the expense of other activities. SENCORP's senior management realized that time for thinking and reflection (realm B) tended to be neglected in most organizations and in their view it should to be given equal prominence with the activities in A and C realms. It was felt that such an approach would encourage employees to engage more actively in decision making as the new management model gave them more time to think about some of the options presented to them by senior management. The A realm was given the responsibility of making sure that there was a balance between B and C realms.

> The model and the reality in which it works uses multiple organizational scales. For example, each of the different realms focuses on different responsibilities in the company, on different levels of detail and on different time frames. C is focused on the short term, whereas B focuses on the medium term and A on the longer term. This basic pattern is repeated throughout the organization from day to day, from on the job activities to long term strategic approaches. Slocum and Frondorf (2000) describe how a president of the company could make a decision that sets a new direction. This is passed on to an employee who has agreed to implement it at the next scale down. This person will create a project designed to think about how best to implement things. This could lead to another project to consider the decision further, or it could lead immediately to an implementation process. Thus the model works at all levels throughout the company. And as Slocum and Frondorf point out, an employee could be involved in a range of projects at different levels and scales. The whole system is based on the activities of individuals and depends for its effectiveness on the free flow of information through all the scales.
>
> (McMillan 2004: 90)

> The model is based upon describing, and therefore improving, individual decision-making in a business setting. We have identified three distinct responsibilities that each individual carries out: to think, to decide, and to act. These are the basic nodes of a system and the information flows between these nodes are the linkages. Therefore, since an organization is an aggregate of individuals (agents in a complex adaptive system), an organization must have the same basic set of responsibilities. Hence the fractal nature of the model.
>
> (Slocum and Frondorf 2000: 238)

The SENCORP story is based on discussions I had with Ken Slocum and Scott Frondorf and their paper (2000) 'Business Management Using a Fractally-Scaled Structure'.

Using self-organizing principles

The ability to spontaneously self-organize and adapt to challenges and changes in the surrounding landscapes has enabled species to flourish and survive for millennia. Nowhere is this ability more evident than in communities of social insects such as ants and termites. Termites, for example, self-organize and construct the most amazing free-form nests that are perfectly adapted to the requirements of the colony and the landscape around them, whilst making best use of the raw materials available locally. These tiny blind creatures are not led by some charismatic leader with a grand vision of the future of the colony, nor a top management team that instructs them on how best to proceed. Instead they operate in a spontaneous and opportunistic fashion, guided in all they do by a strong sense of purpose and direction. If these simple insects are able to create air-conditioned homes that in termite terms are several miles high, without all the paraphernalia of modern management practice, then surely there is much we could learn from them?

Indeed, one suggestion would be that instead of management tightly controlling and directing employees they should instead provide a vision of the future, and a clear purpose for the organization, and then stand back and encourage people to make this a reality. There is an important point to note here. The termites all have a strongly shared purpose: that is the survival of their colony. This enables them to make decisions and prioritize their actions. If managers are serious about tapping into the energies that self-organization can release then they need to ensure that the organization's vision and accompanying purpose is one that is clearly shared by all. The best way to do this, of course, is for everyone to participate in their creation.

The first case study in this section is not one about a business transformation: it is about the transformation of a community but there is a message for business here too. The case study is based on the research of Katrina Wyatt and Robin Drury of Exeter University, as presented to a complexity conference in 2006.

Case study vignette

The Beacon Estate in Falmouth, Cornwall, England, was built to house the many people who worked in the port and the dockyards. By 1995, however, the work in the docks was drying up and many people were out of work. The houses on the estate were badly maintained, many homes were without central heating and a significant number of households lived in poverty. At the time Cornwall was considered one of the most deprived areas in England and the Beacon Estate was one of the most deprived parts of the county. There was drug trafficking, prostitution, vandalism and a high rate of child protection registrations.

People living on the estate felt isolated and abandoned by the local and national agencies. They did not approach them for help and they did not turn to each other for help. One person described how her child had been attacked by a dog and yet the police failed to take action. Properties were vandalized and crimes took place but people did not bother to contact the police as they were convinced the police would not help them. The estate became in effect a 'no go' area and a totally fragmented community.

There were, however, two people who did not give up on the community and who still made visits to people's homes. These were two local health visitors. They saw for themselves the appalling state of the houses which were so cold and damp that mould grew on the walls. As a result many children suffered with asthma. But the parents instead of blaming the state of their houses blamed themselves for the poor state of their children's health. The local people referred to themselves as 'scum'. This was how they believed outsiders saw them. This perception reinforced their feelings of hopelessness and low self-esteem – and so they did nothing to change things.

Then the situation worsened when there were appalling acts of pet torture carried out on the estate. It looked as if the estate would spiral into anarchy and complete degradation and collapse. The two health visitors decided that something had to be done and soon and that it would have to involve the community and the statutory agencies. They spoke to the different agencies and got them to agree to give some support if the people on the estate formed a residents' association. The two health visitors invited twenty of the residents they knew to a meeting – and five came along. The five residents came along because they wanted a better life for their children. They did not want them to grow up in the kind of neighbourhood that was the Beacon Estate. So the five of them visited every home on the estate and asked people what they saw as the real problems. At first people were a little suspicious but gradually they came round and it became apparent that one real concern was the danger of speeding cars. One child had been knocked over already and people were fearful that soon someone was going to be killed.

The health visitors went back to the local agencies and told them that they now had a residents' association. They spoke to the local council about the fast cars on the estate and the need for traffic calming measures. Gradually the statutory agencies offered their support. The police and housing officials became actively involved in trying to improve things. Within a year some £2.2 million had been found and allocated to improve the houses on the estate. Not only was the money allocated but the residents were asked to decide how to prioritise the improvements. Thus traffic calming measures were put in place and substantial improvements made to the housing stock.

The houses on the estate are now comfortable and healthy places to live in, the police and other bodies operate and co-operate there. Health has improved for all age groups. There is less incidence of asthma, no unwanted pregnancies in 1999, and the number of children on the child protection register had dropped significantly. Burglaries have decreased, as has car crime and incidents of assault. Now the estate has after school clubs, courses on life skills and a parent and toddler group. Many people are now proud to live on the estate.

The quality of life on the estate was transformed as a result of the efforts of two individuals who by their small but determined action made things begin to happen (butterfly effect); and who encouraged others to self-organize around key issues. They had felt forced to intervene as they sensed that life on the estate had reached a bifurcation point: it had either to improve or it would collapse into total degradation and violence. It is worth noting too that the five residents who volunteered had come from outside or were returning and had not been pulled into the strange attractor of hopelessness that characterized the area. Once the people on the estate felt listened to then things began to change further. The individuals on the estate began to talk to each other and to reconnect with one another. This also happened to the statutory agencies who began to work together in a co-ordinated way.

Self-organizing leadership: Richard Knowles

Richard Knowles had been a traditional command and control manager for many years until he came to realize that there was a better way of doing things. He refers to the way typical command and control organizations behave as the 'management trap'. This is his description of what happens when new initiatives are announced in this type of organization:

> Those doing the actual, physical work, and trying to make sense of what is going on, get stuck in the unresolved issues. They raise all sorts of questions about unresolved issues while top management pushes to get the work out the new way. As the top people push harder, the people doing the work push back harder. The organization often gets stuck between the need to get the work out and the need to resolve issues . . . If the conflict becomes severe enough, management will reorganize again, and maybe again. Around and around this triangular pattern of issues–structure–work we go. Communication breaks down, people become

isolated, creativity is driven into negative paths. Enormous energy is wasted; our organization is incoherent and floundering.

(Knowles 2001: 117)

Knowles describes how he was able to break out of the management trap in his book *The Leadership Dance* (2002) and in two papers, 'Self-Organizing Leadership: A Way of Seeing What Is Happening in Organizations and a Pathway to Coherence' (2001) and 'Self-Organizing Leadership: A Way of Seeing What Is Happening in Organizations and a Pathway to Coherence' (Part II) (2002). These are the sources for this case study.

Knowles was manager of Dupont's plant in Belle, West Virginia. The plant was more than thirty years old and had a number of serious problems, including out of date pneumatic control processes. The plant had to improve its business dramatically or it would be closed and Knowles was given the task of turning things around. One major change to be made was the replacement of the old pneumatic control system by an electronic one. It was estimated that it would take two years to build the new system and get it operational and it would cost around $6 million to do this. In order to save time and money it was agreed that the new system would not be built in parallel with the old one and that the job would be carried out by the staff at the plant itself. This they would do with the help of the R&D department and the company that sold the equipment. This was a completely new departure for the plant and the management team and they were taking a huge risk. Failure would inevitably mean the closure of the plant and the loss of over 100 jobs.

Knowles and his team realized that they had to involve everyone in the plant if they were to succeed. They began by holding project meetings every week with the plant's operators, mechanics and engineers. Meetings were held in the control room which was on the small side for the numbers attending, but it turned out to be a very fortuitous choice. The reason for this is that everyone had to stand for the meeting (standing on equal terms) and the maintenance and operations staff passed through on their shift system and so kept everyone up to date on progress. Within six months they had two capital projects costing approximately $3 million in total instead of the estimated $6 million. The projects were authorized at the meeting in ten minutes instead of the usual six to eight weeks.

Operators and mechanics were sent away to learn how to use the new equipment and on their return they helped to train their colleagues. A number of self-organizing teams arose as mechanics, operators and engineers from within Du Pont and Honeywell (the equipment supplier) worked together in deciding what to do and then doing it.

During the two-week company shut-down in November the teams came in and worked furiously to get things ready for the change over. It usually took something like a year for such a transition to be fully made. In this case it took five days for the new system to be operating at full capacity and without problems. As a result of this successful transition the plant's productivity increased by 45 per cent, earnings rose substantially, emissions fell by 87 per cent and accidental injury rates fell by 95 per cent. The plant workers did not settle back and enjoy the fruits of their labours but continued to make major changes at least two or three times a month. Everyone had been energized by the changes in working practices.

The successful replacement of the control system and all the many business and employee benefits that accrued Knowles attributed to the development of new working practices. He describes how everyone became fully involved in the project, how trust developed through the project team meetings and how all information was shared. Critically, everyone realized that unless they were able to turn the plant around then it would go out of business and they would be out of work.

As plant manager he learnt to change his whole management approach. He listened very intently at the project meetings and insisted that others did the same. Further, he made sure that ideas and insights were discussed, all questions addressed and that information kept flowing. Decisions were made swiftly and put into action and any changes were made while the work progressed. Trust was paramount.

Knowles writes:

> It is clear from this story that identity, relationship, and information change and interact all the time among people in the organization. This is quite dynamic and enables the organization to function far from equilibrium without coming apart. Self-organizing leadership helps create the conditions where all this comes together successfully.
>
> (Knowles 2001: 122)

I have in this section outlined very briefly the story of how the plant was transformed. I suggest that you read Knowles' book and/or his two papers in order to flesh out his story and gain a better understanding of his concept of self-organizing leadership.

Knowles has described from his own experiences how he evolved a new style of leadership and in so doing provides a new model for managers aspiring to lead using self-organizing concepts. Many effective and intelligent managers will find that they already act according to some, if not all, of Richard Knowles' principles. Knowledge of complexity science should encourage them to continue and to seek to constantly adapt, learn and enhance their skills.

Insect inspiration and other examples of self-organization

Organizations like insect colonies have to survive in highly competitive environments that are subject to innumerable changes. Insects have for millennia successfully adapted to these challenges using self-organization. There is no need for centralized control. Now a number of organizations are successfully using the self-organizing techniques of social insects for competitive advantage. One company faced with an enormously complicated and difficult scheduling and distribution system used a computer programme based on the foraging behaviour of ants to sort out its problems and introduce a very effective new delivery process.

Carl Anderson and John Bartholdi in their paper 'Centralized Versus Decentralized Control in Manufacturing: Lessons from Social Insects' describe how Revco Drugstores (now CVS) achieved a 34 per cent increase in the throughput of its order-pickers at its national distribution centre by using self-organizing principles based on ants foraging behaviour. For example, when an ant finds a source of seeds it collects a seed and carries it towards the colony's nest until it meets another ant which is closer to the nest. It then transfers the seed to this ant and returns to the seed source. The second ant carries the seed towards the nest until it meets another ant. The seed is again passed on to the ant closest to the colony's nest. Ant number two now returns towards the seed source. The third ant carries the seed towards the nest until it meets another ant and so on, until finally the seed arrives at the colony's nest. Revco changed from a centralized scheme to one based on 'bucket brigades'. These follow the same principles used by social ants when collecting food. Using this process meant that the company no longer needed to use detailed planning processes and tight management controls.

Anderson and Bartholdi (2000: 94) write that 'it can be shown empirically, and proven mathematically, that workers spontaneously gravitate to the optimal division of work so that throughput is maximized'. Additionally, 'production is more flexible, agile, and robust than other forms of work organization . . . because the assembly line spontaneously rebalances itself to account for disruptions or changes in work'.

Self-organization has also been used very effectively in other industrial situations.

Case study vignette

General Motors has saved some 1.5 million dollars a year by using a self-organizing approach. It has used this approach for its paint spraying operation at a General Motors plant in Fort Wayne. David Berreby (1996) describes how the painting modules, which are set up to spray the trucks different colours as they roll off the assembly line, are not centrally controlled. Instead, they act as free agents via a computer program which has as its objective the goal of spraying as many trucks as possible, using as little paint as possible. Each module bids for each painting job as it comes up and they bid according to their availability and the associated costs of carrying out each painting job. The booths make high or low bids for work depending on their capacity to carry out the next job and work is always allocated to the lowest bidder.

General Motors have found that they can make large changes to the way the assembly lines produce trucks, or even change the ratio of one colour of trucks to another colour, without any huge changes being made to the paint spraying system. The painting modules are able to deal with the changes and work out the best way of carrying out their new painting tasks.

In an article in *Fast Company* magazine, Paul Roberts describes how 'John Deere Runs on Chaos' by using self-organization.

Case study vignette

John Deere in the USA is the world's largest manufacturer of farm machinery and it is immensely successful both at delivering mass customization and in using self-organization. It uses these two approaches in order to offer its customers a greater variety of products while keeping costs down.

The company's production process uses an assembly line system that is divided into twelve modules or teams of workers. Each team is responsible for building a particular part of the entire product. The company provides them with a constant flow of information on all aspects of the production process. This enables the team to plan ahead and anticipate how best to organize their work. Most day to day decision making is made by the assembly workers. Thus decision making is delegated to those who are most closely involved with local questions and issues.

Each module or team leader is responsible for budgets and for overseeing staffing and maintenance costs. They and the team are given considerable authority, information and incentives to manage locally. John Deere pays its workers according to the number and the quality of the planters they produce. Thus each team has two self-organizing principles. These are: to make as many machines as possible and to make them of a very high quality. The team members are therefore encouraged and motivated to produce large numbers of high quality machines as this will determine the size of their pay packet. This means that team members are highly co-operative and very resourceful, particularly in solving assembly-line problems.

> For example, if Nelsoandra Cole, a 29-year-old assembler, finds something wrong on a planter as it rolls past her module, she deals with it immediately. 'I find the person responsible for the component, and I have it fixed right then and there,' Cole says. 'And if that person can't get to it in time, I find someone who can.'
>
> (Roberts 1998)

Human beings when unencumbered by control mechanisms or traditional authoritarian approaches are innately adept at self-organization. How else did we create village markets, trading nations, global economies, the Internet and Wikipedia? Think of all the great companies around the world. How did they start out? Unless they were specific state-owned initiatives many arose out of the self-organizing actions of one or two individuals. Men and women looking for ways to improve their situation, or simply to make a living, set themselves up in business in a self-organizing response to their environment and circumstances. The case study which follows is a good example of this.

Case study vignette

Boots the Chemists is nowadays a major UK company with approximately 1,500 stores in Britain, outlets worldwide, and its own manufacturing facilities producing medicines, cosmetics and toiletries. It was all started by John Boot an agricultural labourer born in 1815 who became involved with his local chapel in community work trying to help the poor. One way he found he could help was by providing herbal remedies to people who could not afford a doctor's visit and prescribed medicines. In 1849 he opened a shop in Nottingham which sold herbal medicines. It was his way of helping the poor and at the same time providing for his family. He and his wife, Mary, gathered the herbs and prepared many of the medicines themselves. When John died the business was carried on by his wife and his son Jesse. Jesse grew the business such that by the middle of the twentieth century it was a national leader and a major presence on British high streets.

Human beings are able to self-organize to their advantage, to improve their survival chances and especially to counteract any perceived threats to their well-being. Another very potent example of people's ability to self-organize is provided by the fuel protests in the UK a few years ago.

Case study vignette

In early September 2000 at a meeting in Wales a group of local farmers spontaneously decided that it was time to take action over the high price of diesel fuel. The high tax on diesel, which is essential for farm vehicles, was yet another burden on many farmers who were struggling to make a living. Their livelihood was threatened and they felt that they had to do something about it if they were to survive. They took action by picketing a local oil refinery in protest. They were soon joined by local hauliers. The hauliers felt that the high tax on diesel put their businesses at a disadvantage in comparison with other European hauliers. Via mobile phones and word of mouth the news of the protest spread rapidly and gained sympathy and support.

As a result within a week 75 per cent of fuel deliveries had been halted, as refineries and fuel depots across the country were blockaded. The army was ready to be called out, hospitals had to cancel surgery and Tony Blair, the Prime Minister, had a major crisis on his hands. This was all because a group of people had suddenly decided to take action and protest about something that was a threat to their liveli-hoods. They had quickly organized themselves using modern communi-cations technology and learnt how to handle the media and government responses as they progressed.

So the protestors not only used their innate abilities to self-organize but learnt how to adapt and respond to events as the campaign went on. In other words, they behaved as a complex adaptive system on the edge of chaos. Yet once they felt their needs had been addressed the protestors wound down their activities. Self-organizing systems which arise in response to an issue exist until that issue has been resolved or the system loses energy.

Volunteering appeals to people's interests and values and provides them with an opportunity to do something about issues that concern them. It is a self-organizing attribute of human nature. Many charitable organizations flourish because of the support of volunteers who raise money, carry out unpaid administrative work, lobby governments and encourage and sup-port those in need. Other organizations such as Avon, Tupperware and party-plan-type companies run successful businesses using self-organizing volunteers to market and sell their products.

One type of organization which could make good use of self-organizing principles to improve its services to its customers is the retail store. Analysts in the retail sector are always looking to cut costs in order to improve their profits, yet they still appear to embrace a very out-of-date way of working. Most large stores use a hierarchical or quasi command system whereby staff on the sales floor are confined to specific departments or sections, and limited in what they may or may not do. Frequently they have to refer to a supervisor for 'authorization' of a relatively simple problem which often results in a huge queue of customers at a check-out.

I will give you an example from my own experience. One weekend I was shopping in a local department store – a very famous UK retailer. I was on the first floor and there were very few customers. Things appeared to be very quiet. I passed a multiple check-out point where about four young members of staff stood. There were no customers and the young people looked very bored and disinterested. No doubt they were waiting to be told what to do next.

I then moved downstairs to the ground floor area and picked up some items. It was much busier here and when I approached the nearest till point I encountered a long queue of customers waiting to pay for their goods. As I stood there I realized that not every available till was staffed. Further, there were sales assistants carrying out other tasks around the sales floor. The queue moved very slowly. Customers were getting irritated and one lady put her basket down and left the shop, unable to wait any longer. The store is located in a pay-for-parking area and the fines are hefty if you overstep your time limit. No one appeared to notice the long queue of tired customers and no one attempted to solve the problem. No managers or supervisory staff were to be seen.

In this type of retail store if the sales floor staff operated according to self-organizing principles it would operate in this way. First all, 'management' would work with the sales floor staff in deciding what was their core purpose. This presumably would be something like: 'to make sales' (and so have a job). So if making sales is their core purpose then to achieve this they need to keep their customers satisfied. This means that customers come first: before shelf filling and so on. Though the sales floor has to be well stocked too. (And gossiping to colleagues would not be a priority.) Thus if there are customers waiting the priority is to serve them. Which may mean opening up another till, or answering a query, or checking on stock, and so on. And if there are no customers in one area then staff should attend to secondary tasks once they have checked that there are no customers needing their help in other parts of the store. In other words, the sales staff would not be confined to their own department but would roam the whole store making sure that their customers are being attended to and are happy.

People who work in retail have told me how boring it is to be confined to one role for most of their day. Some staff sit at check-outs for very long hours. The work is extremely repetitive and bad for their posture and physical well-being. Working in such a way it must be difficult to remain pleasant and accommodating with customers. Lowly termites do not spend their days carrying out such monotonous routines and yet we are supposed to be the more intelligent species!

I shall end this section by describing an early and significant use of self-organizing principles.

Case study vignette

An early, powerful and well-known example of the use of self-organizing principles is the re-organization of Visa by Dee Hock in the 1970s. The US banking credit card system was in a parlous state in the late 1960s when Dee Hock, who was a vice president of one of the banks, was made chair of a committee set up to sort things out. Hock was a man who hated the hierarchical, command and control models that were used to manage many banking institutions. Instead he was interested in the natural world and the possibility of using biological models to manage organizations. He drew on these ideas when he re-organized the system which was to become Visa International.

The new system, which is still used today, is completely de-centralized and operated on invisible structures and self-organizing principles. This allows for great individual freedom. For example, each bank can set its own prices, create its own markets, offer its own range of services and determine how to attract new customers. All this is done under the Visa aegis. Every bank is self-governing and out to protect its own interests but at the same time they have to cooperate and behave according to shared principles. These include agreed standards on a number of things, such as the design and lay-out of credit cards and most import-antly, the operation of the clearing house system. This is absolutely crucial to the survival of their credit card operations. Thus there is both co-operation and competition within the system which keeps it vibrant and coherent.

Each bank is an autonomous self-organizing agent within the system. Each is able to manage its own affairs, pursue other business interests, make corporate decisions and develop its own strategies. The banks are all in fierce competition with each other – but in the matter of Visa they co-operate for their own advantage. Without this co-operation their customers would not be able to use their credit cards in any store or any bank worldwide. As a result Visa International covers the entire globe and is available and operational in almost all languages, currencies and cultures.

> No way of doing business, dictated from headquarters, could poss-ibly have worked. 'It was beyond the power of reason to design an organization to deal with such complexity,' says Hock, 'and beyond the reach of the imagination to perceive all the conditions it would encounter.' Instead, he says, 'the organization had to be based on biological concepts to evolve, in effect, to invent and organize itself'.
>   . . . 'Visa has elements of Jeffersonian democracy, it has elements of the free market, of government franchising – almost every kind of organization you can think about,' he says. 'But it's none of them. Like the body, the brain, and the biosphere, it's largely self-organizing.'
>
> (Waldrop 1996: 77)

Complex adaptive organizations

Human beings, the organizations they co-create and the societies they form are all complex adaptive systems. Although they are complex adaptive systems, they are not always able to reach their full potential as complex adaptive systems operating on the edge of chaos. Too often circumstances, ideologies, authoritarianism and mechanistic or quasi mechanistic thinking hinder their evolution and full development. So if their existence is not impeded in any way, how should we describe organizations that are able to operate *fully* as complex adaptive systems or as complex adaptive organizations?

Complex adaptive organizations are:

- essentially self-organizing with individual employees spontaneously co-operating and competing according to shared values and beliefs in order to enhance the survival of the organization and protect their own jobs;
- created by individuals who are constantly learning and reinterpreting their roles and their interactions with others for the overall good of the organization;
- places where the organization's core purpose and system of values and beliefs are shared by all – though these may be subject to challenge and change from time to time;
- not subject to any centralizing, controlling authority;
- non-hierarchical – though they may be layered, but every 'layer' will be autonomous or primarily responsible for managing its own 'local' operations;
- able to flourish on the edge of chaos – thus individuals are highly creative and innovative;
- adept at taking risks for the benefit of the organization but never risking too much and tipping over into 'chaos';
- able to respond flexibly to changes in circumstances and to adapt readily and appropriately to these changes;
- ready and willing to adapt and change their structure and their processes in response to learning and environmental changes;
- places where learning and shared learning experiences are valued and viewed as essential to good practice and the future survival of the organization;
- places where individuals learn from any mistakes and there is no culture of blame;
- able to turn events to their own advantage;
- able to create their own visions and dynamic interpretations of the future.

Roger Lewin and Birute Regine in their book *The Soul at Work* (1999) make it clear that they believe that organizations will need to behave as complex adaptive systems operating on the edge of chaos if they are to survive in today's fast-moving and unpredictable world. The traditional mechanistic models may have worked well in more stable times but organizations that operate close to equilibrium, as they did, will find it increasingly difficult to survive in the new age of rapidly shifting global economies and high customer expectation. They suggest a number of guidelines which an organization can use to help it achieve its potential as a complex adaptive system.

- Recognition of the importance of relationships between people as they interact and affect each other both as individuals, in teams and in companies
- There should be few rules which in turn become practices that are shared and which guide people.
- Lots of small-scale experiments are the best way to make change happen.
- Instead of trying to plan detailed strategies organizations should create the conditions for strategy to emerge. 'This includes nurturing the formation of teams and creativity within teams, and in *evolving* solutions to problems, not *designing* them. Furthermore, hierarchic, central control should give way to distributed influence, and a flat organisational structure' (Lewin and Regine 1999: 49).
- Organizations should employ a diverse range of people. People from different cultures, backgrounds, ages and so on. This will enhance the potential for creativity.

According to Lewin and Regine an organization managed as a complex adaptive system will be very focused on its people. It will be 'very human-orientated, in that it recognises that relationships are the bottom line of business and that creativity, culture and productivity emerge from these interactions'. Further, complexity science 'recognises that the intelligence and sources of solutions to business problems are distributed throughout an organisation, and are not confined largely to the top' (Lewin and Regine 1999: 50).

They state, however, that it is not easy to manage in a complexity-based way, especially if a manager is used to the command and control way of doing things.

> It is hard even for those who embrace its principles, because the everyday urgency of business can make time spent interacting and nurturing relationships seem like a waste of time, a distraction from tough business realities. It is hard because it requires constant attention, including constant vigilance of one's own behaviour and the behaviour of others.
>
> (Lewin and Regine 1999: 50)

This is a significant point. Changing from one management style, from one way of thinking to another, will prove very tough for many managers accustomed to a very different way of operating. It may have taken years to assimilate certain practices and responses and similarly it could take years to discard and replace them. It is vital that managers not only observe the behaviour of their people and constantly encourage good complexity-style practice, but that they pay even more careful attention to their own thinking and actions.

Lewin and Regine describe a number of organizations that have sought to manage themselves in a complex adaptive systems way. One of these organizations is St Luke's, a UK-based advertising agency.

Case study vignette

St Luke's was set up as a co-operative in 1995 by Andy Law and David Abraham who wanted to create a company funded on moral principles and shared values. They wanted to show that it was possible to break the mould of traditional management and advertising agency practice. In his book *Open Minds* (1998) Andy Law describes how the company is based on an organizational model that has three separate but totally connected core principles. These are: constant exploration based on the vision of 'open minds'; meeting the needs of their clients with 'fascinating' products which are delivered on time; and being happy and true to themselves and their own values. These three core principles form the three pillars of the organizational structure of the company: Vision; Value; Values. Thus the company has an 'invisible' structure.

When designing St Luke's the two co-founders deliberately ignored the traditional linear structure of most organizations and created a form based on project team working and a 'citizen cell structure'. (See Figure 5.2.) This shows the different features of every cell. Each is composed of about 35 people who manage themselves in a self-organizing way. Thus each cell or part of the company develops in its own way but its micro culture mirrors the overall culture of the company. The cells communicate and know what is happening in each of them by means of a range of shared weekly, monthly and annual events. Each cell is responsible for its new growth and development and if any one cell grows successfully and has more than thirty-five members then it splits and forms two new cells. Thus the organization has a fractal design.

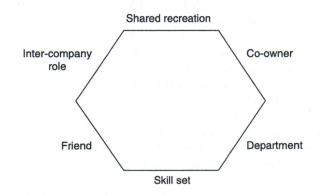

Figure 5.2 Citizen cell structure.

Source: Adapted from Law (1998: 127).

> All employees are co-owners of the company and are able to vote in the six trustees responsible for overall policy guidance and other corporate affairs.
>
> The structure of the St Luke's is designed to supports its dynamic, interactive, team working approach which is 'a perfect example of a complex adaptive system operating in the creative zone' (Lewin and Regine 1999: 105).

In 2001 St Luke's suffered a downturn in its fortunes and made a loss. In spite of this, however, it still continues to survive and thrive in what is a volatile sector.

Another example of an organization behaving like a complex adaptive system on the edge of chaos – for a time at least – is provided by Richard Pascale and his co-authors in *Surfing the Edge of Chaos* (2000).

Case study vignette

During the 1970s and 1980s Sears, the US retailer, lost much of its market share and was struggling to survive when Arthur Martinez was brought in as its new Chief Executive Officer. Martinez was to push the retailer away from its unhealthy equilibrium state and closer to the edge of chaos in order to improve its fortunes. He did this in a number of ways. He challenged his most senior managers to face up to the company's poor performance and deliberately moved responsibilities further down the organization. He set a series of tough targets that he knew could not be achieved using traditional methods and set about building teams of managers trained and energized to push through a number of much-needed changes.

One significant action Martinez carried out was to call a number of big meetings of the sales staff in the company's stores. In this way he involved approximately two-thirds of the company's 300,000 employees in his change programme. At these meetings staff were asked for suggestions on how they could improve customer retention and then were given the task of doing just that. By the 1990s the company was thriving and Martinez received a gold medal from the National Retail Federation for his work at Sears.

Sadly after a time Sears ceased to operate like a complex adaptive system flourishing on the edge of chaos. Pascale *et al.* (2000) point out that Martinez and his senior team did not see the company as a living system and did not realize that it could move back towards equilibrium again.

'Sears, whatever its future, is very much a complex adaptive system. It reflects (1) the ever shifting struggle between equilibrium and inno-

> vation and (2) the unending tension between the preserving forces of tradition and the transforming forces of change.'
>
> (Pascale *et al.* 2000: 57)

W.L. Gore – a complex adaptive organization

In March 2007 *The Sunday Times* announced the name of the company which headed its list of the best 100 UK companies to work for – and the company they named for the fourth year in a row was W.L. Gore. This company is the subject of the penultimate case study in this section and I have drawn on material from the company's website (www.gore.com) and Alan Deutschman's article, 'The Fabric of Creativity' in *Fast Company* magazine (2004).

W.L. Gore was founded in 1958 by Wilbert 'Bill' Gore, his wife Genevieve, 'Vieve' and their son, Bob in the basement of their home in Newark, Delaware, USA. From these humble beginnings producing electrical cables insulated with plastic coatings the company has spread worldwide and develops and manufactures thousands of different products. These include technological products for use in electronics, medical care, fabrics and general industry. The most famous of these products is, of course, GORE-TEX fabric. The company has 7,500 employees worldwide and more than forty-five plants and sales locations. It is a supremely successful company with sales in the 2006 fiscal year of $1.84 billion.

The company has four divisions: fabrics, medical, electronic and industrial – but in other respects it is very unlike traditional US corporations. The company has a president and a CEO and each division has its leader but there is none of the deep hierarchical structure of most large companies. There is no system of job ranking or specific roles and no prestigious job titles. Employees instead develop their roles and skills over time.

Its founder had worked for many years as an engineer in a traditional hierarchical organization and was all too aware of its shortcomings. He had noted that people did not communicate properly apart from informally or in the car pool and also that the only time people really pulled together and made things happen was when there was a crisis. Then a task force would be created and all the usual rules put to one side while things got done. This system worked well so Gore decided to use a similar approach in his own company.

The company was designed as a flat lattice organization. There are no chains of command nor predetermined channels of communication. Rather, associates, as employees are called, communicate directly with each other and are accountable to fellow members of their multi-disciplined teams.

In order to ensure that everyone in his company keeps in good contact with each other the size of each task force team is limited. Each facility employs between 150 and 200 people. By doing this everyone in each facility knows what everyone else is doing and who has the knowledge or skills for a particular job or project.

Without a chain of command or traditional hierarchy where does leadership come from? The answer is that it comes from within, from the culture of the organization.

> People become leaders by actually leading, and if you want to be a leader there, you have to recruit followers. Since there's no chain of command, no one has to follow. In a sense, you become a talent magnet: You attract the talented people who want to work with you. You draw them with your passion for what you're working on and the credibility that you've built over time.
>
> (Deutschman 2004)

Gore has an outstanding record for innovation and for sustained innovation in several fields. It produced GORE-TEX the amazing plastic coating that makes fabrics waterproof and windproof but also lets them breathe. Its revolutionary fabrics are used by astronauts and mountaineers as well as soldiers and Arctic explorers. It has delivered a range of top-notch medical products including heart patches and synthetic blood vessels and superb industrial and electronic products including air filters for industrial plants and fuel cells to convert hydrogen to electricity. It is also famous for its Glide dental floss and Elixir guitar strings. Other companies pour millions into R&D often without any real innovation emerging. Others are highly innovative at start-up or rely on the genius of one man. But according to Deutschman: 'Pound for pound, the most innovative company in America is W.L. Gore and Associates.'

Diversity is key to innovation at Gore as is patience and self-belief. The company deliberately promotes a culture of diversity actively recruiting people from all backgrounds. Its website states that: 'Knowledge, expertise, talents, creativity and hard work are what lead to unique, valuable and profitable products. It is for this reason that attracting, growing, energizing and retaining the best talent is critical to our success.' Furthermore, the company is patient and tenacious in pursuing its breakthrough ideas until they are perfect for the market place – and the market becomes convinced of their value. Also, as a privately owned company, Gore has considerable freedom in that they do not have to worry about share prices and greedy stockholders.

The company and all employees adhere to four basic guiding principles as laid down by Bill Gore. These are:

- Fairness to each other and everyone with whom we come into contact.
- Freedom to encourage, help, and allow other associates to grow in knowledge, skill, and scope of responsibility.
- The ability to make one's own commitments and keep them.

- Consultation with other associates before undertaking actions that could impact the reputation of the company.

(www.gore.com: 2007)

Lewin and Regine offer a set of guidelines which they suggest will enable companies to operate as fully functioning complex adaptive systems. W.L. Gore acts in the ways they suggest. It recognizes the importance of relationships; it has a minimum of rules; it carries out lots of experiments; strategies and solutions are evolved rather than designed; and the company employs a diverse range of people.

Another company which operates as a complex adaptive system on the edge of chaos is Semco, the Brazilian company I have written about earlier in this chapter.

Ricardo Semler and Semco – complex adaptive organization

Ricardo Semler transformed the family business by pushing it away from its traditional and long-standing equilibrium position towards the edge of chaos by restructuring; introducing a new form of order (one without control); empowering his employees and enabling them to self-organize; and in so doing creating a new company culture. In 2000 Semler's paper 'How We Went Digital Without a Strategy' was published. I refer to this to describe the continued success of the company and to provide further evidence of the complex adaptive nature of Semco.

Semler describes how in the last decade the company has quadrupled its income, enlarged its number of employees from 450 to 1,300, and expanded its business so that it not only provides manufacturing (pumps, industrial mixers and dishwashers) but also services to the Internet. How has this been achieved?

- Semler has always refused to define the precise nature of the family business. In his opinion, if you do this then you 'put your employees in a mental straightjacket' and this limits their thinking and the search for new business opportunities.
- The company is able to constantly transform itself and adapt to changes in circumstances and the creation and exploitation of new business opportunities.
- It is able to transform itself naturally and without senior management driving the changes. It does this by giving up control, Semler explains:

> People, I've found, will act in their own best interests, and by extension in their organization's best interests, if they're given complete freedom. It's only when you rein them in, when you tell them what to do and how to think, that they become inflexible, bureaucratic, and stagnant. Forcing change is the surest way to frustrate change.

(Semler 2000: 52)

Semler illustrates how this self-organizing approach to change can work by providing an example of how his employees found an opportunity to exploit which was good for them, and for the business. Semco manufactures cooling towers. The towers were fine but about ten years ago the sales teams kept hearing complaints from their customers about the high cost of maintaining the towers. The sales people proposed that the company started a small business managing the maintenance of the towers for their customers. They would charge 20 per cent of whatever savings their customers made and they would give 80 per cent of this to Semco and keep the remainder as their commission. The company agreed to their proposal and a very successful new business was born.

- Semco encourages experimentation. Semler describes how when his company successfully entered the property management business they came to it 'fresh, with no preconceived strategies, and they were willing to experiment wildly'.
- Semco believes in management without control. Semler states that the company's continuing ability to adapt and change itself is based on the simple philosophy that if people are given the freedom to do what they want, then over the longer term there will be more successes than failures. Thus the possibility that such an approach can lead to failure sometimes is readily acknowledged, but Semler is focused on the long-term benefits.

Semler lists six lessons that he has learnt about creating an adaptive and creative company. These are:

1   Forget about the top line. It is not the size of a business that matters but the length of time it survives. The size of a business should be appropriate to its profitability and the needs of its customers.
2   Never stop being a start-up. Every six months Semco is closed down and in effect starts again. During this time every business is evaluated and all employees too.
3   Do not act like a children's nanny. Do not treat people like children by always telling them what to do otherwise they will never be able to think for themselves.
4   Let talent find its niche. Semco lets people chose where they work and what they will do. This avoids a 'disconnect' between the requirements of the company and the needs of the individual.
5   Make decisions quickly and in the open. Individual initiative is crushed when people have to go through complex bureaucratic procedures. At Semco proposals for new businesses have to meet two criteria to go ahead. First, the 'business has to be a premium provider of its product or service. Second, it has to be 'complex, requiring engineering skills and presenting high entry barrier'.

6   Seek and make partnerships. Help is needed to get new businesses off the ground and alliances and partnerships can facilitate this.

Semler observes:

> If my 20 years at Semco have taught me anything, it's that successful businesses do not have to fit into one tight little mold. You can build a great company without fixed plans. You can have an efficient organization without rules and controls. You can be unbuttoned and creative without sacrificing profit. You can lead without wielding power. All it takes is faith in people.
>
> (Semler 2000: 58)

For more details and further information on the points in this section I strongly suggest you read Semler's paper.

Key questions

- How does a complexity-based definition of organization differ from traditional definitions?
- What are the main features of a complex adaptive organization operating on the edge of chaos?
- How can managers push an organization away from equilibrium towards the edge of chaos?
- How have W.L. Gore and 3M managed to be two of the USA's most innovative companies for so long?
- Why is Semco a good example of a complex adaptive organization?

6 Complexity in action: a case study of the Open University

Key points

- The Open University: the context for the case study
- The New Directions Programme 1993–1996
- The emergence of unexpected processes: feedback loops in action
- Learning and change dynamics
- The programme's legacy and a model for organizational change

This chapter is devoted to a case study of a four-year organizational change process at the Open University, which was the subject of my doctoral research and an independent case study by the Institute for Employment Studies (IES) of Sussex University. It provides in detail the story of how complexity-based principles may be introduced and effectively used in a complex and traditional organization.

The Open University

Some facts and figures

The Open University was founded in 1969 and admitted its first students in 1971. It is a unique university in that it has no entrance requirements once one has reached the age of eighteen and uses distance learning to deliver all its courses. In spite of considerable scepticism about its ability to succeed and deliver quality higher education the Open University has prospered. At the time of writing the University has approximately 150,000 undergraduate and more than 30,000 postgraduate students. It is the largest provider of management education in Europe and is ranked amongst the top UK universities for the quality of its teaching.

The University is governed by two main bodies: the Senate and the Council. The latter is responsible for all financial and employment matters and the former for all academic issues. The chief executive position is held by the Vice-Chancellor. He or she has a senior team made up of some five Pro-Vice-Chancellors (PVCs) each with their own portfolio, the University Secretary and the Director of Finance. The Secretary is responsible for the administration of the University, which at the time of the change process consisted of some eight divisions each with a number of sub-divisions. At that time there were eleven faculties or schools, a huge students' administration division with numerous sub-divisions and a Learning and Teaching Services division that covered media development, publishing, rights and warehousing. Additionally, the University had thirteen regional centres across the UK. The governance structure of the University was set up using classical, bureaucratic notions of organization and as it grew and expanded so did the many, many layers of its centralized, functionally specialized, top-down structure.

During the late 1990s the University had approximately 3,000 full time staff made up of academics, administrators, secretarial and clerical staff, technical staff, and a range of professionals including accountants, surveyors, editors, designers, IT experts and so on. It also employed several hundred skilled and unskilled manual staff including gardeners, electricians, plumbers, warehouse packers, forklift truck drivers, postal staff and porters. Several thousand part-time associate lecturers were also employed to support the local delivery of the University's teaching programme.

Time for strategic action

When it was set up the Open University was funded separately from other Higher Education Institutions (HEIs). In 1993 this changed and for the first time in its history the University found itself in direct competition for its core grants with other HEIs. The competition for core grants was likely to be fierce and it was clear that the more students the University attracted then the more it would benefit financially. On the plus side, the change now meant that the University could manage its financial affairs in a more business-like fashion. Previously any unspent monies had to be returned at the end of the financial year and the University had not been allowed to build up capital reserves. All this added up to a major change in the University's operating environment.

But other significant changes were taking place too during the 1990s. Many HEIs impressed by the success of the University's distance-teaching programmes were now offering their own, sometimes more local, provision. Also new technology had been developing apace and many of the Open University's traditional distance-teaching and learning methods were coming under threat from accessible and exciting new multi-media developments. Thus changes in the University's environment meant that it had a chance to get ahead financially, especially if it could increase its student numbers: but at the same time it was also threatened by other institutions and growing demands for new multi-media experiences.

The University's senior team recognizing the urgent need to handle these challenges put together a new strategic plan which addressed the University's priorities and needs for the next ten years. It also drafted a strategic action plan called 'Plans for Change' which described the major actions that would need to be taken over the next five years if the overall plan was to become a reality. This document provided a set of six 'directions' whereby management and staff could prioritize key activities in support of University strategy. (These are shown in Appendix 1.) Most importantly the document acknowledged that all the staff would be need to be involved if the University's strategic objectives were to be achieved.

The new directions story 1993–1996

See Appendix 2 for information on all the events and activities that took place in the programme. The section that follows is an extract from my book: Elizabeth McMillan, *Complexity Organizations and Change* (2004) published by Routledge, pages 113–19. This narrates the story of the programme as it took place.

The story begins – 1993

In January Geoff Peters, PVC, Strategy asked the Personnel Division for its support in setting up a series of workshops to provide an opportunity for staff consultation over the new 'Plans for Change'. As head of training and development I was thus involved in the programme from the very beginning. This is how I became a participant–observer.

Geoff Peters described how the University needed to double its student numbers over the next ten years and how at the workshops he wanted people to explore both the real blocks and the real opportunities to change. He described two major outputs that he was hoping for from the workshops.

1   'People wanting to change, questioning the *status quo*.'
2   'Insight into attitudes and issues.'

Further, he was looking for feedback from the workshops which he would use to brief his own team, his task groups, and heads of units or divisions. The workshops were designed 'to give staff an understanding of the scope of the change needed, and for staff to tell the University about any problems which our plans pose for them and for their colleagues' (Geoff Peters quoted in *Open House*, April 1994).

It was decided to set up six two-day workshops as soon as possible and to invite some thirty staff to each one. Staff from all categories and locations were invited to attend and their names selected from the internal phone book. In this way it was hoped to have a representative 'diagonal slice' of staff at each workshop. Invitations were sent out and heads of units/departments asked to allow their staff to attend and also to brief them on the University's strategic plans before they attended. Furthermore, they were asked to follow up with a debriefing and to give their support for actions to be taken afterwards.

Six two-day workshops were held in the first half of the year. At first the design of the workshops varied but by the fourth workshop a pattern of process had emerged which was to become the model for later ones. This was as follows:

- initial plenary introduced by Geoff Peters, PVC, Strategy;
- work in small groups on visioning the OU of the future;
- plenary discussion to share these visions and draw out key themes;
- work in small groups to develop an action plan for each key theme;
- final plenary to present action plans to the PVC, Strategy.

In his initial plenary session Geoff Peters described the current situation in which the University found itself, the need to increase student numbers and the need to change the way the University did things if 'Plans for Change' was to become a reality. He also made it very clear that he believed all members of staff had a part to play.

The design of the workshops may look similar to many of the 'away day' type of events that managers attend from time to time. As Stacey *et al.* (2000) point out, typically when managers participate in these events they fail to properly address the real issues and to consider any ideas on a practical day-to-day level. Further, there is a strong tendency to continue doing what they have always done during and after these events and to avoid discussing why their controlling mechanisms so often fail. A number of factors made these workshops quite different, in particular, the mix of people, the facilitators and their approach and the interaction of all these things.

Each workshop consisted of a mix of staff and this mix was replicated in the small groups. A group might contain a clerical worker, a warehouse worker, a junior administrator, a senior academic and a middle manager from one of the professional areas, say, a surveyor. Thus each group had a range of perspectives on the organization, on what was needed and on how to make things happen. For example, in one group session several members discussed how to bring extra courses on line. Then a worker from the warehouse asked how they were supposed to do this when the warehousing facility was already at capacity. This stopped everyone in their tracks and they then discussed ways in which this problem could be sorted out. The warehouse worker was able to keep everyone focused on the practicalities of an expansion in teaching materials. People used to working in different theoretical and bureaucratic domains encountered staff used to working with hard-nosed, practical issues. It was an encounter that enriched the discussions and encouraged the development of multiple perspectives. People discovered that an idea that might have advantages for their area could pose real problems for other staff in other areas. The interconnected nature of people's activities soon became vividly apparent. In some groups departmental antagonisms emerged and the facilitator along with other members of the group would work to resolve things and find a way forward, if at all possible.

Thus by the afternoon of the second day when the groups were asked to put plans for action together a rich learning interchange had taken place which ensured that the suggestions and recommendations made by the different groups in the plenary sessions were founded in fresh realities. Out of these realities came a variety of ideas and practical suggestions for changing many existing practices and introducing new approaches.

Skilled facilitators from the training and development unit played a key role in each group. They were there to encourage and ensure equality of participation and the resolution (if possible) of real issues. Equality of participation was seen as vital if the groups were to work. The University is a hierarchical institution and some members of staff see themselves as junior to others and so on. Furthermore, some staff are used to discussing issues and exploring ideas with colleagues and others are not. Many of the manual, clerical, secretarial and technical staff were not at all used to this kind of activity and they were given support and recognition in the group via the subtle interventions of the facilitators. Additionally the facilitators were briefed to encourage their groups 'to let go', to experiment, to have fun and to see the future as wide open and full of many possibilities. Furthermore, I had recently come across chaos theory and some of its core tenets and I had discussed many of these with the facilitators.

An important feature of the workshops which emerged during the first series was the notion of everyone being empowered to take action. The PVC, Strategy, the facilitators and myself encouraged people to consider what changes they could make themselves in their own areas, no matter how small. Many people were accustomed to being directed to do things, or to having to ask for permission. Thus for a lot of staff taking action on their own behalf and making a change, however minor, was a major step. Over time the programme came to be recognized for its action approach and for the importance it attached to individual action.

By early summer the workshops were beginning to generate interest across the University. Staff began to ask to come along instead of waiting to be invited. In the autumn two more workshops followed which concentrated on specific aspects of New Directions, such as short response times. There was also an effort to increase attendance by academic staff who had so far been under-represented, and also to include staff who were also students taking OU courses, in order to introduce a student perspective. Each workshop was unique in that it had its own mix of staff and thus its own internal dynamics, but they were all characterized by energy and engagement.

In the autumn a letter went out to all New Directions workshops participants asking for volunteers to form a committee to organize a New Directions conference for the coming year. This would provide an opportunity for participants to update themselves, review the outcomes of the workshops, network, celebrate changes and communicate directly with the Vice-Chancellor, and the Vice-Chancellor's top team.

By the end of 1993 there had been eight two-day workshops involving approximately 164 staff and reports/features in three editions of *Open House*, the University's staff newspaper.

1994

This year was to see a significant expansion of the programme and several important developments. Early in the year it was decided to continue the programme of workshops by offering workshops based on key themes which had emerged in 1993. These included considering the need to develop 'an electronic strand' to the University's teaching design and delivery; improving the way the University attracted its students; improving the joining processes and improving internal communications. Each of these workshops was attended by the PVC, Strategy and the senior manager with responsibility for addressing these themes. Some senior managers were more enthusiastic than others at having to share their 'brief' with a random selection of staff and to ask for their views. In the event, however, all these workshops were highly successful from the view of both the participants and the senior manager concerned. Following the model created by the PVC, Strategy, ideas and suggestions from the workshops were fed into the appropriate planning groups for consideration.

An event of major significance during the year was the New Directions conference in May.

The 1994 conference and conference planning team

Some twenty-three staff responded to the invitation to form a conference organizing committee. It was decided that twenty-three was too many to form an effective group. After a lot of thought eleven staff were chosen as a representative cross-section. In the event eight staff regularly attended. There were: two regional academics, two secretaries, a senior editor, a warehousing manager, an administrative assistant and a chief clerk and myself as facilitator and provider of developmental advice and training administrative back-up.

The group first met in March 1994. Its task was to organize the conference so that it represented all staff groups, to pull together all the ideas and experiences to date and to initiate further actions. A provisional date for the conference had been fixed: 18 May 1994. Thus the conference planning team had just over two calendar months to organize everything. The event was organized with five meetings between which there had been an e-mail flow of ideas, discussion and decision making. The conference offered twenty workshops in parallel streams with a mix of internal and external speakers and an exhibition. It was a significant achievement.

> On the day, the University's Training Centre was filled to capacity with over 100 delegates (and there was a waiting list). Participants included secretaries, gardeners, academics, administrators, managers and technicians. The day culminated in the presentation of action plans to the Vice Chancellor, Pro-Vice Chancellors and other members of the OU's senior management team.
>
> (Parsons and Russell 1995: 2)

The conference was very successful, it influenced a range of activities and initiatives and was to make an important impression on those staff who attended. A formal report was written up and circulated to all delegates and senior staff.

The staff survey team

A few days after the conference it was decided to involve New Directions participants in organizing a staff survey for the University. The effective way in which the highly successful conference had been organized by a group of volunteers from the programme had impressed the group charged with delivering the survey. For almost two years the Staff Policy Committee of the University had talked of the need for a survey of staff, to find out what the various staff groups felt about working in the University, but nothing had been done.

A note went out to all the conference delegates asking for volunteers to work with the Director of Public Relations, Les Holloway, on the design and delivery of a staff survey for the autumn. Eleven people volunteered and in the event nine were able to make the first and subsequent meetings. The team consisted of one senior academic, two senior secretaries, one editor, one administrator from the Planning Office, a senior O & M officer, a course manager and the grounds superintendent. I too was a member of the team where I acted in a facilitative role.

During June a revised tender document was prepared and an invitation to tender went out to five companies. The tenders were received by the end of July. Next the team met to decide which company to recommend to carry out the survey and a revised timetable was drafted. In September the team met for a debrief on the qualitative stage of the survey and discussed the draft questionnaire. In October there was a briefing on the results of the pilot survey and discussion of next steps. The questionnaire went out to all full-time staff of the University on 31 October 1994. There was a very good return of 65 per cent.

Meanwhile the conference planning team continued to meet and 'reconstituted itself as a "ginger group" to facilitate, and if necessary carry out the follow-up work' (Parsons and Russell 1995: 2). It was a significant shift in the 'ownership' of the programme. I attended the meetings of this group and found its members had been highly energized by the conference and its success and were committed to building upon the enthusiasms it had aroused. They decided that more staff could become involved in New Directions if events took place in the lunch hour. Thus with the backing of the PVC, Strategy they arranged a series of lunchtime briefings which took place in the autumn. These included a briefing on 'Plans for Change' by Geoff Peters, a session with the Director of Marketing and one with the Director of Personnel. The briefings proved to be very popular with staff and the rooms were usually filled to capacity with deeply interested employees. In a move to involve more regional staff inter-regional workshops were held in Birmingham and London. These explored how regional activities would look in ten years time and produced a wealth of new ideas for both course topics and better services to students.

The group also 'hit upon a novel way of spreading the *New Directions* message . . . they invited staff to enter a cartoon competition on the theme of "the OU of the future" ' (Parsons and Russell 1995: 3). The entries were imaginative and amusing with innovative possibilities for the future. The winning cartoons were used to produce a New Directions Cartoon Calendar for 1995. A thousand calendars were printed and made available to all staff and the winners presented with bottles of champagne. The calendars were rapidly taken by staff and pinned up on walls in different parts of the University. Also in the autumn a simple leaflet describing New Directions, including its principles and practice, was distributed to all staff.

In December the survey team met to discuss the follow-up to the findings of the survey, including presentations to the staff and supportive action in relation to the findings.

Total attendance at the programme in 1994 was approximately 533. It is difficult to quantify precisely the figures as some people attended more than one workshop and no formal attendance records were kept of the lunchtime briefings. There were reports/features on New Directions in five editions of *Open House* in 1994.

1995

In January the first report on the staff survey was presented to the Vice-Chancellor's senior team and the staff survey team members. A series of presentations to different representative groups was arranged and an open presentation to all staff in the University lecture theatre. All staff received a summary report of the findings and all department heads were asked to discuss these with their staff and devise follow-up action plans. The survey team had completed its task and after celebrating over lunch the team disbanded. It had been a highly effective and successful team.

Also in January several members from the conference planning team (now the 'ginger' group) and the staff survey team got together and formed the New Directions 1995 action group. On an away day in January the new group brainstormed a number of ideas which were picked up and taken forward during the year. These included a mistakes workshop, a visualization workshop, a workshop for OU students and series of communications workshops. The idea for a mistakes workshop arose out of discussions about experimentation and creativity. If people were to take risks to change things then the University would need to be a 'safe' place, it was argued. Thus a group of the volunteers got together and designed a 'Make Better Mistakes' workshop. The open invitation to staff to attend the workshop was worded as follows: 'Change at the Open University is bringing new ways of working. Inevitably things will sometimes go wrong. How do you cope with mistakes? Does the University learn from its failures? Can one replace blame by objective analysis?'

The two workshops offered generated enormous interest and were oversubscribed. The visualization workshop arose from interest in conjuring up new images in order to stimulate new ideas and new ways of thinking. Two artists were employed to work with the staff at the workshop and to help them create vivid visual images of a changed University. The communications workshops were a direct response to the call for better communications which came out of the conference. These were organized in consultation with different departments of the

University so that teams of staff from different areas got to together to explore how to improve things. Another calendar was also produced and distributed.

The number of attendees in the programme in 1995 was approximately 387. In 1995 there were reports/features on New Directions in four editions of *Open House* and one edition of *Sesame*, the students' newspaper.

1996

The programme was now in its fourth year. There were three communications workshops and a 'Making Better Mistakes' workshop and in the autumn another conference. This conference organized by the action group was not so ambitious as the 1994 conference but it offered eight workshops in two streams. It also included a 'fair' element that comprised an OU horoscope, a picture gallery of New Directions art work, a graffiti wall and the planting of a symbolic new mulberry tree by the Vice-Chancellor, Sir John Daniel. Thus in its own modest way it made a significant contribution. It showed clearly, by the kind of activities it offered, that conferences on important topics did not have to be serious events composed of lectures and 'talking heads' but that by appealing to the senses as well as the mind people could meaningfully explore strategic issues.

Members of the action group were now finding it more difficult to create the space needed to support the programme and enthusiasm was waning. Furthermore, changes in the external environment were affecting people's workloads and most importantly their morale. In January 1997 the group decided it would take a break and review the situation at a later date to be decided. This was to be the last time that it met.

The New Directions 'volunteers' in the form of the 'ginger' group (some of the conference team) and the 1995 action group (the two teams plus a few others) had been active for over two years and had supported, suggested or helped to design and deliver some six lunchtime briefings; four regionally based workshops; three mistakes workshops; six communications workshops (one of these in Cambridge) two cartoon calendar competitions and a conference. I had worked very closely with the volunteers and provided developmental expertise and administrative support but they had come up with the ideas and backed them with their energies and commitment. It was a significant achievement for a disparate group of volunteers with full time roles in the institution – and a development that had not been expected at the beginning of the programme. It had been a totally spontaneous and unpredicted response.

In 1996 approximately 170 staff participated in New Directions events and there were items/features on New Directions in three editions of *Open House*. Attendance was not recorded at all events in the programme so to arrive at an accurate figure for the number of individual staff who participated in the programme is impossible. But it is estimated that about 23 per cent of the full-time staff were involved. It is important to bear this in mind when considering the impact the programme made on the University and the extent of its influence. The records show that academic staff were in a minority.

The emergence of unexpected processes

The New Directions programme could be described as a top-down strategic change initiative that successfully engaged support from staff at all levels across the organization. The workshops could be viewed as consultative devices to encourage employee support which also enabled senior management to review progress by checking on support for delivery. Further, the programme added another mechanism for change and staff development which reinforced and re-emphasized the pursuit of strategic priorities. (See Figure 6.1.) Thus in a number of ways the programme appears to be a traditional

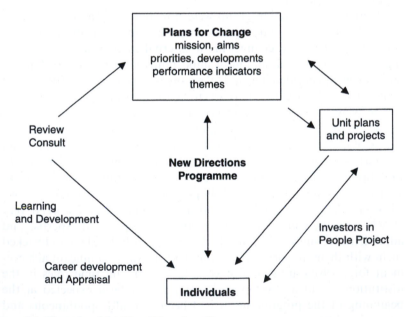

Figure 6.1 The role of the New Directions Programme.

Source: Adapted from G. Peters in McMillan (2004: 121).

change intervention – but there are many significant differences which reflect the use of complexity-based principles. These will emerge as we progress through this chapter.

Interaction and the response dynamic

Not only did the programme give additional support to change and development processes already in place but it provided a feedback mechanism for staff and gave them an opportunity to influence strategic thinking and feed fresh data into the planning processes. Key to this was the PVC Strategy who fed information and ideas from the workshops into meetings of the University's senior management team and also into the official planning processes. Individuals also fed back from events to meetings in their own departments, thus informing their own unit or departmental plans. Thus the programme created individual positive feedback loops which over time have amplifying potential (the butterfly effect).

Participants in the programme in reacting and responding to issues created a unique dynamic which added energy to both old and new feedback loops. This was assisted by reports in *Open House*, discussions along corridors and formal and informal meetings – and more events.

The ways in which people responded to the programme and the way in which it unfolded over a four-year period were totally unexpected and could not have been predicted. One major unexpected response was the way in which a number of the workshop participants responded to events, became more involved and continued to unroll the change process on a voluntary basis. Thus a consultation initiative designed to last for a few months went on to become a University-wide 'movement' for change that ran for a further three years or so. Figure 6.2. shows how the initial response dynamic in 1993 expanded over the next three years as the original organizers listened and responded to participants, who in turn responded to other staff and other participants. Out of this dynamic emerged a partnership between the PVC Strategy's office, learning and development and the staff volunteers. It was a partnership in which the volunteers developed a guiding hand.

How was it that the programme was able to encourage such engagement? An insight into this is provided in a letter sent to the PVC Strategy. In it a member of the regional staff wrote:

> I felt that the informal atmosphere and the friendly welcome established a group environment which was totally unthreatening and which helped everyone to feel able to contribute freely. I came home refreshed, better informed and with the feeling that, however lowly my position. . . . I had been listened to. I was made to feel that I had something to contribute to the future of the OU . . .
>
> I thought that it was a most creative and imaginative idea to choose staff at random from all grades and areas within the OU . . . I felt

Figure 6.2 The response dynamic.

Source: Adapted from McMillan (2004).

privileged to be asked to take part. It has increased my respect for the openness of the OU . . . From someone who never wins a raffle I felt this time, at least, I had won one of the major prizes.

(McMillan 1999: 260)

The letter was typical of the enthusiasm of many junior staff who were normally unable to participate in the University's consultation processes.

A people's movement with its own distinct style

After a time the New Directions programme came to be described by many of its participants as a 'people's movement for change' which had action as its prime focus. Right from the beginning the programme had encouraged people not only to think about the changes needed, but also to make them happen. Geoff Peters wrote in 1995: 'New Directions is also about action. The activities are designed by staff volunteers and emphasise practical results. The over-used phrase "think globally act locally" really does fit the New Directions activities. Staff sort out where the University needs to go and then they take action to help get there' (McMillan 1999: 259). In an organization where permission was often needed to do things differently this was a huge departure from normal protocols. Such an approach was designed to cut away at the bureaucratic heart of the institution that stifled many attempts at personal initiative and individual creativity all in the name of due process.

From the beginning the workshops had set the tone. It was to be informal, open, inclusive, involving and different, and from these early foundations arose the programme's three key behavioural hallmarks: creativity, humour and experimentation. These gave the programme its own unique style, creating its own strange attractor. At workshops and other events staff were encouraged to be as creative as possible both in exploring and considering issues and in presenting their ideas and conclusions. People produced drawings, poems, street theatre and even their own version of the *News at Ten*. One manager described the programme as being a 'bit zany'. Allied to the use of creative processes was the use of humour as a way of encouraging discussion and debate. One member of staff described how the programme used 'a sense of humour to get over the serious issues'. The calendar competitions used humour to get across the idea that the University had to change and that the future would be very different. The IES study commented that:

> As the programme progresses, it emerged that the way to unlock people's creativity, to get them to speak openly and equally at all levels of the organization was through the use of unusual techniques, an informal atmosphere and creative facilitation. Individuals were encouraged to work with people they do not know, to have fun, to loosen up, to explore the use of metaphors.
>
> (Tamkin and Barber 1998:18)

Hand in hand with the use of creativity and humour went experimentation. A very good example of the experimental approach was the decision to hold Mistakes Workshops. The New Directions volunteers had decided that staff would not be willing to make changes if they felt at risk if things went wrong. It was important that a learning climate was created and a blame-free culture. People needed to be encouraged to learn from all that they did, including any mistakes. *Open House* described the idea as 'a revolutionary-for-the-OU workshop'. The organizers of the workshops realized that if the University was to change significantly then it had to develop a more positive attitude to risk as a prerequisite to innovation and inspired change. These workshops proved to have very broad appeal as the following quotes illustrate.

> I came away feeling that my ideas and input had been harvested. I would certainly recommend anyone who needs to re-energise their 'UMPH' to attend the next one.
>
> (Training Assistant)

> I'll never feel the same ... When I go back I'm going to say 'go for it girls'.
>
> (Assembly Operator)

It really was amazing how all these different types of people just get together and start working ... for me it was the OU style from its beginnings, but looking at the future. Wonderful.

(Senior Lecturer)
(McMillan 1999: 258)

There was one response to the programme that was not unexpected and that was opposition from some managers. Some were sceptical of the value of New Directions, others were antagonistic and even openly hostile. One or two senior managers thought that the Vice-Chancellor and his senior team were taking far too much notice of the views of more junior staff and some even thought that 'revolution was in the air'. Others tried to stop their staff attending. This could all be interpreted positively as the programme having a real impact on the organization, particularly those areas dominated by hidebound, traditional management values. A good example of the attitude of many senior managers is contained in a letter of complaint.

I cannot see that getting together a group of staff, most of whom do not sit on decision-making committees and none of whom are in positions of management, can genuinely influence the policy changes that need to come about. I feel it would have been more productive to convene groups of staff who share similar perspectives and concerns.

(McMillan 1999: 261)

At the same time there were a significant number of senior staff who were very supportive and welcoming of the programme and its involvement of their staff.

When one considers the impact and influence 'the people's movement' was having then it comes as no surprise that those managers who held traditional views with a vested interest in maintaining the *status quo* were hostile. The ideas that were generated in the early workshops were particularly influential, as Geoff Peters noted.

The ideas were so prolific that they have generated papers which have been discussed twice by the Vice-Chancellor's weekly meeting, a summary paper went to SPRC [Strategic Planning and Resources Committee] last month, and at the last meeting of the OUs, senior team managers were able to talk through some of the issues and to hear a very interesting report of how Operations and some other units had been bringing their new directions people together to consider change in their area.

(McMillan 1999: 264)

The workshops on major strategic themes enabled staff to input their ideas directly to the senior managers involved and to influence the University's strategic planning processes.

So for example, when earlier this year we were drafting an international strategy, we held open workshops on the 'OU going global'. The results were then fed straight into the preparation of a first draft and those who attended the workshop were able to comment knowledgeably on the thinking as it developed further.

(Geoff Peters, *Open House*, July 1995)

Learning and change dynamics

If learning results in change and change may be an outcome of learning then there is much evidence to suggest that a range of learning–changes were taking place for both those involved in the programme and others as has already been described.

It should also be borne in mind that the programme and its distinctive approach affected not only those who attended events but also their colleagues. In summary, staff at the University described how the process:

- made them think about the University and its situation;
- encouraged discussion about strategy and strategic issues;
- acted as a catalyst for change; and
- had a therapeutic effect.

As a result of the New Directions initiative, significant numbers of employees were now engaged in reflecting on the University and its strategic situation. This for the majority was a completely new experience and a whole new approach to their role in the organization. As one senior manager put it: 'it got people to understand some of the environmental issues the University was facing and to engage with them and to recognise that the world had changed' (McMillan 1999: 275). It was also a new experience for the organization as a whole, but one that resonated with its open values.

People claimed to have a much wider view of the University and their part within it. The IES study comments that the OU and the retail company also in their study, were the only two out of the five organizations they studied where interviewees 'spontaneously mentioned that they had learned about their organization' (Tamkin and Barber 1998: 32). Participants in the programme 'found a greater appreciation of the University's structure, the work of colleagues in different parts of the organization, the workings of the committee system and an appreciation of how others viewed their own department' (Tamkin and Barber 1998: 28). Junior staff, especially, had gained a better understanding of how their colleagues perceived them and also a better understanding of how the University worked.

The study also notes that because many of the participants in New Directions were in relatively junior positions they found the opportunity of mixing with people from other areas very valuable and insightful. Some managers changed their style as the result of feedback from subordinates during the workshops becoming active co-learners in the process.

A significant number considered that their participation in the programme had directly changed the way they carried out their job. They cited:

- improved communications in their own areas;
- a managerial style that was now more personal;
- being more tolerant and analytical of own mistakes;
- making better provision for the development of their own staff; and
- reading more on complexity science and applying some complexity-based ideas to their work

The degree and depth of any changes that the programme influenced or inspired varied considerably from individual to individual and area to area. The IES study noted that some of the barriers to change remained – and that many of these barriers were people who had helped to create the University and were wedded to the *status quo*. In spite of this though the study found that there was 'considerable commonality of response, describing an organization that had become more flexible and less hierarchical, more sharing and more open with information'. It was noted too that this reflected the New Directions approach which sought 'to enhance communications and create a more open organizational culture' (Tamkin and Barber 1998: 48). One interviewee stated:

> I think the University is changing a lot at the moment, some of it is attributable to New Directions, perhaps only a small amount. New Directions had been a good oil, making it go more smoothly, it was an outlet for individuals at any level to voice difficulties and uncertainties, to vocalise those in a non-threatening way.
>
> (Tamkin and Barber 1998: 48)

The study concluded that New Directions together with the University's management development programme resulted in: 'a move away from an organization that was resistant to change to one where there is a growing awareness of the need to change. There is also a perception that it had become more open' (Tamkin and Barber 1998: 18). As one member of staff put it succinctly: 'I believe that it shifted the University out of its complacency' (McMillan 1999: 276).

Significant numbers of staff believed that they had learnt or discovered something as a result of their participation in New Directions. Many spoke of mindsets being affected and even shifted (double-loop learning). Here are some examples of both single- and double-loop learning:

- One secretary described how the confidence she had gained as a result of running a workshop at the conference had spurred her on to take some management courses. Also, she had met with the Director of Personnel to discuss some of the issues that had arisen from the conference.

- An administrator was encouraged to continue trying to make changes in his own area.
- One manager had realized that before the programme his view of the University had been too narrow. His horizons had stretched and he now saw new ways he could contribute to his role. As a result he was now involved in National Vocational Qualifications as an assessor and verifier and was involved in writing national standards for the Royal Society of Arts.
- One secretary had learnt about facilitation skills from her participation in the programme.
- One middle manager unused to participating in such wide ranging discussions told how now he was able to participate more effectively in all kinds of group situations.
- One senior manager, with over ten years at the University, thought he had learnt more about the values of the University and its subcultures.
- An academic described how the conference had made a significant impact upon his thinking and his learning had led to action and change. He recalled how 'the telling example' of a secretary not being allowed to take out an inter library loan had influenced his thinking, especially in the context of the University as a learning organization. He had attended the Rover workshop and had been inspired to make a bid for research funding to set up a similar learning programme at the University. Further, he had written a paper on the 'OU and the Learning Society' which explored the Open University's contribution to learning in the UK.

The 1994 conference – rich flows of change

The section that follows is an extract from my book: Elizabeth McMillan, *Complexity Organizations and Change* (2004) published by Routledge, pages 130–33.

The 1994 one-day conference is worthy of special consideration as it is a microcosm of the whole New Directions programme. It created a change process within a change process and like a fractal reflected the overall pattern of the programme. But how did it contribute to the New Directions change processes?

The planning team decided that the conference would try to stimulate people to become involved and to take individual action to change the University. There would be speakers from other organizations to introduce new ideas and share their experiences on change, interactive workshops, and opportunities for the staff to come together pool their knowledge and ideas, and put their recommendations to top management. The staff of the University responded positively to the call to join in the conference. Employees from all areas, categories and levels of seniority attended. The opportunity to participate was highly appreciated and especially the opportunity to express views directly to top management, and the atmosphere on the day was described as 'buzzing'.

Speakers from other organizations that had undergone major changes included Rover and the Metropolitan Police and the feedback comments on these sessions were exceptionally positive. The OU has many cultures but exposure to stories of changes in other organizations served to introduce a measure of challenge and diversity into the existing cultural perspectives of some of the conference delegates. The speakers from the external organizations also introduced new information into the organization which is essential if creativity and change are to flourish (Nonaka 1988).

Table 6.1 summarizes the main issues to emerge from the group 'action' sessions which were drawn together and presented in the final plenary session. These indicate how staff from all walks of working life, were aware of the challenges the University faced from its external environment. But a major thread running throughout was the importance of addressing internal issues too, and especially staffing concerns,

Table 6.1 Conference issues and outcomes

Issue/theme	*Outcome/follow up*
Staff policy: equalization of staff terms and conditions; more staff development; need for a Pro-Vice-Chancellor for staff	Significant progress made
Marketing strategy: need to improve; importance of customer research and corporate identity	Significant progress made but more needed
New technology development: fear that University was being left behind; need for multi-media developments	Very significant progress made
Need for improved communications: better bottom-up communications and more effective and appropriate information giving.	Significant progress made but more needed
Low staff morale: due to conflicting messages; barriers between staff; working on a treadmill	No progress
Need for leadership and for better people management skills	No progress
Need for a flatter organization structure and better co-operation between departments	Some progress

Source: Adapted from McMillan (2004).

if effective change was to be achieved. The emergence of what could be described as a 'democratic strategic action plan' is discussed further in the next sub-section.

The conference as part of New Directions sought to bring about changes in the University. Thus progress on any of the issues raised provides a conventional measure of how effective the conference and New Directions had been in influencing and even changing aspects of the University. It had raised issues that may well have already been under consideration but in doing so it had turned a spotlight on them and raised their profile. Table 6.1 shows that of the seven issues raised significant progress was made on four of them, some progress on one of them and no progress on the remaining two. Details of how these issues were followed up is provided in Appendix 3.

Participation in the conference made a major impression on a number of people. One manager, for example, had been 'really recharged' by the conference and believed it had encouraged her to become more politically active, to approach the General Secretary of the Association of University Teachers at their council meeting shortly after the conference, and to join the National Executive. Other staff were so enthused that they had decided to take action themselves. One secretary in the marketing team had approached the PVC Curriculum Development to talk about the need to market things differently.

Because there was widespread representation of staff at the conference so word spread around different levels and in different areas of the organization. This spread of involvement added to the existing response dynamics and further amplified existing feedback loops as well as creating new ones. All this contributed to the energy for change within different areas of the University.

The conference was reported in *Open House* as 'an outstanding success' and Geoff Peters notes that 'already a number of developments have taken place as a result'. The report listed several follow-up activities including:

- the setting up of the team of volunteers from the conference to form the staff survey team;
- the production of a user friendly version of the Staff Policy Committee Action Plan to be circulated to all staff;
- an invitation to all staff to input to the next stage of the New Directions programme.

All staff were recommended to read the conference report as it would provide them with 'some valuable insights as regards the information exchanged and ideas shared' (McMillan 1999: 298).

To summarize, the conference had been a New Directions one-day event with a 100 delegates which had sought to stimulate visioning of the future and ideas for changing the University. It had made a considerable impression on many of those there and appeared to exert a range of influences on some other staff too. Some of the positive aspects of the conference were as follows:

- It influenced or gave an impetus to a number of significant and recognizable changes.
- It boosted the flow of change within the University.
- It enabled the grass roots of the University to articulate their views and be heard by senior and top managers.
- It encouraged and inspired many staff to take actions of their own.
- It provided a fertile learning environment.
- It was a successful landmark event that put New Directions on the University map.

Some of the mainly negative aspects were as follows:

- It raised anxiety levels for those staff who felt threatened by changes, especially in new technologies.
- It failed to reach most of the regional staff.
- It added to the irritation some managers felt about New Directions.
- It increased the perceived marginalization of academic staff.

Democracy at work?

The final plenary session of the conference had asked the delegates to make presentations to the Vice-Chancellor and his senior team under the heading of 'Strategic Recommendations for the Future'. At this session the delegates had produced a realistic strategy for future action with clear time scales – either now or in the future. In effect a collection of staff from a range of roles, at all levels and from all areas of the University had created a democratic or 'grass roots' version of the University's official strategic action plan ('Plans for Change'). (See Table 6.2.)

Table 6.2 shows a predominantly internal focus that puts people or staff-related themes at the core. As a strategic action plan it sees internal issues as a priority. Although there is a strong internal focus important external aspects are also listed as critical for future success. The importance of developing new technologies is highlighted and the danger to the University if it falls behind in this respect. This is a critical issue for an organization that uses distance methods to deliver its products. The focus on marketing recognizes the importance of reaching out to its students/customers and ensuring that new

Table 6.2 Democratic strategic action plan

Issue/theme	Focus	Issue core	SWOT	Time focus
Staff policy: equalization of staff terms and conditions; more staff development; need for a Pro-Vice-Chancellor for staff	Internal	People and equality	Weakness	Present
Marketing strategy: importance of customer research and corporate identity	External and internal	Marketing and income	Opportunity	Present and future
New technology development: fear that University was being left behind	External and internal	Technology and multi-media	Opportunity and threat	Present and future
Need for improved communications	Internal	People/organ-ization management	Weakness	Present
Low staff morale	Internal	People management	Threat	Present
Need for leadership and for better people management skills	Internal	People management/ development	Weakness	Present
Need for a flatter organization structure	Internal	Organization structure	Weakness	Present

Source: Adapted from McMillan (2004).

markets are reached, while existing ones are kept satisfied. It is also about developing a strong corporate image, very necessary if the University is to succeed in increasing its student numbers.

The SWOT analysis highlights five areas of weakness and two of opportunity, one of which could also constitute a threat if not addressed. The University is seen as having some significant weaknesses and limited opportunities. This is not a very healthy profile and the time focus makes it clear that present action is required. The plan does not rely on structural or procedural changes as part of a planned management exercise. Instead, it is a strategic action plan that sees the involvement of people as the necessary means of achieving it. As the text from one of the conference slides explains: 'The importance of achieving the University's goals lies with the commitment, motivation and enthusiasm of its staff.'

A wide range of staff from across the institution had participated in New Directions events and had swiftly learnt how to participate effectively in an organizational wide change process and to contribute with clarity and perspicacity to the University's strategic agenda, culminating in the development of a clear strategic action plan. Given the right environment and support individuals were demonstrating their capacity to act as effective complex adaptive systems.

Self-organizing teams in action

Two very important features of the programme were the two volunteer teams: the conference planning team and the staff survey team. These teams delivered very effectively on their projects and together with the 1995 action group influenced and affected the design of the programme and further energized the dynamics for change.

People volunteered to join the teams and to add to their workloads. They did this because they wanted to do something active to support change and reinvigorate the University and they had been encouraged by their experience of the programme and even 'inspired by the conference' to do so.

The volunteer teams worked very well for a number of reasons. One significant reason was that everyone was enthusiastic, highly motivated and committed to their project. One drawback faced by team members, however, was having to squeeze time out of the working week to participate.

Working in a team made up of a mixture of staff drawn from all categories and grades proved to be very advantageous. People learnt more about other areas of the university and about different working roles. There was a valuable exchange of views, a sharing of ideas and significant listening. Working with people they did not normally come into contact with was appreciated as a new and very worthwhile experience.

Both teams worked effectively as coherent and efficient groups with their own distinct style. The conference team was especially spontaneous and creative in its way of working, whereas the survey team was more focused on the delivery of the survey. This suggests that the nature of the projects affected the way the teams worked. Ideas and creativity were needed to design the conference, whereas the delivery of the survey required information gathering and exploration of both staff issues and survey methods.

An important feature of both teams was the lack of political or departmental agendas to snarl up progress. There was the potential for hierarchical patterns to emerge and predominate encouraged by existing roles in the University but this did not happen. The teams operated as groups of equals. They also broke with tradition in that they did not have a formal chair or traditional leader. Instead there was a collective or shared leadership approach which arose out of the open, democratic style of the teams and their strong sense of shared purpose. Initially I acted as a facilitator or guide in each team but this role diminished as the teams grew together. In another break with University tradition decisions were arrived at quickly and were often made on the basis of action. In other words, if someone was willing to carry something out then the team would back them. One team member described decision making this way: 'What seemed to be the best idea always came out on the top of the pile and everybody swung behind it.'

The two teams that were put together at random with no thought for the provision of complementary skills and attributes but they operated like a group of co-learners and supported and encouraged each other. A clerk on one of the teams observed that 'everyone developed the skills needed during the life of the team'. Many of the team members still kept in touch and still formed part of a supportive network of colleagues long after the lifetime of the team.

In summary the teams were quite different to other OU project teams because:

- they were informal.
- they included a wide cross section of staff.
- they were much more open.
- there was no hierarchy 'not even a relaxed hierarchy'.
- there was no person who overruled others in the team.
- there was 'no desperation' that arose from people coming along with different agendas.
- everyone shared a common aim, and therefore:
  - they were purposeful and directed.
  - there was a great deal of energy.

(McMillan 2004: 137)

The next chapter discusses in detail the self-organizing attributes of the two teams and how they differed from more traditional teams.

The legacy of New Directions

By the 1990s the University had become a very successful, well-established, highly respected academic institution with a world wide reputation for excellence in its teaching and learning provision. But as the senior management team realized at the time the University had to change and change significantly if it was to sustain its position in higher education. There was an air of self satisfaction in many quarters – the University had achieved the impossible and that was enough. This was accompanied by a sense of complacency and a belief that the institution knew best. This led to intense and sometimes acrimonious debate over the needs of students and the notion of the students as customers. Overall it appeared that most people, especially long serving employees, felt that there was no need for the University to change the way it did things.

However, some staff as well as the senior team realized that the University needed to change if it were to continue to prosper. The New Directions initiative gave them an opportunity to voice their concerns, to contribute their ideas and to use their energies to change things. It also awakened many staff who had not appreciated the strategic position in which the University now found itself. Several hundred staff were encouraged to think about change at a number of levels, to reflect on change and to take action themselves. As a result the University changed, as the IES study confirmed, and became an organization that was more ready to change and to embrace new ideas. The debate over students as customers was resolved and other issues arose and were debated and resolved as the organization moved on. Many of the programme's new ideas, such as the lunchtime briefings, were taken up and became part of the formal processes. New ways of working had developed and a lot of new initiatives continued to come on stream. For example, several faculties now produce courses twice a year instead of only once a year as previously.

In a conversation some years later, Geoff Peters described how people were still talking positively about the programme, including one of the new Pro-Vice-Chancellors. In his view there had been significant changes in individuals, a new general readiness to change, to do things more flexibly and a 'breaking down of organizational structure and work . . . a general broadening of roles in the OU. People more willing to consider organizational change'.

It is my view that the University changed in many ways as a result of New Directions and its influence. Yet paradoxically at the same time much did not change. The complex hierarchical structures still remain and new initiatives have to deal with cumbersome bureaucratic approaches. There has been progress on the six new directions set out in 1993 but the University's structure, most of its procedures and endemic bureaucratic thinking (strenuously denied everywhere!) still exists.

> Geoff Peters acknowledged that towards the end of the programme New Directions had rocked the boat too much for some. The top management team had developed many misgivings and he felt it necessary to try and tone down its activities and gradually withdraw his involvement. It seems to me that the programme was thus effectively disturbing the organization's equilibrium and beginning to make real changes in hearts and minds when people lost their nerve, or ran out of energy or were overtaken by other events.
>
> (McMillan 2004:139)

In 1999 another series of strategic workshops called 'Shaping the future of the OU' was organized which used some of the approaches developed in the early ND workshops thus continuing some features of the programme's legacy.

New Directions as a model for organizational change

As a strategic change model the New Directions programme began as a top-down model that adopted a deliberate semi-prescriptive approach to strategy but which was influenced by the need to engage all the staff at the University if strategic plans were to turn into strategic action. The consultation workshops were part of the participation and engagement plan – but as they took place, so the strategic approach became less imposed and more emergent and unintended and strategic learning took place. Further, the programme did not pause to solidify things as in Lewin's model, instead it unfolded in a free form way. The self-organizing nature of this is discussed in more detail in the next chapter.

The New Directions programme was not intended as a learning approach to strategy but one emerged out of real-world experiences as events unfolded and the University's strategic thinking was developed and revised in response to the programme. Feedback, interactive responses and real learning at all levels and in many areas contributed to the development of a process of continuous organizational learning.

> Involving people in strategic action planning and giving them a voice in their own future can create powerful positive emotions. The programme boosted the confidence and self-esteem of those involved such that they were able to make their own changes. This suggests that by creating feelings of excitement and optimism a change intervention can stimulate learning and energize individuals and groups of people to do things differently. This is to act directly and appeal positively to the emotions of people rather than to ignore how people will react to strategic planning and then deal with the emotional fall-out when it arises. Such an approach recognizes the importance of the emotions as well as the intellect and incorporating them into the change process, so rejecting reliance on the traditional, rational, logical approach.
>
> (McMillan 2004: 140)

The use of a visioning style as a key part of strategic management was very fashionable in the 1980s and is still used today, yet it has been criticized for often only delivering cosmetic changes. This approach was adopted at the workshops and other events in the programme and it encouraged people to think about future possibilities and as Pedler *et al.* (1991) point out, why should people change unless they have a new vision that will not become a reality unless changes are made and learning takes place? Further, the need to bridge the gap between the present vision and the future reality led to enthusiasm for change amongst many of the programme's participants.

> First order change is a feature of the bureaucracy (Dale 1994) but not second order change. This is because in Morgan's (1986) view bureaucratic organizations tend to operate in a way that actually impedes second order change or double-loop learning. But the programme was able to provide an environment which overcame many of the factors which hindered the development of deep level learning. It encouraged participants to think for themselves, to challenge long accepted norms and facilitated the development of relationships across departmental

boundaries. Participants developed a wider vision of the institution and their role within it. The programme demonstrates how an organization such as a bureaucracy can facilitate the development of double-loop learning as Morgan (1986) suggests by:

- encouraging an open approach to the discussion of strategic change.
- by facilitating the exploration of issues from many perspectives.
- by recognizing that people can make mistakes and can learn from them.
- by encouraging a bottom up approach to the strategic planning process.

(McMillan 2004: 141)

As a model for organizational change, the New Directions programme shows how a traditional, hierarchical organization can involve all employees in strategic level activities and so draw on all the knowledge, experience and intelligence residing in the organization. Such an approach moves an organization closer to behaving as a complex adaptive system on the edge of chaos. Figure 6.3 uses icebergs as a metaphor to show how a traditional, hierarchical organization may change while it is undergoing such a change process.

The icebergs represent the different staff layers in a hierarchical organization. Junior staff are the largest group at the bottom of the pyramid, above them is middle management (MM), then senior management (SM) and finally the top team or board (TT). Both icebergs, and their staff, are affected by a sea of everyday activity which usually engulfs them. In other words, they are so busy with their roles that they give little or no time to thinking about strategic issues. They do not monitor or reflect on changes in the external environment and the implications these may have for the future of the organization. Strategy is not their prime concern – that is the job of the top team and senior management.

The iceberg on the right shows how, when an organization adopts a New Directions style approach to strategic change, then all levels of staff are engaged in considering strategic issues and watching the external 'sky'. Thus the sea of everyday activity recedes from time to time. As a result of this many more employees better understand the challenges faced by the organization and are able to contribute to the evolution of strategic directions and supportive actions. This engagement process is particularly important in times of major change. As all levels of staff in the organization are engaged, so richer and more diverse possibilities for the future emerge. Further, as people from different areas and roles come together and learn from each other so a co-learning community may arise and also a strong sense of shared purpose. The organization is now drawing on all the ideas, insights, energies and collective wisdom of everyone in deciding how best to work with the 'weather' of the external environment to ensure the future survival of the organization.

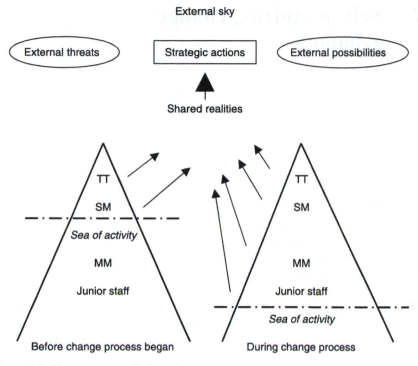

Figure 6.3 Change process 'icebergs'.
Source: Adapted from McMillan (2004).

Key questions

- The New Directions Programme could be described as a conventional change intervention that successfully encouraged a bottom-up process – how accurate and complete is this description in your view?
- The programme brought together people from all levels, roles and areas of the University – how did this affect them, their working life and the University?
- The 1994 conference is described as a microcosm of the whole programme – why is this?
- How significant is learning as part of an organizational change process?
- How much did the University change as a result of New Directions?
- How did the programme engage people and how significant is the role played by the volunteers?
- What are the characteristics of the New Directions strange attractor?

7 Self-organizing change dynamics

Key points

- Letting go to self-organize
- Effective self-organizing teams
- Team working in organizations
- A complex adaptive change process?

This chapter draws on research and experiences of the New Directions programme to further consider how complexity principles, especially self-organizing principles, can be applied in stimulating change dynamics.

Letting go to self-organize

No one could have predicted in the early spring of 1993 that a short series of consultative workshops in support of 'Plans for Change' would have resulted in the emergence of a people's movement for change which rolled out spontaneously over another three years or so. How did this happen? The answer I believe is that the organizers were prepared to let go of the reins of control and see what happened. They had trust in the staff of the University and were convinced that they too had the future success of the University in their hearts. An opportunitistic approach developed whereby ideas or suggestions which arose were either rejected or built upon in an unplanned, self-organizing fashion.

Since the inception of the programme I had been building up my knowledge of complexity science by reading widely and by attending a number of informative seminars. These included presentations by distinguished scientists like Brian Goodwin and Steven Rose, the science writer Roger Lewin and complexity expert, Ralph Stacey. As a key player in the delivery of the programme I was ready to try out the new way of thinking I had discovered. I deliberately introduced these new concepts into meetings, team discussions and various events and sought to influence the thinking of those involved in the programme whether formally or informally. A number of those I spoke to came on board and explored these new ideas for themselves. The PVC

Strategy had been a senior lecturer in systems and he too was familiar with notions of self-organization and emergence. He was also very relaxed about the self-organizing aspects of the programme and prepared to let go in a very supportive way. For example, he attended the opening minutes of the first meeting of the conference planning team and said simply that its purpose was to organize a conference for the programme in May 1994 and that the rest was up to them. Then he added that whatever they chose to do he would support them. I know of very few managers of such seniority who would take such a risk.

Fractals and butterflies

The New Directions programme has a number of fractal aspects. One notice-able one is the way the workshops developed similar structures and evolved similar patterns of process. At each workshop there would be a mix of staff from all categories, levels and locations and part of the process would involve using small groups to vision the future via free flowing discussions. These 'visions' would then be fed back from the small groups to everyone at the event, including a senior manager who could take the ideas forward. The content or the theme at each event may have varied but the processes always followed a recognizable pattern as did the style and behaviours of the facilita-tors. The conference in 1994 was in many ways a scaled-up version of the workshops. Further, recognizably similar repeating behaviours arose creating a distinctive style which came to be associated with the programme, as dis-cussed in the last chapter. This style permeated all events and combined with the visions and values of the participants, which were consistently held across the programme, led to the creation of a temporary New Directions strange attractor. This and the spontaneous, unplanned, free-form nature of the pro-gramme suggest that it was essentially self-organizing and fractal in nature.

I was very enthusiastic about complexity science and the possibilities it offered managers as it mapped so well onto the reality of my managerial experience. I have no doubts that my enthusiasm infected others and I created a small but influential butterfly effect. Other individuals too made an impact as they changed the way they did things and influenced others around them. The programme also deliberately set out to encourage a host of individual changes and 'to let a hundred butterflies take flight' as someone put it.

A map of the programme

Figure 7.1 encapsulates in diagrammatic form the self-organizing way in which the programme unfurled over some three years. The map was created by Carol Russell, a key member of the conference planning team, in the autumn of 1996. It is possible to see waves of activity spreading out from the original pre-planned beginnings in April 1993. The formation of the volunteer teams was key to this – as the map clearly illustrates.

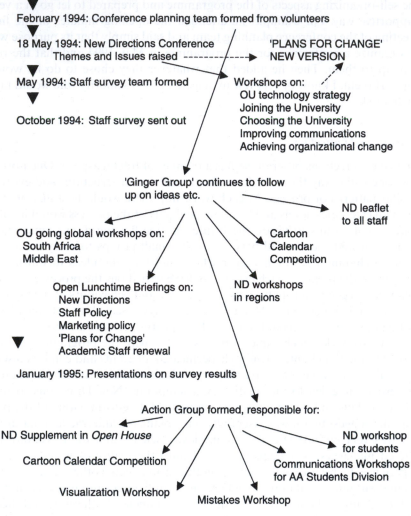

April 1993: PVC, Strategy and Head of Training and Development set up series
of consultation workshops for staff on 'Plans for Change'
▼

February 1994: Conference planning team formed from volunteers
▼

18 May 1994: New Directions Conference   'PLANS FOR CHANGE'
Themes and Issues raised ----------▸ NEW VERSION
▼

May 1994: Staff survey team formed   Workshops on:
▼   OU technology strategy
                                            Joining the University
October 1994: Staff survey sent out   Choosing the University
                                            Improving communications
                                            Achieving organizational change

'Ginger Group' continues to follow
up on ideas etc.

                                                                ND leaflet
                                                                to all staff

OU going global workshops on: Cartoon
South Africa   Calendar
Middle East   Competition

Open Lunchtime Briefings on: ND workshops
New Directions   in regions
Staff Policy
Marketing policy
▼ 'Plans for Change'
Academic Staff renewal

January 1995: Presentations on survey results

Action Group formed, responsible for:

ND Supplement in *Open House*   ND workshop
                                                       for students
Cartoon Calendar Competition
                                            Communications Workshops
                                            for AA Students Division
Visualization Workshop   Mistakes Workshop

Action Group: Planning commences for 1996 events including a Conference.

Figure 7.1 Map of activities.

Source: Adapted from a map drawn by Carol Russell in McMillan (2004: 144).

The teams had formed in response to the programme and were encouraged
to act and create informal new flows of activities and fresh responses. These
in turn stimulated other employees, encouraged learning and the formation
of informal networks of programme participants. The volunteers acted in
a self-organizing way by reacting spontaneously and opportunistically to

events. As one of them stated: 'At several New Directions events last year, staff had suggested we should also be asking students what kind of OU they'd like to see in the future. So in the usual New Directions fashion, we decided to get some students together and ask them' (McMillan 1999: 344).

The map also shows how the ideas from the conference led to a fresh series of workshops which fed ideas and suggestions on key topics into a new version of 'Plans for Change'. Note too the wide scope of the workshop topics, from internal issues of staff policy and academic renewal to global concerns with workshops on the expansion of university teaching into South Africa and the Middle East.

As I pointed out in Chapter 6 the programme began primarily as a deliberate strategy but became more an emergent or consensus strategy as described by Mintzberg and Waters. As they state a consensus strategy is one which is driven not by top management but evolves through the 'results of a host of individual actions' (Mintzberg and Waters 1989: 13). An 'emergent strategy means, not chaos, but in essence unintended order' (Mintzberg and Waters 1989: 17). Thus emergent or consensus strategies with their notions of many individual actions and unintentional order resonate strongly with notions of self-organizing systems.

The programme did not descend into disorder or anarchy as some senior managers feared because it had structure and both planned and unplanned features. The content was put together spontaneously and the structure evolved over time in support of the activities and the ethos of the programme. It was also constrained by the requirements of 'Plans for Change' and the six core new directions contained therein. Further, the University's values and core purpose: to provide high-quality higher education via distance teaching, provided a sound guiding framework for activity. One senior manager described the programme as having 'structured spontaneity'. It evolved in a 'more free-wheeling' fashion as it went on, but there was still 'a structure within it' like 'a self-imposed hierarchy'. Thus the programme was able to operate as a self-organizing system on the edge of chaos. It had no need of traditional command and control mechanisms as it was able to create its own patterns of internal order.

From the very start the programme had a very strong sense of purpose: to change the University and to do so by involving all its employees in making the changes. A strong sense of purpose is essential if a system is to be self-organizing. As the programme continued so fresh objectives emerged but still within the framework created by the programme's overall purpose. Again these objectives were not pre-planned but were a spontaneous response to events.

Self-organizing networks

The University like many large, traditional, bureaucracies has a large number of informal systems or networks which facilitate the flows of activity and creativity and work around the log jams in the system. The New Directions programme encouraged and facilitated the formation of more of these informal systems – which are essentially self-organizing as they usually arise in response to an issue or specific situation. The workshops, by bringing people together from all areas of the University, provided the right conditions for the creation of more self-organizing networks. Some were essentially social in origin, others were work or task based.

The volunteer teams proved to be very strong self-organizing systems and members spoke of friendships which continued to flourish long after the end of the programme. The creation of self-organizing networks is essential if an organization is to survive. This is particularly true of an organization that is close to equilibrium or stability, as these can help move it further towards the edge of chaos. These self-organizing systems challenge the *status quo* where necessary to get things done, learn rapidly from events and create and grab passing opportunities. They bring additional energy, innovation and achievement into an organization. They also give employees a chance to use their skills and knowledge in engaging with the future of their organization – which is their future too. The Edge of Chaos Model discussed in a later chapter explores this notion in some detail.

Self-organizing teams

Ralph Stacey provides a description of the essential characteristics of self-organizing teams in his book *Strategic Management and Organisational Dynamics* (1996). He describes them as groups which arise spontaneously around specific issues, communicate and co-operate about these issues, reach a consensus and give a committed response to the issues. This description matches that of the teams which arose from the New Directions programme: the conference planning team and the staff survey team.

In his book Stacey examines and defines self-managed or empowered teams and self-organized teams. Research on the programme indicates that both project teams could be described as self-organizing, although the survey team also had significant attributes of a self-managed team. I would suggest that this reflects the nature of the project which it was carrying out on behalf of the Staff Policy Committee.

Team working in organizations

Table 7.1 shows a comparison between Stacey's definition of a self-organizing team and my own definition based on my own research on the programme and a literature search. My definition of a self-organizing team operating in an organizational context, is as follows:

- It knows what it has to do.
- It holds meetings that are loosely structured.
- Its core purpose influences the structure of meetings.

Table 7.1 Self-organizing teams

Team	Stacey's (1996) definitions – match (%)	My definitions – match (%)	Overall match (%)
Conference planning team	70	80	75.5
Staff survey team	46	63	54.5

Source: Adapted from McMillan (2000: 186).

- It has decision making processes that are mainly spontaneous.
- There is freedom in its meetings to explore lots of ideas.
- Lots of ideas arise spontaneously.
- It is full of energy and enthusiasm.

Overall the conference planning team closely matched these definitions but the survey team less so.

My case study research provided additional data on team working which added to and built on Stacey's definitions of self-managed and self-organized teams. From this work has evolved the team working model shown as Figure 7.2 This shows different approaches to team working set against the organizational contexts of four simple models of organizations.

Stacey's definitions of self-managed and self-organized teams provide the first eight descriptive statements in Figure 7.2. The final six descriptions in italics are based on my own research. The other definitions of committees or traditional teams are based on my own observations and research and in relation to the definitions for self-managed and self-organizing teams.

The line at the top of the figure illustrates the changing flow of team working from the very formal committee system on the left to the very informal self-organizing team on the right. At the bottom of Figure 7.2 a line represents the changing nature of organizations, from the bureaucracy on the left to the emerging twenty-first century or complex adaptive organization on the right. The organizations of the 1980s and 1990s are referred to as 'modern/traditional' because although many adapted their structures and updated working practices many still thought in a traditional way about people and processes. In reality in most organizations the teams will not fit neatly into any one category but will display attributes from one or more team types. However, the characteristics of the teams do relate strongly to the nature of the organizational context in which they operate and give a good indication of the essential nature of the organization.

The 1995 New Directions action group

The New Directions action group was a self-organizing group which formed early in 1995 in a spontaneous response to the issues that had arisen from the

Committee	Traditional team	Self-managed or empowered team	Self-organizing team
Part of formal structure		Part of formal structure	Not part of formal structure
Formal and permanent		Formal, temporary or permanent	Informal and temporary
Not spontaneously formed		Not spontaneously formed	Spontaneously formed
Controlled by senior management		Indirectly controlled or steered by senior management	Boundaries influenced by senior management
Managers decide 'who' and 'what'		Managers decide 'who' and 'what'	Team members decide 'who' and 'what'
Represent and reinforce the hierarchy		Replace the hierarchy	Often in conflict with or constrained by the hierarchy
Represent senior management		Empowered by senior management	Empowered by team's members
Strongly shared culture		Strongly shared culture	Cultural difference provoke and constrain
Little or no sense of shared purpose		Some sense of shared purpose	Strong sense of shared purpose
Order via controlling, formal processes		Order achieved via recognized processes	Inherent order emerges
Behaviours governed by procedures and roles		Behaviours influenced by procedures and roles	Behaviours predominantly spontaneous
Strong sense of role commitment		Strong sense of team commitment	Strong sense of personal and team commitment
Low levels of energy and enthusiasm		Variable amounts of energy and enthusiasm	High levels of energy and enthusiasm
Little or no learning possibilities		Possibility of some learning	Co learning community

Bureaucracy — Traditional organization ·········· Modern – Traditional ·········· Complexity organization

20th century ·········· 21st century ··········

Figure 7.2 Team working in organizations – a fluid spectrum of process.

Source: Adapted from McMillan (2000: 191).

1994 conference and the staff survey. It saw itself as a group dedicated to keeping the programme going in order to facilitate change in the University by encouraging local action. The group aimed to listen to staff views and ideas, to keep them informed on the progress of issues raised and to empower them to take action.

At its first meeting it forged its identity not by formal discussion but by using brainstorming techniques and seeing what emerged. They discussed what they believed the New Directions programme stood for and devised their own vision of the OU of the future, before moving on to listing priorities for action. Seven projects were identified for the coming year and people signed up to them. Of the seven projects listed four were achieved during the year. Figure 7.1 shows the activities carried out by the group and how they added to the ripples of change across the University.

At its meetings the action group adopted the processes and the action style of the other two volunteer teams. They explored the issues, made decisions via consensus and agreed actions and allocated responsibilities on a voluntary basis. In other words, they behaved as a self-organizing team and along with the other two project teams demonstrated the effectiveness of such a way of working even within the constraints of a traditional, hierarchical organizational setting.

A complex adaptive change process?

How well does the New Directions programme map onto our knowledge of the behaviours of complex adaptive systems when applied to organizations? In Chapter 5 I listed seven ways in which managers could achieve change without using command and control methods. How well does New Directions score? On the first three points the PVC Strategy, his support team and others involved in the formal side of the process score highly. They let go, recognized that the future is unpredictable and sought to understand the unfolding of events in a non-predictive way. I am not sure that they sought for evidence of patterns, flows of similarities, fractals or evidence of strange attractors. But these were all part of the programme. Notions of order and disorder were accepted as part of the process – though at times somewhat nervously. Also the idea that transformation can be uncomfortable and even painful was accepted, as was the notion that people had to learn to work with upheavals and not try to stifle them, as they could be precursors of beneficial changes for the University.

In Chapter 5 I also listed thirteen key attributes of a complex adaptive organization operating to its full potential, that is, on the edge of chaos. How well does the Open University undergoing the New Directions programme map onto this list of definitions? The evidence suggests that the programme itself and those participating map onto many of the attributes described as follows:

- The programme was essentially self-organizing (point one) once it had responded to the feedback from the first series of workshops.
- The volunteers working with the PVC Strategy's office, my department and many of the programme's participants were constantly learning from their experiences of the programme and from each other (point two) from which the University benefited.
- They and many staff not involved in the programme keenly shared the OU's core purpose and values (point three).
- The programme itself was not subject to any centralizing, controlling authority. It had been instigated by the PVC Strategy, Geoff Peters, who could have imposed a centralizing control but at no time did he attempt to do so. Many of the New Directions participants, however, may have been subject to such in their own areas (point four).
- The programme was non hierarchical (point five) although the University as a whole most certainly was.
- For a time the programme did enable individuals and some areas to operate and flourish on the edge of chaos facilitating pockets of innovation and creativity across the organization (point six).
- The New Directions action group proved to be adept at taking some risks – for example the Mistakes Workshops. The PVC Strategy and the organizing support team took a significant risk in letting go of the proposed consultation exercise and seeing what happened next (point seven).
- Everyone involved in the rolling out of the programme and many of the staff involved seemed able to respond flexibly to changes, to adapt to them and to be willing to change in response to learning (points eight and nine).
- The programme along with the University's staff development programme provided places and opportunities for learning and shared learning experiences which were valued and seen as essential for good practice (point ten).
- Within the shelter of the New Directions programme there was no culture of blame and people were encouraged to learn from their mistakes – but this did not apply to the University as an institution (point eleven).
- It is very difficult to know how well people involved in the programme were able to turn events to their own advantage. In some cases, employees were able to do this and to improve their career or to take up new and interesting options but it is not possible to assess how well the University did as a whole (point twelve).
- The participants in the programme were very able to create their own visions and dynamic interpretations of the future as was the University's top team (point thirteen) but how widespread this was is hard to say.

Thus at the time the programme was at the peak of its influence on individuals and some areas of the University it accorded with many of the attributes of a complex adaptive organization operating at its peak.

Ikujiro Nonaka (1988) uses his research on Japanese companies to describe some of the ways an organization can deliberately create chaos in order to transform itself. The New Directions programme mirrors several of his ideas for pushing an organization away from equilibrium and closer to the edge of chaos as indicated:

- It used workshops and events to offer strategic visions of the future which were open to interpretation and debate. This encouraged creativity.
- New information was introduced into the University via the use of external speakers at the two conferences.
- The programme promoted creative discussions between different groups of staff and encouraged experimentation.
- It encouraged employees to change their point of view and to work together co-operatively.
- It set up self-organizing teams which were protected by senior management (the PVC, Strategy).

Nonaka's (1988) observations of renewal in Japanese firms convinced him that an organization needs a strategic vision which is open to interpretation if it is to create renewing chaos. Further, it needs processes which encourage 'creative dialogues' between groups of staff regardless of status, and opportunities for experimentation and debate. These factors create fluctuations in ideas and points of view which if amplified by a series of feedback loops and fed back into the organization stimulate waves of change. The University's strategic action plan provided the strategic vision around which the workshops created a flow of dialogue and debate which was amplified via a variety of feedback systems and over time set up waves of change across those areas of the institution involved in the programme.

(McMillan 2004: 156–157)

Key questions

- What are the key self-organizing attributes of the New Directions programme?
- How do the two New Directions project teams differ from conventional teams?
- What evidence is there to suggest that during the life of the programme the University moved closer to behaving as a complex adaptive system on the edge of chaos?

8 Essential principles for introducing a complexity-based change process

Key points

- Twelve suggested principles for introducing a complexity-based change process
- Necessary environmental features, required ethos, desired values and activities
- Supportive beliefs and behaviours

If a senior management team is considering making deep-seated and effective (second order) changes at all levels, strategic and operational, and they want to use complexity-based ideas, then how are they to proceed? Similarly, how do middle managers, supervisors and team leaders introduce changes and new ways of working in their areas of responsibility and influence using complexity? This chapter contains twelve principles which provide answers to these questions and suggest significant steps along a change journey for a traditional organization that wants to transform itself using complexity principles. Application of these suggestions should create flows of changes across an organization. Some will be surface changes with perhaps evidence of single-loop learning, others may be second-order change flows accompanied by double-loop learning experiences, together they have the potential to transform an organization.

The twelve principles are derived from experience of the New Directions programme, research into organizational change, long experience and consultations and discussions with managers at all levels and in all sectors.

Twelve principles for introducing a complexity-based change process

Each of these principles or ideas for action is interlinked and interdependent. In other words, they all work together and the more that are used, then the more effective they will prove. I have listed them randomly and not in any order of priority. I have split this section into two parts. The first part lists twelve suggestions for action for managers who work at the strategic level in an organization and who consequently are involved in strategic thinking and proposals for action that may affect an entire enterprise. They have the most influence and the most resources at their disposal – but other more junior managers can make a huge difference to the effectiveness of an organization and any attempts to introduce change. As they too are key to any organization-wide transformation – and its ongoing development – I have reinterpreted these principles in a way that I hope they will find useful and practical.

Twelve Principles for Senior Management / Strategic Level

1 Use the butterfly effect. Think about all the people in the organization and the impact they can make if they all make small improvements. Small changes constantly happening at the micro-level can affect the macro-level. This is the butterfly effect in action – it can be very powerful – and it requires very little in the way of resources. Encourage all employees regardless of their role and status to improve their way of working and to suggest ideas for more improvements. If people are used to asking per-mission to do things then it may well be some time before they respond to any change in the 'rules'. At the same time it is important to recognize that everyone works in a unique way in a unique environment – sensitive dependence on initial conditions – so that outcomes will vary across the organization. Additionally, these outcomes may well prove to be totally unexpected. Support junior and middle managers in their efforts to achieve changes and more effective ways of working.

2 Expose everyone to a strong flow of information and ideas from other organizations – even other sectors. This will stimulate discussion and debate and lead to innovation and new thinking. It will help to keep the organization on the edge of chaos. Do this by:

- setting up schemes whereby employees can visit other organizations or even do a spell of voluntary work.
- inviting speakers from other organizations and other sectors to speak to groups of employees.

I once was involved in the organization of a 'Lunch Club' for senior man-agement. After a pleasant but quick lunch an outside speaker would talk about his or her job and some significant, sometimes humorous, experi-ences. Speakers included a football club manager, a prison governor, dir-ector of a global motor vehicle manufacturer and a police chief, to recall a few. There is no doubt that listening to their experiences opened up the minds of the listeners and stirred up new ideas and perceptions. It also led to exchanges between senior staff whose paths did not often cross, if at all. So it was a pleasant way of spending a lunch-time – and a very valuable one too.

3 Provide an internal secondment scheme so that employees can move around the organization gaining a global perspective, learning new skills and deriving new insights. This will reinforce the flow of ideas and

information and encourage fresh thinking and new approaches to old problems – as well as creative thinking. It will help to keep the organization on the edge of chaos.

4 Arrange a programme of consultation/participation workshops for a substantial number of employees to discuss with them the future plans of the organization and any proposals for change and to ask for their participation and support. Ensure that each workshop brings together a mix of staff from all categories, levels and areas. They should preferably be chosen at random. The workshops will:

- alert employees to both the opportunities and the threats the organization faces.
- encourage employees used to thinking operationally to think strategically.
- provide an opportunity for enthusiastic people to contribute to future strategy development. (There may be a significant pool of untapped talent in your organization that you may discover via the workshops.) This may ultimately lead to the unfolding of a democratic action plan as happened with the New Directions programme.
- help with the creation of fresh flows of information across the organization which can disturb 'equilibrium' organizations and keep energy and ideas flowing.
- provide employees with an opportunity to meet people from other areas and other roles and so develop new perspectives on their jobs; learn more about the organization and so engage in active learning experiences. (This is all about enabling individual complex adaptive systems to flourish, contributing to the development of a complex adaptive organization operating on the edge of chaos. It is all about long term survival. The Complex Adaptive Process Model in the next chapter will provide more information on this.)
- engage a wide range of people in strategic processes and the future of the organization and this will help create multiple change dynamics at many levels and in different areas. These have the potential to bring about significant changes over time – the butterfly effect.
- surface grudges and possibly long-held grievances as well as good ideas. These 'old wounds' whether individual or collective need to be 'dressed' and 'healed' if the organization is to move on.
- surface opposition and challenge to strategic proposals and current management practice. Opposition may emerge from unexpected quarters. Some managers may resent the involvement of their junior staff in the workshops. This is useful information highlighting as it does their attitude to democratic change processes and possibly even fear of being left behind. Do not dismiss lightly opposition from individuals. There may be very good reasons why people are in opposition – they are not necessarily misfits or awkward characters.

In one programme in which I was involved there was one particular 'awkward character' who proved very argumentative and difficult. The points he raised were debated by the senior manager and others who were present and although a consensus was not agreed, a truce was reached. He was then invited to come on board and join one of the change teams. He joined the team and for a time was a very enthusiastic supporter of the project. It is always better to harness energy rather than oppose it – though this is not always possible – sadly, some people enjoy conflict too much.

- The experience of the workshops creates the right conditions for the emergence and development of self-organizing networks of participants which will challenge ineffective old formal systems and facilitate change. Additionally, this strongly connected 'web' of interactions and responses will speed up the flow of vibrations within the 'web' of the organization and create fast flows of information and ideas that will disturb the *status quo*. Co-learning communities of practice may even emerge. All this helps an organization to flourish on the edge of chaos.

5   It is very important to involve a significant number of senior managers *who must be prepared to let go and leave behind their command and control tendencies.*

- Attendance of a senior manager with strategic responsibilities is necessary at every one of the workshops. Their role is crucial. It is to brief people on current strategic plans, to carefully listen to ideas and recommendations for action from the staff, to feed these into the strategy-making processes and to encourage people to make their own local changes. This creates fresh feedback loops and rich information for the strategy-makers. All this disturbs the equilibrium of the organization and keeps it alive.
- As with any radical change process, powerful support is needed to make sure that the programme is able to make a difference and is not stifled at birth by those fearful of any disturbance of their comfort zone and defenders of the *status quo*.
- Many employees will be experienced management 'watchers' and will be watching the senior people in the organization to see if their actions are backing up their words. They may well hold back until they are convinced that the senior team and other managers are genuine in wanting them to become involved.

6   The workshops should explore the 'gap' between visions of the future and today's reality, with a strong focus on exploring the 'gap' and 'bridging' across it. This exploration can produce creative tensions out of which new energies can arise. This energy will only arise, however, if the organization acts positively to close the gap and make visions a reality. Failure to act can lead to frustration and negative and unproductive tensions.

7   Create a number of self-organizing project teams by asking people from different areas of the organization to volunteer to work on specific short-term projects that involve making changes. Encourage people to come forward whether they have expertise or not in the project topic and regardless of status. The teams will encourage a self-organizing change process and stimulate more changes as they move ahead on specific tasks. Also, each team has the potential to create a co-learning community as people share learning experiences. This is using self-organizing principles very effectively to achieve specific goals. The previous chapter provided information on the key attributes of self-organizing teams.

8   It is crucial that skilled and trusted facilitators are used in key aspects of the change process. They should be used in:

   • all group discussion processes at the workshops in order to ensure equality of involvement and to help overcome any cultural and hier-archical barriers which could hinder the democratic nature of the process and block equality of participation;
   • setting up self-organizing teams. Their role will be to encourage the development of a co-learning community and the emergence of group adaptation. The facilitators should be well versed in under-standing the principles and processes that underpin self-organizing groups.

9   Self-organizing change processes will not emerge and flourish unless the right environment is provided. Such an environment includes:

   • safe organizational 'space' for experimentation and learning;
   • recognition of the role that humour can play in creativity and innovation – leading to effective changes;
   • equality of participation so that everyone's voice is heard and every-one's contribution is valued.

   Table 8.1 summarizes the kind of environment needed in relation to ethos and values and activities. 'Environment' in the table does not refer specifically to the physical environment but rather to the cultural,

Table 8.1 Environment, ethos, values and activities

Environment	Ethos and values	Activities
Safe	Egalitarian	Fun
Stimulating	Open	Experimental
Responsive	Democratic	Challenging
Supportive	Reflect those of the organization	Use eclectic staff groups
Non-political		Offer a variety of learning
Inspirational		opportunities

Source: Adapted from McMillan (2000: 188).

behavioural environment. It should be noted, however, that the physical environment of an organization plays an important role in the creation of cultural ethos and management styles. For example, if an organization has one eating place for its senior executives and another for everyone else then it can hardly expect a democratic culture to prevail.

10 To create energies for change processes within the organization – change processes which should be ongoing – tap into the energies and interests of individuals. These are often those employees who want to play a role, however minor, in creating a future for the organization. One way to do this is by encouraging people to come forward at workshops or other events, as well as via well-established processes. Construct mechanisms whereby people can self-select or volunteer to become involved in new initiatives or the self-organizing project teams. (It is important that they self select and are not 'volunteered' by others.) Such mechanisms create an opportunity for people who need outlets for their energies and ideas. The organization benefits by making extensive use of all the knowledge, skills and experience within it. If highly talented people are involved and invigorated by their role in the organization they are less likely to be poached by competitors too.

11 If a management team wants to facilitate the growth of self-organizing change dynamics it will need not only to provide the right kind of organizational environment but also the right set of organizational beliefs and behaviours. Table 8.2. suggest some important management beliefs and behaviours. How difficult or how long it may take for these to

Table 8.2 Management beliefs and behaviours

Beliefs	*Behaviours*
The future cannot be predicted	Relaxed
Expect the unexpected	Responsive
Human networks and interactions create change dynamics	Listening
Humour and fun can encourage changes	Feeding back
Individuals can make small changes which may be very valuable and should be encouraged	Communicating Letting go
Experimentation goes hand in hand with innovation	Trusting
Energy and enthusiasm in people are a real resource	Supportive
Change is both seen and unseen and cannot be easily measured	Sharing Adaptive
Real change will probably feel very uncomfortable for a time but it is part of an ongoing learning and adaptation process for everyone in the organization	'Walking the talk' Restraining controlling tendencies Resolute Encouraging others to let go

Source: Adapted from McMillan (2000: 188).

become accepted practice and accepted thinking will depend very much on the depth of the prevalent management style and the current organizational culture – although these will vary from area to area across any firm.

'The future cannot be predicted.' It is not possible to know the outcome of any sequence of events over the longer term and to predict how things may unfold but this is not to suggest that managers only engage with the present. They need to think of the future, to anticipate the many possibilities it may hold, to accept that they have no way of knowing how events will turn out and be ready to respond and adapt to many eventualities.

'Change is both seen and unseen and cannot be easily measured.' There are many ways managers can carry out quantitative measurements of change but to make qualitative measurements can be less easy. Observable changes like increases in production, the number of inquiries handled or a rise in the monthly sales figures are readily measured. It is more difficult to measure changes that are less tangible such as the changes in someone's thinking or attitudes, or the acquisition of new interpersonal skills. These will affect observable processes over time but in themselves are not easily measured, especially using quantitative forms of monitoring and analysis.

'Letting go.' This does not mean abdicating management responsibilities and duties but rather the removal of constricting command and control management attitudes.

12 It is not easy to readily understand the many concepts of complexity science and its potential application in organizations and management. I have encountered a number of managers who have attended a one-day introductory event on complexity and then rushed off and started to introduce these notions into their companies. This has not always been successful. In too many instances the application aspects have been misunderstood and even mixed up with long-held mechanistic notions of management – which is not a good harbinger of success. It is therefore vitally important that there are several key people who properly understand the core concepts of complexity and their use in organizational settings. They will not only make sure that the 'old ways' do not corrupt any complexity-style thinking but will also encourage employees to let go of their controlling impulses and to feel comfortable not trying to predict future events.

Twelve Principles for Middle Management, Supervisory Levels

1 Use the butterfly effect. Everyone should be asked to make improvements to their working practices. They will need support if their promising new ideas are to be implemented. Small changes can over time lead to major improvements that can benefit the whole organization. Managers must

lead the way by making small but possibly significant differences themselves – people will be watching to see if they are practising what they
preach. They will not be impressed if management is 'all talk'.

2 How often are managers and their staff exposed to new ideas and different viewpoints? Arrange for people from other areas of the organization
and from other institutions to visit and talk to everyone about their role
and their experiences. This will help keep people up to date, stimulate
discussions and encourage innovation and ideas for more effective working. It will help to keep teams and departments on the edge of chaos.
How often do staff meet the colleagues they 'talk' to via email or telephone? Ensure that they have the opportunity to meet these people personally and so strengthen working relationships, widen perspectives and
improve performance.

*A departmental secretary in a large organization with a number of
regional offices arranged for her secretarial staff to take it in turns to visit
some of the offices they had most contact with. This led to better communications, increased understanding of the problems they all faced and an
overall improvement in working practices. Most importantly, it led to better
staff morale as the secretarial staff felt more valued, given that they were
not usually allowed to go on visits.*

3 Good use should be made of any secondment scheme and staff encouraged to take part. If there is no such scheme then approach senior
management and suggest that one is introduced as it can offer many
short-term and long-term benefits. It will help to keep teams operating
on the edge of chaos.

4 Encourage and support participation in any strategic change workshops
arranged by the organization. (See point 4 above.) Organize a series
of team or departmental change events, possibly in collaboration with
other sections or departments. Such events could include discussions on
improving specific aspects of policy or practice with staff asked to contribute their own ideas. They could also involve problem solving sessions
or new ideas sessions. Again, these could encourage staff to exchange
ideas and put proposals forward. Good ideas could then be put into
effect. If employees are not used to being consulted then it may take
some time before they are willing to contribute.

5 Ensure that a senior team or departmental manager attends each of
these locally organized events. They should be able to describe and report
on organization wide initiatives, listen to ideas and suggestions from
everyone and encourage people to make their own local improvements.
Anyone attending company wide events in support of strategic change
should have a proper opportunity to report back in some detail. This
should then be discussed and any supportive actions agreed and carried
out. In this way horizons are broadened and people encouraged to
think more strategically in relation to their own areas of work and
responsibility.

6   It is vital that action is taken to deliver on any proposals for the future. Employees can be inspired by visions of the future and work to make them a reality – as long as the reality is not too distant and apparently unreachable. Failure to create or reach these future realities can lead to frustration and disenchantment.

7   Look for useful projects that will improve a team or a section's performance and ask for volunteers to join a self-organizing project team to carry out the work. Try to get a mix of people from different areas and roles and ignore status issues – in these teams everyone is equal. Be very clear about the aims of the project and the specifics. For example, the project may be to improve a particular process. Set a clear timescale for delivery and what, if any resources will be provided and any financial requirements; for example it must save £x. Then let the team get on with it only consulting with management when they need to. Chapter 7 provided details on the key features of self-organizing project teams.

8   Use skilled and trusted facilitators who have a good knowledge of complexity science principles to:

- ensure that any workshops or special change events are truly participative and enjoyable occasions that use creativity and 'safe' experimentation to encourage fresh thinking and a letting go of any entrenched mechanistic thinking and behaviours;
- support the self-organizing teams, helping to build group confidence and cohesion, encouraging the formation of a co-learning community and the emergence of democratic decision making.

9   People will not engage in self-organizing change activities unless they work in a 'safe' environment. They will not try out new ideas if they are wary of being censored or blamed if things go wrong. Ensure that mistakes are viewed as opportunities for real life learning and work together to put them right. Table 8.1 shows the kind of environment, ethos and values needed to allow a complexity-style change process to take place. (See the comments on this table made in the previous section.)

10   Encourage employees to volunteer and get involved in a variety of change initiatives in an area or in the organization at large. This will add to their learning and enrich their skills base. It will also provide an outlet for their creative energies which may otherwise be frustrated.

11   Management style is a crucial factor in enabling a complexity inspired change process to take place in a department or section. Table 8.2 lists some key beliefs and behaviours that are essential. (See the comments on this table in the previous section.)

12   Managers should learn about the use of complexity science and its application in organizations and management. It is not an easy topic to master and many unwittingly espouse complexity principles but still practise the old mechanistic ones on a daily basis. Keep a check on behaviours and thinking and encourage colleagues to explore complexity ideas. A group

of committed 'complexity managers' will give each other support and make sure that old-style command and control thinking does not creep in and corrupt things.

Key questions

- What actions as part of a change process can help a traditionally managed organization operate on, or closer to, the edge of chaos?
- How useful is knowledge of the butterfly effect or sensitive dependence on initial conditions in introducing organizational change?
- How may managers at all levels seek to engage their colleagues in an organizational change process?
- How important is the cultural and behavioural context of an organization when considering introducing a complexity-based change process?

9 Innovation and changing: Models for experimentation and adaptation

Key points

- Transition Strategy Model
- Complex Adaptive Learning Model of Strategy
- Complex Adaptive Process Model
- The Edge of Chaos Assessment Model
- The Fractal Web

Managers and researchers alike seem to favour the use of models to capture and explain the essential essence of a theory or a process. They can provide a useful visual short-cut of explanation. Today the use of computers has enabled researchers and others to produce models and simulations of highly complex systems and their interactions. Many of these have helped move forward our understanding of complicated phenomena and contributed to the body of knowledge that is complexity science. This chapter offers five different but inter-related models that have been developed without the aid of computer technology. Instead they are based on research, both theoretical and real life, and discussions and trials with managers at all levels and in both public and private sectors. These models are a work in progress as they are constantly modified as I learn more from my work within organizations. They are included in this chapter as they provide visual maps designed to help managers navigate different situations and environments using complexity science as their guide. Some are more theoretical than others. The Transition Strategy Model, the Complex Adaptive Learning Model of Strategy and the Fractal Web are essentially conceptual models. The other two models, the Complex Adaptive Process Model and the Edge of Chaos Assessment Model, though they are firmly based in the science of complexity, arose from research and discussion with managers and others. They have been tested in the real world and found to have real value. But as with all models they are representations and approximations of reality and should not to be confused with the real thing. They are to be used to facilitate thinking and to assist managers in the application of complexity science principles in organizations – and as the title of this chapter points out – they are for experimentation and adaptation, as each organizational context and each individual manager or group of managers is different.

The Transition Strategy Model

It is possible to begin a change process in support of strategic objectives using a deliberate approach to strategy, as was shown in the case study of the Open University, which can then unfold into an emergent or consensus strategy. Thus traditional organizations may adapt their traditional planned approaches to strategic change by being prepared to respond and learn as events unfold. In this way they may easily move from a planned, highly rationalized and partially (or fully) predictive strategic stance to a more unplanned, intuitive, non-predictive stance. By behaving in this way they move gently from the mechanistic to the non-mechanistic and by so doing avoid excessive shifts of style that both individuals and organizations often find hard to handle. This makes it a useful 'transition' model of strategy which is illustrated by Figure 9.1.

The top of Figure 9.1. shows the flow of 'explicate' or observable changes that are occurring as we progress through the twentieth century to the twenty-first century, as indicated by the long arrow at the bottom of the figure. At the beginning of the twentieth century we have a predominant 'old' (Newtonian–Cartesian) world view and a machine model of organization, which underpins the traditional forms of organization. But as the model indicates these traditional organizations conceived from a classical scientific paradigm perspective undergo a transition period during the late twentieth century. This transition period is heavily influenced and enriched by ideas and practices from the learning organization approach to management and by innovative and radical thinking. As already discussed the notion that change and learning are two sides of the same coin underpins learning organization thinking – and complexity thinking too. In a learning organization all employees are encouraged to learn and to view learning and changing in response to learning as essential for organizational survival. In the same way complexity

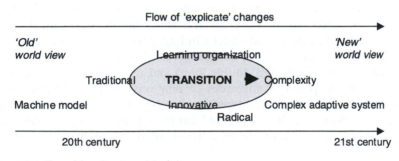

Figure 9.1 Transition Strategy Model.

Source: Adapted from McMillan (2004).

science considers group learning and adaptation skills as vital for the survival of a species.

> Thus these two approaches both support a symbiotic notion of change and learning. Individuals in groups learn from each other and from the complex series of interactions that is always taking place in their group. Socially organized insects, birds and mammals all engage in complex, adaptive learning activities in order to survive. Organizations can use this model to improve the learning, adaptation and therefore the survival chances of their own species, the organization. By creating richly diverse groups they provide a complex range of new interactions and experiences that stimulate learning. By using mixed groups an organization can help to raise the levels of complex learning for individuals and groups and thus the level of adaptive skills within those parts of the organization where they have significant influence.
>
> (McMillan 2004: 165)

The concept of the learning organization is well accepted in the management community and there are many examples of good practice which managers can draw upon when considering organizational change. But as the model indicates, and as you will already be aware, many learning organization ideals map onto complexity science principles when applied to organizations. Thus already many organizations are moving towards a complexity-style approach to management. This is indicated in the model.

Writers like Charles Handy and Gareth Morgan have had a huge impact on the way we conceive our organizations and they have introduced many challenging ideas to rock the traditional boat, as I have indicated in the model with reference to 'radical' and 'innovative'. Handy has pointed out that organizations need to think and act very differently if they are to flourish and survive in the future. Managers will need to learn new skills in order to reframe their world and to adapt to the waves of change. Morgan too has written that managers will need to learn new skills if they are to cope with the rapid flow of uncertainties that are now a feature of modern life. He suggests that examination of the self-organizing behaviours of termite colonies can teach managers a great deal about how to deal with dramatic changes and upheaval. Shared understanding, personal empowerment and a culture which values discussion and debate at all levels are prerequisites for effective learning (single and double loop) and real (second order) change. Both writers are powerful advocates of new ways of thinking and of the central place of learning and adaptation in ensuring organizational survival and success. As I have already pointed out their writings provide many signposts towards a complexity science-based approach to management and change.

The transition model shows how managers and organizations may build a bridge between traditional notions of organization, which were based on the machine model and move towards a complex adaptive system model derived from the new complexity science world view. Already learning organization practice and other innovations have edged organizations away from traditional frameworks and in the direction of an emerging complex adaptive model of organization. Use of the twelve principles described in the last chapter will help to move an organization further towards achieving this.

Once a transition process is underway using these principles then a number of change dynamics should arise. A communications dynamic should emerge as information and ideas circulate and create new patterns of response and reaction. This is linked to a responsiveness dynamic. Most importantly a powerful learning dynamic should arise that strengthens and intensifies as learning experiences increase and connect across the human community. All three dynamics feed into each other enriching the process and circulating energy throughout the organization. These dynamics will disturb the normal equilibrium of a traditional organization and push it away from stability and closer to the edge of chaos.

Complex Adaptive Learning Model of Strategy

Much of the thinking in this section and the development of the complex adaptive learning model of strategy are based on a research collaboration with my colleague Ysanne Carlisle.

As I have previously pointed out strategy and strategic thinking were for many years heavily influenced by classical science (Newtonian–Cartesian) concepts. These suggested that change was an evolutionary, incremental process that took place over long timescales. This was supported by accepted Darwinian theory and an apparently stable world. Newer interpretations of evolution, however, showed that life on earth developed not only incrementally but also unexpectedly and accompanied by massive shifts. Complexity science considers this to be the result of interactions and responses on different scales taking place amongst complex adapting systems as they competed and collaborated in order to survive over long time scales.

The influence of classical science can be seen when one considers the prescriptive schools of strategy and the separation of formulation / thinking from implementation / action. As Mintzberg *et al.* (1998) point out this reflects traditional notions of rationality whereby diagnosis is followed by prescription and then action. From a complexity perspective thinking and action are synchronous and to separate them is to create a false dichotomy and a false version of reality. As human beings we learn from our experiences and from the consequences of any actions we take. Thinking – acting – learning – is a vital ongoing survival process and it is absolutely necessary that managers engage in it if they are to develop key strategic skills. These skills offer better possibilities for the long-term sustainability of an organization than rational, overly analytical approaches.

The complexity paradigm advocates a vibrant model of strategy that exists within a dynamical and unpredictable framework. This is very different to the essentially static models advocated by the traditionalists. From a complexity perspective strategy is seen as a real-world, real-time process which emerges from organizational interactions and responses infused with learning, innovation and creativity. It is conceived as a learning and adaptation process shared by all in the organization.

The Complex Adaptive Learning Model of Strategy is a conceptual model which attempts to capture this approach to strategy. It shows the organization as a complex adaptive system existing on the edge of chaos in relation to strategy and strategic action. (See Figure 9.2.) The figure shows the organization avoiding the extremes of no novelty/stability or too much novelty/ instability and the attendant consequences of either ultimate ossification or disintegration.

This is an organization which resonates with many aspects of learning organization theory and practice and supports the learning school of strategy. An organization seeking to operate as a complex adaptive system on the edge of chaos would engage in retrospective sense making and single- and double-loop learning, with an emphasis on the latter (indicated by the double lines of the box). This, as the model shows, is part of an ongoing cycle of continuous learning and adaptation. Strategy and strategic activities

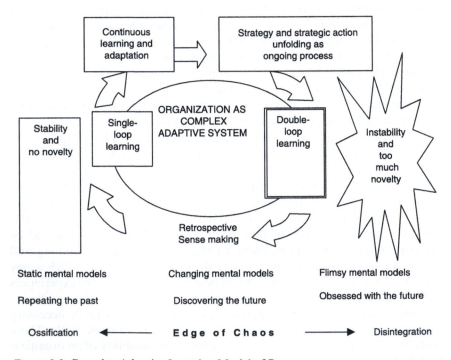

Figure 9.2 Complex Adaptive Learning Model of Strategy.

are fed by this cycle and unfold in a continuous process which itself feeds the continuous learning and adaptation cycle. This cycle is fuelled by single- and double-loop learning experiences which are found throughout the organization. With an emphasis on double-loop learning the organization is constantly engaged in changing its mental models via learning. Static mental models may continue to exist but only as long as they offer value. Most are likely to be replaced over the longer term as the internal and external environment changes. The organization also seeks to balance itself between the past and the future. The past and learning from past experiences is highly appreciated and made use of but a complex adaptive organization when it is balanced on the edge of chaos does not live in the past nor does it endlessly repeat it. Management action is solidly rooted in the present with the future viewed as a source of endless possibilities to be discovered and constantly explored both theoretically and in practice.

Strategic direction is replaced by a strategic 'roving' process where the organization roves opportunistically over many 'landscapes', internal and external, seeking competitive advantage and opportunities for experimentation and learning. In this model all employees would be engaged in this process, not just senior management. The organization would be making use of the individual and the collective capabilities of everyone in order to maximize its survival chances. The role of senior management would be to ensure that there is a constant flow of fresh information and opportunities for creative and innovative activities that provide the right amount of novelty. This would be balanced by the provision of sound frameworks which would ensure that it did not drift towards chaos and disintegration. A strongly shared culture and a clearly articulated (and shared) core purpose with attendant processes would provide such a defence. Additionally, these could also be provided by traditional means, for example, sensible and responsive legal, accounting and auditing procedures.

The model shows how the use of a complexity science approach to strategy supports the notion of organizations as adaptive and vibrant communities of continuous learning and adds further credence to the strategy as learning school.

Complex Adaptive Process Model (CAP)

The Transition Strategy Model shows how to build a bridge between old and new thinking and between traditional, controlling, predictive approaches to strategy and a complexity science-based approach. The Complex Adaptive Learning Model of Strategy provides further elaboration on the strategic aspects of moving into this new organizational form. These two models, although conceptual, suggest a number of application possibilities. This next model, the Complex Adaptive Process Model offers a rich list of practical suggestions for managers as they shepherd their organization towards a complex adaptive form of organization. (See Figure 9.3.) All three models can be

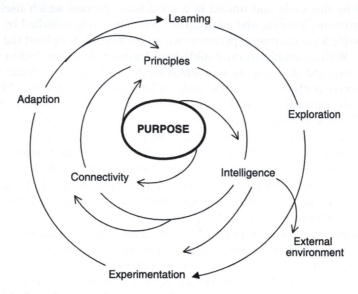

Figure 9.3 Complex Adaptive Process Model.

(© Elizabeth McMillan 2005)

elaborated upon by managers to suggest new ventures or to experiment with innovative practices.

Socially organized insects, mammals and many other living species, including humans, engage in complex, adaptive learning activities in order to increase their chances of survival. Organizations, composed as they are of complex adaptive humans, can use this model which is based on the core attributes of complex adaptive systems, to improve their chances of survival and success.

About the model

Complex adaptive systems are always *exploring* their environment seeking for new opportunities to exploit and for fresh information (*intelligence*) to inform their actions in the present and to construct new models of the future. They *experiment*, trying out new ideas and new structures as they interact, *adapt* and *learn* from their other activities and from changes in their environments. The agents or individuals in the system are closely *connected* and interact in a non-linear fashion. They are able to self-organize without any centralized control because they have a shared *core purpose* and simple underlying *principles* that guide them in their everyday actions.

The model which is based on research and consultancy practice is a fractal one and therefore can be used at any level of scale whether individual, team, department, or organization.

Purpose

The purpose circle is the starting point whenever the model is used. It is a reminder that self-organizing systems (complex adaptive systems are self-organizing) are guided in all that they do by a clear sense of purpose. Deciding upon purpose and principles are the first two things to be done when using the model. Thereafter there is no prescribed sequence of activities. Users of the model should be guided by their own judgement and experiences.

Principles

The second step in using the model is to identify the principles that will be used to achieve the core purpose. Self-organizing systems are open to their environments and have no centralizing controlling hierarchy and any agreed principles should reflect this. They have to operate and survive within the constraints of their environment and this should be reflected by principles relating to 'environmental' considerations such as budgets, time scales and resources as well as values and behaviours. For example, I read of a North Sea oil platform built using self-organizing principles. The group that sat down to plan the task were told how much money they had and how long they had to get the platform ready. These formed the first set of guiding principles to which they then added principles of their own. These were that the platform had to be of the highest quality as regards build and safety. With their core purpose set i.e. to build an oil platform and their guiding principles agreed the team knew exactly what it had to do, how and by when. It completed its task within budget and before time. Sometimes there may be an overlap between principles and core purpose. What is important is that they are clear and strongly shared by all involved. In some circumstances they may be modified in the light of experiences.

Intelligence

Intelligence concerns the ongoing collection of data (by exploring, experimenting and connecting) and its interpretation in the light of knowledge, learning and experience. It is data that has been discussed, reflected upon, challenged and shared. It is rich knowledge that has been gathered in from all environments, via formal and informal systems and is essential for the survival of a complex adaptive system. In business terms this could include a stream of knowledge about strong competitors and their changing status as rivals, new market possibilities or the impending resignation of a senior manager in a collaborating company.

Exploration

Exploration of its many 'landscapes' is an essential feature of a complex adaptive system. It has to explore to discover what is happening in the world around it and to come across new ideas, unexpected opportunities and possible threats and dangers. Thus exploration requires that old and new territory are scanned and explored. This may be conceptual territory (ideas, theories, themes) or physical/geographical spaces and environments. It could also be an exploration of behaviours and consequences. It interlinks and often overlaps with experimentation.

Experimentation

Experimentation is about trying out new ideas and new ways of thinking and behaving. Such behaviour is at the heart of radical innovation. Stepping outside of comfort zones is one way in which people can experiment as well as the more obvious choices of trying out a new process or product.

Connectivity

Connectivity is about effective communications. It is about communication in many forms: formal and informal, local and global, face to face, paper-based and electronically. The richer and more diverse the patterns of communication, then the better will be the quality of information or intelligence. For communications to be effective there has to be active 'listening', accurate and perceptive interpretation and appropriate responsiveness – when this constantly takes place then there is connectivity.

Learning

Learning has to be gleaned and acknowledged from every activity. There should be both single- and double-loop learning taking place. Experimentation may mean that mental models and long-held ideas are challenged and displaced. Exploration may lead to simple discoveries and new knowledge. Learning must be a valued and ongoing activity with time for reflection and sense-making activities. Communities of co-learners should be encouraged and cherished as adding value to any enterprise.

Adaptation

Hand in hand with learning goes adaptation. This is learning put into practice and given value. Without the ability to learn and adapt a complex adaptive system would fail to thrive and survive. Organizations need flexible management systems if they are to adapt to changes in their environments and benefit from gathered intelligence and learning experiences.

Using the model

The Complex Adaptive Process Model may be used in five different but complementary and overlapping ways: as a conceptual model; as a model for comparison and analysis; as a guide to action and a model for introducing organizational change; for project management; and for monitoring and evaluation.

Conceptual

The model shows in simple diagrammatic form the ongoing key activities that an individual, a team, a department or an organization should be constantly undertaking if they aspire to behaving like a complex adaptive system on the edge of chaos.

Chapter 3 listed the attributes of complex adaptive systems and the model encapsulates these as follows:

- *they consist of large numbers of agents interacting in a non-linear way creating higher and higher levels of complexity* – the model is non-linear and designed for individuals (agents), groups or organizations to use thereby creating varying levels of reaction and response. Each type of activity has the potential to generate its own dynamic as different employees engage in the process. As responses and reactions arise from all the different activities so dynamic and increasingly complex interplays emerge.
- *there is no central controlling mechanism* – 'purpose' is at the centre of the model but its function is not controlling. There is no controlling mechanism but the model has its own internal order which arises from the guiding framework created by 'purpose' and 'principles'. It is underlying 'principles' and core 'purpose' which enable self-organizing systems to know how to respond to different situations and to better their survival chances. Further, once purpose and principles have been decided upon then there is no linear sequence of activities. The circularity of the model and the arrows indicate its non-linear responsive nature.
- *they are constantly learning* – learning is shown as an essential ongoing activity.
- *they learn to adapt to changing circumstances* – adaptation is shown as an essential ongoing activity.
- *they actively try to turn events to own advantage* – although not shown specifically this is an implied aspect of learning and adaptation.
- *they constantly revise and change their structures as they learn about the world* – this is a feature of learning, specifically double-loop learning.
- *they anticipate the future* – 'exploration' refers not only to physical/ geographical journeys of discovery but also conceptual/intellectual ones including speculation about the future. 'Learning' and 'intelligence' too play a role in this.

- *they are self-organizing* – through its activities the model is open to all its environments. Energy and matter is acquired via the gathering of 'intelligence' and the energizing nature of internal feedback. New structures and new forms may emerge as a result of spontaneous learning and adaptation responses to other processes.
- *they seek to exist on the edge of chaos* – this is the overall aim of the model.
- *they have emergent properties* – this is an implicit outcome in the model and use of the different ongoing activities within the overall process.

Comparison / analysis

The CAP model can be used to compare individual or group behaviours with those of a complex adaptive system. To do this an individual, for example, would insert 'comparison of self with CAS' into the 'purpose' circle. Then they need to ask themselves the following questions: What are the principles I live/work by? Am I constantly exploring? Connecting? Experimenting? Learning? Adapting? Gathering and creating intelligence? They would also need to consider in some detail how effectively they are engaged in these activities.

For example, are they effectively exploring all the many 'worlds' that they should? They need to consider intellectual/cerebral exploration and emotional/behavioural exploration as well as physical and geographical 'journeys'. Is there an imbalance, for example? Perhaps they are spending too much time in travelling (physical exploration) at the expense of doing something different like reading about a new management topic (intellectual exploration). There may be an imbalance in one particular aspect. For instance, managers may spend a great deal of time visiting company offices around the world but not walking around their own building.

And is it sufficient? Some time should be spent reflecting on each part of the process and what it means for his or her organizational setting. How diverse are their experiences? Complex adaptive systems thrive on diversity.

A guide for action / for organizational change

Reference to the model as suggested above should suggest new possibilities for action including introducing organizational changes. Again an appropriate purpose should be inserted in the central circle and some principles established. Then all the different activities on the model commenced as an ongoing and totally interconnected process.

Sometimes the very act of using the model to establish and clarify purpose can lead to important changes. As the following paragraph indicates.

One chief executive officer used the CAP model to transform his company. His airline industry business was over twenty years old and had changed over time but it soon became clear that the business stream it was pursuing was going

*nowhere. The CEO and his team had lots of ideas as to where the airline indus-
try was going and they knew that they had considerable capabilities which they
could use to add value to the business. In spite of this, however, they found
themselves struggling to decide what to do next and how to make it happen. The
CEO was introduced to the model and how it could be used. He wrote: 'The
turning point was recognising from Elizabeth's model that "Purpose" needed to
be at the centre of our thinking and then become the driver of our actions. Once
this became clear the rest fell into place and a direction emerged which everyone
understood.' The model remained pinned above the CEO's desk as a simple
reminder of what was important in determining business strategy.*

Project management

The model may be used to set up projects, deliver them and later appraise
them. A project team would begin by asking what are the guiding principles
by which everyone operates? These could be financial, legal, ethical, time
based, behaviour based and so on. For example, if a group of friends wanted
to open a new restaurant then the project 'purpose' circle would say 'open a
new restaurant'. The principles which the team would have to suggest and
willingly agree to might include: budget, time scale, operating openness and
value for money. Thus 'intelligence' would require the collection of information on anything related to the project, including other value for money
concepts, other successful restaurants in their locations, etc. This links closely
to 'exploration'. This could involve travelling around to view different locales,
looking at different building types, as well as thinking about original ideas
for cuisine. 'Connectivity' suggests close communications with anyone who
might have an interest in the project, have information, ideas or experience.
This includes, of course, communication within the team itself. The team
should 'experiment' in a number of ways. They might try approaching people
who are not within their normal circle of contacts (links to exploration) and
try out new concepts and ideas. It may consider radical new furniture or an
untried chef. As the project progresses so the team would need to keep checking that they are learning and adapting to their experiences as they proceed.
The model may be used to appraise the project by comparing the team's
activities with those required by the model. There may have been an over-
emphasis on one aspect at the expense of another or too little attention paid
to learning and adaptation. It may be that the 'principles' changed as a result
of learning. The model should used to encourage flexibility, responsiveness
and new thinking.

Monitoring and evaluation

As was suggested in the above paragraph monitoring and evaluation of
a project or a process may be easily undertaken by comparing espoused and
proposed actions with realized, actual actions firstly in relation to core

purpose and principles and then in relation to the different 'labels' on the model. Then adjustments should be undertaken as part of an agreed ongoing learning and adaptation process.

The Edge of Chaos Assessment Model

The Complex Adaptive Process Model is closely entwined with the Edge of Chaos Assessment Model and they are highly complementary. Each is particularly effective when used in conjunction with the other.

The Edge of Chaos Assessment Model can also be used at a number of levels: individual, team, department or organization. It too may also be used in a number of different ways. It can be used to discuss management styles and performance, in counselling situations, as an aid to mentoring, to assist in maintaining work – life balance and to identify factors contributing to stress. (See Figure 9.4.) This shows the model at the level of an individual. The model is still under development which is why at the time of writing there are only six attributes shown.

Individual level

There are five columns in the model each representing a different position on the spectrum from 'totally stable' (no novelty) on the left to 'chaotic' (too much novelty) on the right. In the centre of the figure is the 'edge of chaos' zone which is where a complex adaptive system aims to exist and where, it is suggested, individuals should also seek to operate. Beneath the three main headings is a list of attributes associated with each position on the spectrum. An individual may find that they are at different places on the spectrum in relation to the different attributes but it should give them an overall indication of how near they are to either stability, the edge of chaos or instability (chaos). This position can vary from day to day and week to week and even hour to hour. What matters are the overall position and the degrees of fluctuation and movement.

The statements below the 'edge of chaos' arrow indicate the likely outcome for an individual who remains for too long in any of the three major positions. All individuals, of course, should aim to behave as a complex adaptive system operating on the edge of chaos. This may mean dipping into either of the extreme zones if needed but not lingering there. The model may be used by an individual personally for private consideration and reflection or it could be used in discussion between an individual and their manager, or an individual and a trusted colleague or mentor – or at home with a family member or a good friend to consider, for example, work–life balance. It may even be used in group situations as part of a supportive feedback process.

By identifying where they are on the model at any given time an individual can consider the ways in which they might move towards a better position or maintain their current healthy situation. If, for instance, a person finds that

Totally Stable No novelty	Stable Aspects	Behaving as a Complex Adaptive System	Chaotic Aspects	Chaotic Too much novelty
Ultimate couch potato		Moving around, active, exploring		Ultimate headless chicken
No real learning	Single-loop learning	Engaged in single- and double-loop learning. Sense making and reflection.		No sense making.
Inadequately connected to environments, data flow lacks energy or real value.		Well connected to all environments, internal and external, with a steady flow of reliable and useful data.		Over connected and over whelmed with data of variable quality.
Life too structured, too rigid and inflexible.		Flexible structures and strong guiding frameworks.		No reliable structures or guiding frameworks.
Is a slave to routine, rigidly bound by own set of values whatever the circumstances.		Has flexible routines for working and social/family life. Clear values and guiding principles for living.		Has no routines. Values and guiding principles subject to sudden changes. Like a rudderless ship in a storm.
Stuck in the past. Repeating past behaviours to the detriment of the present and the future.		Values the past, envisions the future, lives in the present.		Obsessed with the future to the detriment of the present.
		Edge of Chaos		
Lack of interest in living – little or no discernible life force		Healthy, active, fulfilled individual		Highly stressed, breakdown (mental/physical/emotional) seems inevitable

Figure 9.4 Edge of Chaos Assessment Model – individual.

(© Elizabeth McMillan 2007)

they are 'inadequately connected to environments' with data flows of little value then they can make real efforts to communicate better and connect more effectively to their internal and external environments. Use of the CAP Model may prove helpful. It is important to note, however, that the model may also provide information on the organization in which the individual is working and poor connectivity, for example, may have more to do with the structure and culture of an organization than an individual's behaviour. Every individual exists in a complex web of macro- and micro-level environments that influence and affect everything they do whether inside or outside their workplace. Thus although the model is focused at the individual level it inevitably links to these other contexts. It may, for example, reflect helpful aspects of the organizational culture, underline deficiencies in the prevalent management style or highlight tensions between personal and work life.

The model may be used as a simple 'health check' at the individual level. How well is an individual managing? Are they struggling to cope with too many initiatives (novelty overload)? Are they bogged down in rigid routines that are of their own making or are they a design feature of their organization? The health check has been found to be useful in considering work–life balance. It is important to recognize that the model can tell someone a great deal about the environment in which they are currently managing (or living) as well as their own behaviours. Below are some examples from healthcare managers who used the model as an individual health check.

Totally stable

- Three managers wrote under the 'Couch Potato' heading: 'Fed-up'; 'bored and un-stimulated'; 'comfortable and complacent with the situation'.
- One manager identified with 'No real connectivity' and wrote: 'Distanced, alone, stuck.'
- Another manager found herself 'Stuck in the past' but this was not as a result of her own management style. She wrote: 'Can't get colleagues to stop saying: "It never happened like this years ago." '

Chaos

- Several managers identified with 'The ultimate headless chicken' and wrote: 'Oh no! Not another crisis, my schedule is full!'; 'always charging around, completing so many pieces of work at one time'; 'it's all gone pear shaped!'
- Under 'No sense making' one stated: 'Too much to read and absorb – not taking in information'; and another noted: 'no time to reflect.'
- Under 'No reliable structures' two managers wrote: 'Pulled in all directions'; and 'No Structure. Constantly changing.'
- One manager under the 'Obsessed with the future' heading wrote: 'Obsessed re future possibilities, prevents activity now.'

Edge of chaos

- A number of managers identified with 'Learning in lots of ways' they wrote: 'Realising could be more than one way of doing something – but having the courage to try something new'; 'sufficient learning and stimulation'; 'learning is appropriate and is being implemented'.
- One manager stated under 'Flexible structures and guiding frameworks: 'Solid structure, but flexible.'
- Under 'Values the past etc.' one manager observed that she/he: 'Reflects on the past and enjoys the present.'

I have only provided quotes from managers who identified with the three main headings but over half of those who took part in the exercise found themselves under 'Stable Aspects' or 'Chaotic Aspects' and drifting either towards stability, chaos or the edge of chaos.

The case study which follows describes one person's experiences and how the model proved useful.

Case study vignette – an individual's experience

The opportunity for a four-month placement to cover a secondment on the senior management team of my part of a higher education institution was one that seemed too good not to take up. Being encouraged to take the placement by key staff was an act of support and faith in my abilities. It made me feel on a path onwards and upwards in my career. I said 'yes' although I had little time to think about the practicalities and had too little experience to ask questions about the situation. I had no thought that it would be anything but valuable to my career and enjoyable.

The placement was located at a geographically distant site so I found myself leaving my home, husband and two children and spending three hours commuting each way at first, though I later found a B&B locally. I realized quite quickly that I was in at the deep end. The duties I had expected were only a fraction of what needed to be done and there was a backlog of work and associated ill-feeling. I had little or no experience in most of the areas of work. I found myself in a politically and culturally difficult environment, and seen as imported talent by the existing staff, one of whom quite clearly wanted and should have had the post. My original job was not backfilled, so I found myself with two jobs not one. The post put a strain on my home and family life.

I found myself succumbing to the stress of the situation fairly quickly and as the months progressed became ill and unable to cope. I survived the four months but some months later became very ill and needed time off work. The conclusion by others was that I was the problem – having a low ability to manage stress. My health, confidence and self esteem were very badly damaged. Slowly and with great difficulty I started the task of regaining my health, confidence and self-esteem. The sense of personal failure was very great.

About six months after finishing the placement I became involved in a small research project looking at using tools based on complexity science in management work. Being introduced to the edge of chaos model had a major impact on my understanding and ability to cope with the feelings about and recovery from my disastrous placement experience. It was a key turning point in coping and moving on.

The model clearly enabled me to see how this situation had arisen and that I was not the only reason for the outcome. Prior to taking the placement I had felt under stimulated and at the stable end of the model. The placement offered me the chance for more exploration, learning, connection, flexibility and a situation in the present whilst looking to the future. Using the model I could see that what had actually happened was not a move to the edge of chaos, but a move into the chaos zone. I was the overloaded headless chicken. The situation itself was chaotic, without adequate structure or sense. Without support and good management to provide this I was destined to fail. The inevitable disintegration happened.

The model has enabled me both to analyse what happened and why. It has relieved me of the sense of it all being due to personal failure and enabled me to realise the importance of the context and the role of others. Effective placements require good organization and management to be effective. I have learnt lessons as an individual and as a manager. I keep the model on hand to think about my own situation and the impact of decisions I make. I have used it to coach and support other staff.

Organization level

Figure 9.5 shows the model at the organizational level. Again there are five columns in the model each representing a different position on the spectrum from 'totally stable' (no novelty) on the left to 'chaotic' (too much novelty) on the right with the 'edge of chaos' zone in the central column. Beneath each heading is a list of attributes associated with each position on the spectrum. An organization may find that they are at different places on the spectrum in relation to the different attributes but it should give them an overall indication of how close it is to stability, the edge of chaos or instability (chaos). This position may vary over different timescales.

The statements below the edge of chaos arrow indicate the likely outcome for an organization that remains for too long in any one of the five different positions. The model may be used by managers to consider different aspects of an organization's performance in relation to 'behaving as a complex

Totally Stable *No novelty*	Stable Aspects *Little novelty*	**Behaving as a Complex Adaptive System**	Chaotic Aspects *Lots of novelty*	Chaos *Novelty overload*
Tight, rigid management controls		Management by self-organizing principles, shared processes		No co-ordination or organization. Management confused and without coherence
Change can be organized but does not occur		Constantly changing and adapting as needed		Change cannot be co-ordinated
Totally inflexible and unresponsive structure and frameworks	Inflexible and largely unresponsive structure and frameworks	Flexible, responsive structure with supportive frameworks	Insufficient structure or frameworks	No discernible structure or frameworks
Inadequately connected to all parts of the system. Little or no flow of relevant, clear and useful information, often inaccurate and untimely	Adequately connected but information flow is spasmodic, often of poor quality, often not relevant or difficult to understand	Well connected to all necessary parts of the system. Flow of relevant, good quality, important, information that is useful, timely and readily manageable	Over connected to all parts of the system and receiving an overload of information some relevant and some irrelevant. Struggling to handle it	Highly overly connected to all parts of the system and receiving an overwhelming overload of information relevant and irrelevant – it is impossible to handle and make sense of this
Decisions deferred and delayed to serious detriment of system	Decision making slow and cumbersome and sometimes too late	Able to make effective, timely decisions using information flow and contacts	Decisions rarely made on a well-informed basis, of poor quality, fudged or not taken at all	Decision making chaotic and to detriment of system
Single-loop learning only Static mental models		Lots of double-loop learning and single-loop learning too		Double-loop learning but disconnected from reality and frantic. No sense making
Trapped in the past to the detriment of the present and the future		Aware of the past, taking advantage of past experiences and aware of future possibilities		Obsessed with the future to the detriment of the present
Ossification certain	Ossification likely	Survival chances are high	Disintegration likely	Disintegration inevitable

Edge of Chaos

Figure 9.5 Edge of Chaos Assessment Model – organization.

adaptive system'. Thus the model is especially useful in carrying an organizational 'health check'. Once the current or predominant positions have been identified, perhaps via group discussion or extensive employee consultation, managers may use the model to improve an organization's current position or to help maintain an existing one. Use of the CAP Model can assist in this. It is worth remembering that different parts of an organization may be operating too close to chaos and others too close to stability and the tension between these may be affecting the overall organization and keeping it in a healthy position. Should this be the case then managers need to ask themselves what would happen should something shift the position of one of these key areas? Further, they also need to consider how healthy it is to have parts of an organization existing at the extremes.

The model is still under development and thus currently seven attributes are available. The following list shows the key attributes against which managers can compare the 'health' of their organization:

- management and management systems;
- ability to change;
- flexibility and responsiveness of organizational structures and frameworks;
- connectivity and quality of information flow;
- quality and effectiveness of decision making;
- types of learning; and
- time horizons / focus.

The model may prove of real value in strategic activity providing as it does possibilities for present and future action. It also may be used as a yardstick for innovation and creativity given that complex adaptive systems operating on the edge of chaos are at the height of their creative and innovative powers. As with the CAP model the Edge of Chaos Assessment Model has many applications at different levels and over different timescales and managers should use them in ways that they find most useful and enlightening.

Organizations exist in complex, dynamical and highly changeable environments and when using this model or any of the other models presented in this chapter managers need to bear this in mind. These environments are described as 'macro-scale bundles of contextual influences' which can be 'successfully unpacked into micro-scale dense networks of complexly interacting, mutually influencing and multiple causally-ambiguous considerations' by Ray Cooksey in his 2003 article ' "Learnership" in Complex Organisational Textures'. Cooksey lists four main areas or macro-bundles each interconnected with the other and each with their networked micro aspects. In my view, considerations of these will help managers to conceptualize the richness and complexity of any context under discussion. These are as follows:

- *Environment*. This includes: society, global, industry, information, physical, professions and government.
- *Organization*. This includes: roles and expectations, resources and support, policies and procedures, culture and diversity, structure and design, history.
- *Individuals*. This includes: past experiences, current work situation, emotional, cognitive, physical, needs and goals.
- *Groups*. This includes: peers and colleagues, family and friends, communication practices, work group development and dynamics.

The Fractal Web

As was pointed out in an earlier chapter the classical science (Newtonian–Cartesian) world view affected many aspects of early industrial life, including organization design and the architecture of the physical working environment. This approach is still reflected in many aspects of modern organization design. One common example is organization charts which are still predominantly linear in nature. There is the linearity of the hierarchies of management and the vertical linearity of formal communications and chains of responsibility, command and accountability. Further, reductionist thinking ensures that corporate tasks are broken up into separate compartments and functions which often results in the creation of non communicating 'silos'. Such structures tend to be very inflexible and not readily able to adapt to rapid changes in circumstances. Uniformity tends to be the cultural order of the day. When one company takes over another then one or other has to conform and merge in with the values and norms of the other. The perception appears to be that if everything is the same then it is easier to understand and control. This does not facilitate a rich diversity of response to any situation, especially a crisis.

Organization design is, in my view, a rather neglected area of management theory and practice but an organization's form can significantly affect its strategy, culture, technology, environment and ability to respond appropriately to events. For an organization to be effective and sustainable in the long term then it must have a form that is both appropriate to its core purpose and enables it to maintain maximum performance in changing circumstances. As Peter Senge (1994) makes clear, what is the point of the captain of a ship asking his crew to turn to starboard by sixty degrees if the rudder will only turn to port, or if it takes the ship six hours to respond to his command? Richard Pascale and co-authors (2000) go further stating that: 'design is the invisible hand that brings organizations to life and life to organizations'.

At the end of the twentieth century there were a number of attempts to break away from conventional organization design as many organizations responded to business and other pressures by experimenting with structural changes. Some sought to reduce bureaucracy and become leaner and fitter by cutting out layers of management. Sadly, in many cases organizations did not capitalize on this and introduce more effective systems of working. Additionally, they failed to take into account the loss of valuable skills and experience as they shed staff. Structures were modified or changed but in most cases the basic linear design remained in place. This was because managers were still influenced by quasi-mechanistic thinking and failed to understand the importance of the relationship between organization design and human interactions.

Organizations themselves may have experienced real difficulties in realizing effective changes in their structures in practice but in theory there was an important shift in notions of design criteria. Ashkenas *et al.* (1995) report that the new success factors for organizations were speed, flexibility, integration and innovation. These replaced size, role clarity, specialization and control. This change resonates well with many of the principles that arise from a complexity science approach to organization design. Table 9.1 compares classical science principles of organization design with those inspired by complexity science.

What kind of organization form emerges if one uses complexity principles to inform its design? The Fractal Web is a model of how an organization might look if one used the complexity science principles shown in Table 9.1, along with notions of adaptation, learning (complex adaptive systems), patterning, rhythms and flow. Most importantly, it was conceived by thinking about the fractal nature of many biological forms and the human heart and circulatory system in particular. Fractal patterning is a key design principle in the natural world where physical structures are in harmony with necessary activities. The model is based on a simple web pattern which is created by a ring of circular 'arteries' which are criss-crossed by other arteries. (See Figure 9.6.) In this section we consider the model as representative of an organization but it may be replicated on different scales from individual to global. The design ensures that the core purpose and accompanying principles are reflected and understood at every level of the organization. Regardless of how you slice through it, the structure is a fractal one.

Table 9.1 Organization form and design principles: a comparison

Classical science principles	Complexity science principles
Linear	Non-linear
Hierarchical	Non-hierarchical
Reductionist	Holistic
Controlling	Self-organizing
Inflexible	Flexible
Uniform	Diverse
Centralized	Networked
Closed	Open

Source: Adapted from McMillan (2002: 130).

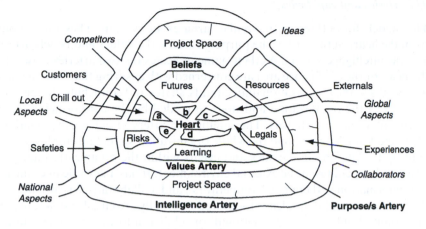

Figure 9.6 The Fractal Web.

Source: Adapted from McMillan (2002: 133).

The structure of the web has been designed to encompass all the key attributes of a complex adaptive system by encouraging learning and experimentation and acknowledging the key role they play in facilitating dynamic adaptability and responsiveness to change. The organization is able to unfold as it learns and to develop its structure in response to its own activities and events in the external environment. The notion of continuous flow has been incorporated into the design as essential to nourish the organization. Thus ideas and knowledge flow throughout in waves of changing depth and speed as they respond rhythmically to internal and external landscapes.

The heart and inner chambers

The 'heart' of the web represents the core purpose of the organization which gives all employees focus and the five inner chambers, a, b, c, d, e (the number may vary), contain or represent the essential principles of the organization. At the Open University, for instance, these principles are based on the notion of openness: openness to people, to places, to methods, to environments and to ideas. The heart is the confluence area where all the main arteries come together and flow into each other. The heart is 'nourished' by the knowledge and experiences conveyed in the main arteries and it in turn 'nourishes' the organization with a rich mixture of purpose and principles. This circulates through all the system energizing activities and giving clarity to direction and decision making.

The arteries and capillaries

The model shows three main circular 'arteries' or systems. They radiate out from the heart in this order: the purposes artery, the values and beliefs artery and the intelligence artery. As their name indicates the two arteries closest to the heart or the confluence area are concerned with ensuring that every person who works in the organization understands, shares and contributes to the core purpose of the organization and does so guided by the core principles and attendant values and beliefs. The intelligence artery circulates information, ideas and knowledge around the whole organization so that all employees are kept up to date on all activities and events within the organization and are aware of happenings in the external environment. It has a key role in ensuring that information gathered on 'competitors', and 'collaborators' is available to the right areas and that 'ideas' discovered externally are circulated, as are any important chunks of 'local', 'national' or 'global' information. The arteries that run horizontally and vertically across the organization represent intelligence gathering activities and relationships with other organizations and the external landscape. The larger the space then more small capillaries are connected to it to ensure that organizational flow continues. If a number of small vessels join then a new small artery is formed. All the arteries, with their network of 'capillaries', work together to make sure that everyone in the organization is well informed, has clear operating guidelines and understands the organization's aims and their role in making that a reality.

The cells or spaces

The areas between the arteries are areas of specific activity that are necessary to achieve the overall purpose of the organization. The number and size of the different spaces will vary at any given time, depending on how much work is required in that area, the number of people involved and the amount of resources required. All the spaces are dynamic as they respond to the needs of the organization and its employees. Thus changeability is built into the design. Some spaces are needed so that an organization can meet specific requirements such as legal, audit, health and safety obligations and financial and human resources. Thus:

- *Legal*: this space would ensure that the organization met all its statutory requirements as well as any covering anything that had legal implications / aspects for the organization.
- *Safety*: this space would be devoted to ensuring that the organization operated safely with high standards of employee welfare. It would cover ergonomics, counselling, Health and Safety at Work (in conjunction with Legals) building and equipment maintenance, and so on.
- *Resources*: this area would be responsible for the provision and management of all financial, capital and human resources.

These three spaces cover a wide range of conventional functional areas and all would work very closely ensuring there were no 'gaps' in provision. Their 'labels' were deliberately chosen to reflect a wider view of their role than is usual for such functions. They provide a sound procedural framework for the organization.

The model shows that the organization (or the individual if the model is viewed at that level) currently has two major projects underway. One of which is considerably larger than the other. These may be short term projects or major ones that have a lifetime of several years. The project spaces are able to expand or contract in response to changing circumstances. The projects themselves may have arisen as a response to intelligence circulated around the organization. Employees would be encouraged to form self-organizing project teams in a proactive and positive response to information and ideas flowing through the organization. Thus the structure enables people to respond spontaneously to events guided by an overall sense of direction and purpose – a self-organizing response.

Other spaces are provided for the following reasons:

- Learning: this acknowledges that learning is highly valued and ensures that everyone participates in a range of learning experiences.
- Futures: all employees are encouraged to think about the future of the organization and how it may continue to thrive over the longer term.
- Risks: this is an organization without a blame culture. Everyone is encouraged to innovate and come up with new ideas for the benefit of the organization. This means that everyone is able to take appropriate risks and experiment with new ideas and new ways of working.
- Externals: everyone in the organization is aware of the crucial role the external environment has on the organization. Thus all employees are encouraged to gather information about what is happening in any area of the external environment that they may come into contact with. There will be some employees who will be dedicated external environment watchers.
- Experiences: this organization values and shares experiences, past and present.
- Chill out: this acknowledges that human energies and rhythms can fluctuate in response to events. People are not machines and sometimes they need to slow down, or step aside for a time. This space is not about pampering employees – it is about recognizing that relaxed, healthy employees are good for the effective working of the organization.
- Customers: this space is all about maintaining very strong links with existing customers, looking for new customers, in fact anything to do with customers and the organization's relationship with them. The fact that they are built into part of the organization design recognizes the importance of this relationship and this is true whether they are retail customers or health-care patients.

Employee roles

People are moved around the organization, spending time in different spaces, and several spaces at one time too, even if they are specialists. An accountant, for example, will always spend a percentage of his or her time in the 'resources' space but he or she will also be active in other spaces too. In this way they spread their knowledge and expertise around the organization and learn about the work that goes on elsewhere. All employees will be required to contribute to the flow of 'intelligence' around the organization. This means that they have responsibility for ensuring that 'nutrition' flows around and feeds the whole system. People would also be required to spend time gathering intelligence from outside sources such as competitors and others as indicated in the model. This will encourage them to develop a rich perspective on life outside the organization and its relevance to the organization's core purpose. The taking on of different roles will facilitate connectivity, encourage learning and a sound appreciation of how the whole organization works.

Leadership

There is no hierarchy of authority to take a strategic lead or to direct the activities of others. Leadership would be expected to emerge as a self-organizing response to events. Leadership would be distributed throughout the organization on a day to day basis as all employees should be knowledge-able enough to make most operational and non strategic decisions. Strategic level decisions would be shared collectively but individual leaders or a leadership group might emerge in response to specific issues or organizational needs. A group of employees, for example, might be created to question and test the organization's core purpose and principles. Their role might be to ensure that these were still relevant and appropriate to existing circumstances. Membership of this group might be long term but not permanent and members would be volunteers who had the support of others. If a crisis arose then people would self-organize into a group to deal with it. If this was a major financial crisis, for example, then a team of volunteers (including financial specialists) would take the lead in searching for a solution. They would continue to lead until the crisis was resolved. Then the group would disband. No one person would lead the organization on a permanent basis although a number of people may emerge over time who frequently acted in a leadership role. The emergence of effective leadership through the learning dynamics of an organization is discussed further in the next chapter.

Flexibility

The Fractal Web design offers a very flexible organizational form that can adapt to changing circumstances very readily without jeopardizing its existing functions. If the organization needs to expand then it adds more arteries or extends existing ones and so creates more spaces (activities) – whatever is needed. If it needs to contract then it narrows the arteries or reduces their length. The organization is thus able to adjust its size by contracting or expanding in such a way that it still maintains the integrity of the overall structure. For example, if the organization decides to expand by entering a major new market it will need to create additional spaces for activities directly associated with this new venture. One way it can do this is by pushing the intelligence artery further out and increasing the size of spaces between the values and beliefs artery and the intelligence artery. 'Safeties' and 'Experiences' may not require additional activity so their spaces can stay more or less the same. That frees up space for more 'Projects', more 'Resources' and more 'Customers' in support of the new venture.

> The Fractal Web is a product of the imagination but it was an imaginative process that drew on knowledge from hard science, real life research, long time observations and experience of organizational life. It is a speculation, and I would argue that researchers and writers should not be afraid to play with their ideas and their intuitions in a way that is unconstrained by current notions of what constitutes validity. To do so is to join distinguished company, for Albert Einstein is renowned for his observation that: 'Imagination is more important than knowledge. Knowledge is limited. Imagination encircles the world.'
>
> (McMillan 2004: 174)

Key questions

- How might a traditional organization use the Transition Strategy Model to think about moving towards a complex adaptive system model of organization?
- How does the Complex Adaptive Learning Model of Strategy bring together notions of strategy from the learning school and notions of a complex adaptive system operating on the edge of chaos?
- In what different ways may managers use the Complex Adaptive Process Model?
- What aspects of performance are considered when using the Edge of Chaos Assessment Model at the individual level?
- How might the Edge of Chaos Assessment Model when used at the organizational level highlight problems with an organization's structure and culture?
- The Fractal Web is a speculative model of organization design. In what ways does it differ from most models of organization design?

10 New perspectives, opportunities for innovation

Key points

- Leadership
- Radical innovation
- Experimenting
- The age-old tussle
- Change dynamics

In this final chapter I present more ideas drawn from complexity science and from management with a view to weaving together a picture of future possibilities that will transform organizations and inspire innovative and radical management thinking and practice based on an understanding of human dynamics as complex responsive interactions.

Leadership and the new 'managers'

What are the implications for leadership and management in an organization using complexity science-based principles? In Chapter 5 I proposed a numbers of ways in which managers could achieve their important objectives without using mechanistic controlling methods. This was attained by challenging prevalent notions of predictability and dropping the use of control to eliminate the unexpected. It was about breaking free from any domination of quantitative, analytical, rationalist approaches and using qualitative information and approaches too. It was about reviewing notions of order and disorder and acknowledging that disorder is a natural part of our world and sometimes contributes to a transition process. In conclusion I suggested that like the captain of a ship in a storm managers should use their skills and experience to learn to ride the waves and to flow with the ocean currents. Too many managers with mechanistic tendencies would soon sink their ship if they disregarded the force of the waves and expected their vessel to sail on regardless of the natural elements.

Chapter 5 also suggested some key ways in which managers could change their focus and their style and Chapter 8 was devoted to describing the essential principles needed to introduce a complexity-based change process. It included a range of actions that could be taken by managers at different levels of seniority and influence and recommended that particular attention was paid to providing the right kind of organizational context for complexity-based approaches to flourish. This included developing and supporting a certain sets of beliefs with accompanying behaviours and creating a 'safe' but stimulating environment that encouraged and sustained a number of specific values and related activities. Use of these principles should enable managers to move across the 'transition' phase of the Transition Strategy Model towards a complex adaptive systems approach to management. Dedicated use of the Complex Adaptive Process Model should further reinforce this approach and offer more guidance. The Edge of Chaos Model could be used in a number of ways to check out how an organization or an individual manager is performing in relation to behaving as a complex adaptive system on the edge of chaos. This model also provides useful insights into organizational issues and contexts.

For those managers wishing to adopt a complexity science approach to management this book offers a number of signposts which can help them on their journey. How long and how difficult the journey will prove to be will depend on the individual and their current position and the contexts in which they are working. The approach taken in this book has assumed that most managers will be working in an organizational context that still has some type of management hierarchy and a good sprinkling of traditional if not mechanistic attributes. Thus this book has presented considerations of how managers use their roles and authority to create new environments that are more 'complex adaptive system friendly'. This assumes that they have the authority to do this. But would they always have such authority in a complexity-style organization which has no traditional status-based hierarchy? The answer is no they would not. The Fractal Web offered a speculative model of organization in which there were no managers in the conventional sense, so the question arises: what happens to leadership if there is no clear hierarchy?

Self-organizing learnership

Ray Cooksey in his paper ' "Learnership" in Complex Organisational Textures' (2003) offers a new view of leadership derived from an evolved blend of organizational learning and self-organization. Cooksey points out that single- and double-loop learning at individual, group and organizational levels are necessary if organizations are to cope with all the complex challenges posed by the many contexts in which organizations have to exist. (These contexts are macro and micro bundles of influences which were referred to earlier in Chapter 9.) Organizations which learn in this way should be able to continuously add to their knowledge and experiences and so constantly enhance their ability to respond and adapt to changes in their circumstances. There is, however, a danger that such organizations are so devoted to the pursuit of learning that it detracts from their achievement of core business goals. This can be avoided, Cooksey suggests, by the cultivation of 'learnership' by as many employees as possible: ' "Learnership" can be defined as a developed capability to know when, where and how to best engage in the collective learning process to maximise the chances of successful organisational adaptation to rapidly changing circumstances' (Cooksey 2003: 207). This involves being actively responsible for one's own learning; trusting and relying on the learning abilities of others; facilitating and supporting others as they learn; awareness of one's own limitations and how to overcome them; readiness to promote learning even in difficult situations.

Various individual and organizational influences contribute to the development of this learning process which is essentially cyclical in nature. The process involves all employees in the creation of new meanings which are juxtaposed and tested against old meanings, and out of which new actions arise. These in turn create new meanings and so the cycle goes on. In this way an organization facilitates the development of 'learnership' in everyone and an organization that truly learns will emerge. But what of the role of leaders? In traditional learning organizations the leader's role would be to create and support the conditions for learning to arise and flourish but Cooksey believes that something more is required. He argues that effective leadership should not just be 'an add-on pre-condition' to successful organizational learning. Rather, it should be viewed as:

> an essential dynamic component, inseparable from the learning process itself. In this light, the concept of 'learnership' implicitly embeds leadership as a fundamental energising force behind learning and this embedding evolves within every person who develops 'learnership' as a capability (an idea similar, but not identical with, Johnson's (1994) concept of 'self-directed leadership' as an outcome of genuine empowerment.
>
> (Cooksey 2003: 208)

Thus 'learnership' is not about leaders showing the way but rather about all learners having the potential to evolve into leaders. Thus over time leadership shifts out of the hands of the few and is diffused into the hands of the many. Employees are no longer dependent on guidance and encouragement from above to stimulate their learning as they are all actively responsible for their own learning. As a result the distinctions between leader and learner roles become increasingly blurred. In these organizations leaders become learners and learners become leaders and eventually blend together and become indistinguishable. The notion of leaders and followers disappears. All are leaders. Thus:

> When the evolution and diffusion of these processes has reached a critical mass (such mass would likely be uniquely different for each business), one would say that the people within the business have achieved and can

action true 'learnership' in pursuit of adaptive behaviours that ensure the continued survival, profitability and vibrancy of the business. At this point, the business can achieve true self-organising status – something that cannot be traced back to the influence of any single individual or group.

(Cooksey 2003: 209)

Cooksey's notion of 'learnership' leadership fits well with the self-organizing and transient leadership idea offered by the Fractal Web model of organization in Chapter 9. Both notions suggest a way forward whereby all in an organization are able to contribute to strategic and operational thinking and action thereby creating a 'super adaptive intelligence' that works for the long term benefit of an enterprise.

Radical innovation – pre-adaptation

Step back a few years and most managers would not have envisaged, even in their wildest dreams, some of the immense changes that have taken place over the last couple of decades. Now in the early years of the twenty-first century we all recognize that change is very much a fact of organizational life and that it can happen suddenly and on a massive scale. So how are managers to anticipate and prepare for these immense shifts and upheavals? How can they innovate and adapt to rapidly changing circumstances?

The distinguished biologist Stuart Kauffman offers some suggestions in an article published on the *Scientific American.com* website in October 2006. First of all he points out that the business community has found it very hard to adapt to unexpected changes and he puts this down to a dependence on economic models with a focus on market equilibrium. Many economists have been influenced by physics and he cites the Black–Scoles model devised by physicists to predict volatility on the stock markets. Thus a non-living science is being used to explain living phenomena. Kauffman suggests that economists should consider the living world and draw on biology to understand business 'because the biosphere and the living things in it represent the most complex systems known in nature'. Kauffman argues that gaining a better understanding of how species evolve and adapt could bring profound and radical insights that could help businesses to adapt and improve economic growth.

Kauffman proposes that the way forward is to use a modern evolutionary theory: pre-adaptation. Use of this theory could lead to significant innovation and preparedness for change. But what is pre-adaptation? Apparently a living organism has features which could in other circumstances develop in a totally novel and useful way. For example, lungs were once swim bladders which helped fish to maintain their balance in the water. When some fish began to move out of the water and onto the edges of the land their swim bladders acquired a new function – to act as reservoirs for oxygen. Thus swim bladders were pre-adapted to become lungs. As Kauffman explains: 'Evolution can innovate in ways that cannot be pre-stated and is non-algorithmic by drafting and recombining existing entity for new purposes – shifting them from their existing function to some adjacent novel function – rather than inventing features from scratch' (Kauffman 2006).

The prehistoric fishes that slowly made their way onto the land did so to achieve some kind of evolutionary advantage which they could not have achieved without major adaptation. They did the unthinkable and they did this by making use of what they had to hand, so to speak. They used their existing attributes in totally unpredictable and amazing ways as part of a response to significant changes in their circumstances. This carries an important message for managers pondering innovation. Think with your wildest imaginations in relation to creating advantage out of changes in organizational and economic contexts. As hot new economies emerge all around the world creating new products, new services and new markets, so the opportunities for innovation increase. As Kauffman explains:

> A species' suite of adaptive features defines its ecological niche through its relations to other species. In the same way, every economic good occupies a niche defined by its relations to complementary and substitute goods. As the number of economic goods increases, the number of ways in which to adaptively combine those goods takes off exponentially, forging possibilities for all-new niches. The autocatalytic creation of niches is thus a main driver of economic growth.
>
> (Kauffman 2006)

Evolutionary biology suggests to organizations and their management that there is a world of infinite possibilities for adaptive innovation out there. Further, the more markets arise, the greater are the choices and possibilities for innovation. The likelihood too is that those organizations that exist on the edge of chaos will be those that are best able to adapt to a changing world through the discovery of novel innovations.

As Kauffman indicates: 'The path to maximum prosperity will depend on finding ways to build economic systems in which new niches will generate spontaneously and abundantly' (Kauffman 2006). The message for organizations and their management is create an environment for their activities in which ideas for new 'niches' (products or services or both) constantly arise.

Experimenting

Embarking on a complexity approach to management would be for many an experimental venture. Experimenting can be dangerous and have massively unpredictable outcomes but without it we would not have evolved to our current state of knowledge nor indeed have been true to our complex adaptive nature. Only by experimentation and exploration and the taking of risks did our ancestors evolve and survive. I would suggest that organizational evolution too has to take risks to change and thrive. I have referred to a number of organizations and individuals that have taken an experimental leap and successfully pioneered new ways of managing. There are probably many, many more out there, especially small businesses led by confident entrepreneurs, but there is one outstanding pioneer that I should like to add to the list of those already written about: Tim Smit.

Tim Smit is renowned in the UK as the man who discovered and restored the Lost Gardens of Heligan and who successfully built the ecological masterpiece of the Eden Project. This is a complex of vast translucent domes which house botanical treasures from all over the planet and which is located in a disused china clay pit in Cornwall. The Project has breathed new life into an economically depressed area and attracted millions of visitors who have been entranced and inspired by the beauty and magnificence of the plants. As Smit himself once put it, the Project houses 'the only rainforest in captivity'.

The restoration of the gardens and the building and operation of the Eden Project have been incredible achievements and Smit's approach owes nothing to conventional management techniques. His management philosophy is based not on notions of control but on openness and a belief in the ability of individuals. Smit talks about his 'monkey business' approach to management. In his view most ideas about management consist of getting the 'monkey' off one's back and onto someone else's. In other words, the work is shifted around an organization and major decisions are not made and things not dealt with. Smit has some 'rules' which are used to ensure that no 'monkey' management occurs in his enterprises. He aims to constantly rip the blinkers from people's eyes so that they are always seeing things afresh. He wants his employees to get out and about and to do things differently. Some of the 'rules' he applies are as follows:

- All employees are expected to read one or two books a year which are outside their normal reading patterns. (Exploration and experimentation)
- Employees have to prepare a meal for their co-workers once a year. (Connectivity)
- Employees are encouraged to carry out acts of kindness or to give a gift to someone who is not expecting anything. (Connectivity)
- Senior management use 'gang trials' where they give each other direct feedback on performance in a supportive atmosphere.
- Applicants for senior appointments are interviewed by everyone who would work for them. Thus a prospective Finance Director would be interviewed by the complete Finance team.
- Employees are empowered to contribute their ideas and can earn the right to redeem earned capital.
- Everyone has the chance to work in cross functional teams and demonstrate their abilities – this provides opportunities for employees to

operate outside their normal roles. (Experimentation, exploration, connectivity, learning, intelligence)
- No one is criticized for making mistakes – but failure to take responsibility or to do one's best is criticized.

Experimentation and exploration are encouraged, as is connectivity, adaptation and learning. (See the notes in brackets based on the Complex Adaptive Process Model.) Furthermore the uniqueness of each individual and their potential is recognized.

The business is now extremely successful and Smit is determined that people do not become complacent. In order to keep the original excitement of the start-up going, he will occasionally engineer chaos. This approach ensures that there are ongoing streams of change that stimulate innovation and creativity. Without apparently being aware of it, Smit is using notions that map onto a complexity science-based approach to management to sustain an inspirational enterprise.

The age-old tussle

The age-old tussle between the emergence of radical new ideas and the maintenance of the *status quo* continues within the management community. Ricardo Semler travels the world extensively talking to organizations about his company, exchanging ideas and discussing the future of business. In 2000 he wrote of how he had encountered a number of new companies in Silicon Valley, USA which were infused with the same approaches as those he introduced at Semco. These visionary organizations had eschewed bureaucracy and the traditional hierarchies of management in favour of openness, experimentation and 'a respect for individuals and their ideas'. These organizations were recognizing the potential of all individuals in their organization to contribute to the success of their enterprise and knowingly or not were enabling individuals to play to their inherent evolved strengths. In other words, they were working with and not against the individual complex adaptive systems that are their employees. Semler also noted that there were worrying signs that some new businesses forced by investor pressure were reverting to more traditional ways of doing things. Semler provides this depressing picture:

> CEOs from old-line companies are being brought in to establish 'discipline' and 'focus'. Entrepreneurs are settling into corner offices with secretaries and receptionists. HR departments are being formed to issue policies and plot careers. Strategies are being written. The truly creative types are being caged up in service units and kept further and further from the decision makers.
>
> (Semler 2000: 58)

Yet in spite of these mechanistic tendencies many aspects of mainstream management practice are supportive of some of the ideas that complexity science indicates management should pursue and develop. A recent article 'Standing in the Way of Control' in *People Management* (2007) by Stephen Wood reports on a number of surveys carried out by the University of Sheffield into innovatory management practices in a range of organizations in both the public and private sectors. The surveys concluded that employee empowerment was 'the single most effective HR practice in terms of increasing value added per employee in manufacturing companies, closely followed by extensive training and development' (Wood 2007: 40). Empowerment was discovered to be important because it encouraged employees to take a broader perspective on their roles in the organization and to be more flexible and more proactive, as follows:

- Employees who were empowered were more likely to understand how their jobs fitted into the wider organizational framework and to 'share their knowledge with colleagues and customers'.
- 'Managers whose roles give them discretion are more likely to take charge of situations without waiting to be asked to do so.' Also production workers would take a proactive role in problem solving.
- Giving employees discretion promoted a 'sense of ownership of the organization's strategic goals'.
- Empowerment was found to directly affect 'skill utilisation and learning' which lowered people's anxiety levels as they found they were better able to cope with their jobs.

Empowered employees are not self-organizing employees but they are freed up from many controlling processes in a way that enables a number of self-organizing abilities to emerge for the benefit of the organization. Table 7.1 in Chapter 7 compared the attributes of traditional teams with empowered or self-managed teams and self-organizing teams. In my view, this study demonstrates the benefits of a loosening of control and a move towards a complexity-style organization. Large numbers of organizations have experimented with empowerment, most notably via total quality management, complexity science would encourage them to build on these foundations developing a self-organizing model of team working and moving towards creating a complex adaptive organization.

As I have already pointed out learning organization concepts resonant very powerfully with complexity science-based notions of organization and they too are established in the mainstream of management thinking and practice. But as the Transition Strategy Model indicates, these organizations have to move further away from notions of organization derived from classical (Newtonian–Cartesian) concepts if they are to become complex adaptive organizations living on the edge of chaos. In my view unless organizations continue to shift towards this new twenty-first-century model of organization, they will not thrive in the global turbulence of the modern world.

We are currently at the beginning of a process of discovery and creativity as we think about how best to design organizations so that they may evolve successfully in a world of rapidly changing contexts. One thing is clear and that is that old ideas based on notions of a predictable stable universe will not suffice. We cannot engineer our organizations to operate smoothly like clockwork nor should we endeavour to design and operate them in that way. Michael McMaster in his book *The Intelligence Advantage: Organizing for Complexity* (1996) makes some interesting and insightful observations. He writes that all the organization founders he has met agree that their businesses came about by chance. They arose as the result of a chance interaction between events and their own efforts. Thus he supports the notion that businesses emerge from self-organizing interactions as was discussed in an earlier chapter. (It should be noted that state created organizations do not fall into this category.) McMaster goes further, suggesting a new theory of organization. Organizations are complex adaptive systems and emergent phenomenon each with their own characteristics, own culture, own ability to learn and even their own intelligence. Thus:

> This theory implies that these qualities exist independently of the founder, management, and people currently in that corporation. Even though some of the specifics that were intended and planned by individuals can be traced to individual personalities or to the results of specific historical accidents, what now exists has a life of its own.
>
> (McMaster 1996: 9)

Managers therefore need to recognize that the universe is a dynamic self-organizing system in which organizations and ecologies constantly interact with each other and that the machine model is out of date and unreal. McMaster proposes that managers need to behave like horticulturists in a rain forest with responsibility for the survival of a particular plant species within the forest. If they look after their 'plants' well then the species will flourish but if they fail to look after them then the species will weaken and its place in the forest will be taken by other species. This approach to management is a far cry from traditional approaches.

Change dynamics

If we are to transform our organizations and so transform our societies and enhance our way of life then we have to discard the lingering inadequacies of the machine model and the Newtonian–Cartesian view of life. Change is constantly happening on every level from the universal to the microbiological and it is a rich river. Its waters are created by many slim trickles that may be barely discernible and also by the huge swells that result from heavy rain or deep snows. Sometimes the waters are clear and tranquil and at others they flow fast and are full of disturbed sediments so that little can be seen. However much this river changes it is still the same river and it is one we can better understand and observe by using a complexity science perspective. Managers need to recognize the nature of this 'river' and learn to understand its dynamical nature rather than trying to control the flow and direct its energies.

Change is not always observable or traceable and linear cause and effect analysis of its origins (if you can be sure of your subject) is unlikely to be accurate. The use of quantitative measurements and statistical data can capture changes in production processes and various inputs and outputs but managers should not rely on such approaches to tell them the whole story. Significant changes may be taking place that are not readily observable and would certainly elude traditional measurements. These are changes in human behaviours and the rich interactions of human responses. The dynamics of change are created by human activity as feedback amplifies and reverberates across the web of the organization. Single-loop learning may be easily identified but double-loop learning is not so readily detected, especially if traditional methods are employed. Managers need to look for flows and fractals. They need to look for flows of learning and adaptation behaviours, for flows of new information, for flows of ideas, flows of innovative thinking and practice. All these flows indicate the presence of deep and significant processes. In other words, they may indicate the operation of complex adaptive humans operating on the edge of chaos.

Human learning and adaptation is constantly affecting an organization and a complexity style approach to management advocates that managers tap into this rich survival source and work with it rather than trying to stifle it.

In my view, the literature on managing change is overly focused on prescriptive strategies and the use of 'rabble rousing' showmanship put across as inspirational leaders presenting exciting visions of a brave new organization. It is thrilling and also frightening when one leads from the front into an unknown future, but these leaders tend to thrive on such challenges. Recent research indicates that those at the top of organizations suffer considerably less stress than those who have to answer to their call. It is the leaders who live longest. Can this be the way we want to run our democracies and the organizations that sustain them?

The chances are that change will be forced on organizations in the richer societies by a new generation of managers and employees who have higher expectations of personal satisfaction and career fulfilment. This new generation may consider 'learnership' the norm and view 'leadership' as outdated, unsatisfying and quaint. As Charles Handy points out in a recent article in *Sesame* (2007)

> Our young people are growing up in an affluent society. They probably don't feel the tremendous pressures we did to stay in a job. They probably don't like or accept hierarchies as much as we did . . . Who's going to run our organisations if the best people peel off in their 40s?

> (Handy 2007: 33)

Human beings are paradoxical creatures. They long for harmony and order and at the same time enjoy excitement and challenge (disorder). How best do we manage this paradox in our organizations and continue to thrive? To date organizations have depended too much on controlling and prescriptive systems that have unbalanced the paradox and been constantly disturbed and challenged by human needs and behaviours. A complexity-style approach to organizations takes into account the human factor and shows how self-organization can create its own order. It shows managers how they can harmonize intrinsic human needs with those of the organization and prepare strongly for the unfolding of unknown futures.

In Handy's view: 'The purpose of business is not to make a profit. It is to make a profit to enable it to do something more or better. Organisations are not machines. They are living communities of individuals' (Handy 2007: 33). This view will not be accepted in many boardrooms and will possibly be laughed at in some quarters but the world is changing and such closed attitudes may soon have to change too. We are too closely connected, too closely packed in, too closely reliant on each other on this planet to continue to exploit each other and treat the world as a never ending source of plenty. Fortunately complexity science offers organizations a way to transform thinking and practice that should enable managers to abandon their selfish and mechanistic attitudes and facilitate a more harmonious future.

Key questions

- How does a 'learnership' approach to leadership spread responsibilities and decision making out to all in an organization?
- Can notions of pre-adaptation lead to truly radical innovations?
- In what ways is Tim Smit using complexity science ideals?
- Are organizations machines or rainforests?

Appendix 1

Plans for change

New directions 1993–1997

1   From long to short response times
2   From complexity to simplicity
3   From provider-led to customer-centred provision
4   From an expenditure to an income culture
5   From centralism to subsidiarity
6   From quality control to quality assurance

(from McMillan 2004)

Appendix 2

Diary of events

1993

April	New Directions Workshop – 'How to achieve Quality Growth for the OU of the Future' × 3
May	New Directions Workshop × 2
July	New Directions Workshop × 1
November	New Directions Workshop × 1
December	New Directions Workshop × 1

1994

January	Electronic Strand Workshop × 2
February	Joining the University Workshop × 1
March	Choosing the Open University × 1
	Conference planning team formed
April	Improving Internal Communications Workshop × 2
May	NEW DIRECTIONS CONFERENCE
	Staff survey team formed
June	Achieving Change Workshop × 1
August	New Directions Cartoon Competition announced.
October	Lunchtime Briefing – Geoff Peters, PVC, Strategy. New Directions and 'Plans for Change'.
November	The Regional Centre of 2001 – Birmingham Region
	Lunchtime Briefing, Philip Marsh, Director of Personnel.
	The OU Going Global Workshop – Office for International Collaboration.
December	The Regional Centre of 2001 – London Regional Office
	Lunchtime Briefing, Ted Atkinson, Director of Marketing,
	Calendar Cartoon Competition prize winners receive prizes from Geoff Peters, PVC, Strategy.

1995

January	*New Directions Action group first meeting*
	The Regional Centre of 2001 – Newcastle Regional Office
February	OU Going Global Workshop – Office for International Collaboration.
	The OU in the 21st Century Workshop
May	Lunchtime Briefing, Geoff Peters, PVC, Strategy. The new 'Plans for Change'
June	Workshop for OU students in R04 – Birmingham
	Making Better Mistakes Workshop
	Lunchtime Briefing, Geoff Peters, PVC, Strategy. The new 'Plans for Change'
July	Communications Workshops for AA (Students) × 2
	New Directions 1996 Cartoon Calendar Competition announced
September	Lunchtime Briefing, Tim O'Shea, PVC, Quality Assurance and Research, and Academic Staff Renewal
	Visualization Workshop
October	Communications Workshops for AA (Students)
November	Making Better Mistakes Workshop
December	New Directions 1996 Cartoon Calendar Competition winners receive prizes from Geoff Peters, PVC, Strategy

1996

February	Communications Workshop for AA (Students)
May	Communications Workshop for Centre for Modern Languages
July	Communications Workshop, for Cambridge Office
September	New Directions Conference and Fair (80 participants)
November	Making Better Mistakes Workshop

1997

January	*New Directions Action Group disbands*

(from McMillan 2004)

Appendix 3

Conference issues

Staffing issues

Within two months of the conference *Open House* reported that talks were taking place on addressing 'unjustified' differences in terms and conditions which had been a major issue raised at the conference. A schedule of differences had been drawn up by personnel division and sent to the trades unions and further discussions were due to take place in the autumn. The decision to go ahead with a staff survey was seen as a response to the staffing issues raised by the conference. A Pro-Vice-Chancellor with responsibilities for staff matters in the strategic context was appointed four years after the conference.

Marketing

This issue has been progressed with a reorganisation and the setting up of OU World Wide with the posts of development manager and marketing manager as key roles. There had been a lunchtime briefing session on marketing. However, it was felt that more work was needed on market research and on what was described as an amateurish approach.

New technology development

Significant progress has been made on the development of new technologies and a great deal has changed. There was general agreement that these actions may have already been under consideration but that the conference had given them a major impetus.

Improved communications

Several activities were seen as directly attributable to the conference and New Directions including the provision of Lunchtime Briefings for all staff on strategic issues. These were mainstreamed as 'Off the Record' lunchtime briefings by the public relations department. A series of communications workshops had also been organized by the New Directions action group in response to the conference plea for better communications.

Low staff morale

It was felt that no progress had been made on the issues of low staff morale, and that the downturn in the University's financial situation during 1996–1998 had further lowered staff morale.

Need for leadership and for managers with better people skills

Leadership was not an issue identified by those who were active in the programme. They had felt empowered by the conference and by the programme to take action themselves. However, some of the non-activists were expecting changes to be made for them. Their view of management drew on traditional notions of leadership where senior managers were meant to plan for the future and to direct their staff towards it. This they did not think their managers were doing and thus they articulated the need for leadership.

Need for flatter organization and better co-operation between departments

It was felt that there had been some progress as there were now more *ad hoc* groups in the University and more recognition of the need to cut across formal structures. Inter-unit contracting had also changed attitudes between departments. Apart from the *ad hoc* groups the conference and New Directions were not seen as directly contributing to these developments.

(from McMillan 2004)

Bibliography

Allen, P.M. (2001) 'A Complex Systems Approach to Learning in Adaptive Networks', *International Journal of Innovation Management*, 5(2): 148–180.

Anderson, C. and Bartholdi, J.J. (2000) 'Centralized versus Decentralized Control in Manufacturing: Lessons from Social Insects', in McCarthy, I. and Rakotobe-Joel, T. (eds) *Complexity and Complex Systems in Industry: A Conference Proceedings*, Warwick University, Warwick, September.

Anderson, P. (1999) 'Complexity Theory and Organization Science', *Organization Science*, 10, May–June: 216–232.

Ashkenas, R., Ulrich, D., Jick, T. and Kerr, S. (1995) *The Boundaryless Organization Breaking the Chains of Organizational Structure*, San Francisco: Jossey-Bass.

Berreby, D. (1996) 'Between Chaos and Order: What Complexity Theory Can Teach Business', *Strategy and Business*, spring.

Bohm, D. (1980) *Wholeness and the Implicate Order*, London: Routledge and Kegan Paul.

Brown, S.L. and Eisenhardt, K.M. (1998) *Competing on the Edge. Strategy as Structured Chaos*, Boston, MA: Harvard Business School Press.

Capra, F. (1983) *The Turning Point*, New York: Bantam Books.

Carlisle, Y. and McMillan, E. (2002) 'Thinking Differently about Strategy: Comparing Paradigms', Proceedings on CD-ROM of Australian and New Zealand Academy of Management Conference, La Trobe University, Beechworth, VIC, December.

Carlisle, Y. and McMillan, E. (2006) 'Innovation in Organizations from a Complex Adaptive Systems Perspective', *Emergence: Complexity and Organization*, 8(1) 2–9.

Chandler, A.D. (1962) *Strategy and Structure: Chapters in the History of American Industrial Enterprise*, Cambridge, MA: MIT Press.

Clippinger, J.H. III (ed.) (1999) *The Biology of Business*, San Francisco: Jossey-Bass.

Cooksey, R.W. (2003) ' "Learnership" in Complex Organisational Textures', *Leadership and Organization Development Journal*, 24(4): 204–214.

Cooksey, R.W. and Gates, R.G. (1995) 'HRM: A Management Science in Need of Discipline', *Asia Pacific Journal of Human Resources*, 33(3): 15–38.

Coveney, P. and Highfield, R. (1995) *Frontiers of Complexity*, New York: Fawcett Columbine.

Dale, M. (1994) 'Learning Organizations', in Mabey, C. and Iles, P. (eds) *Managing Learning*, Routledge in association with the Open University.

Dent, E.B. and Goldberg, S.G. (1999) 'Challenging "Resistance to Change" ', *The Journal of Applied Behavioral Science*, 35(1): 25–41.

Deutschman, A. (2004) 'The Fabric of Creativity', *Fast Company*, 89: 54–60.

Durcan, J., Kirkbride, P. and Obeng, E. (1993) 'The Revolutionary Reality of Change', *Directions – The Ashridge Journal*, September: 4–9.

Eccles, T. (1993) 'Implementing Strategy: Two Revisionist Perspectives', in Hendry, J., Johnson, G. and Newton, J. (eds) *Strategic Thinking: Leadership and the Management of Change*, Chichester: John Wiley.

Foss, N. (2000) 'Internal Disaggregation in Oticon: Interpreting and Learning from the Rise and Decline of the Spaghetti Organization', 5th revision, LINK, Department of Industrial Economics and Strategy, Copenhagen Business School. Available online http://www.cbs.dk/departments/ivs/staff/njf.shtml (accessed 4 February 2003).

Fowler, A. (1997) 'Let's Shed a Tier', *Personnel Management*, Chartered Institute of Personnel and Development, March: 21.

Fuller, T. and Moran, P. (2000) 'Moving Beyond Metaphor', *Emergence*, 2(1): Lawrence Erlbaum.

Gleick, J. (1993) *Chaos*, London: Abacus.

Goodwin, B. (1997a) 'Life Living at the Edge of Chaos', Valedictory Lecture, Open University, 16 July.

Goodwin, B. (1997b) *How the Leopard Changed Its Spots*, London: Phoenix, Orion Books.

Gribbin, J. (1999) *The Little Book of Science*, London: Penguin Books.

Gribbin, J. (2002) *Science, A History 1543–2001*, London: Allen Lane, Penguin Books.

Hampshire, S. (1956) *The Age of Reason*, New York: Mentor Books, The New American Library.

Handy, C. (2007) quoted in 'The Future of Work', *Sesame*, Milton Keynes: The Open University, Summer: 33.

Johnson, P.R. (1994) 'Brains, Heart and Courage: Keys to Empowerment and Self-directed Leadership', *Journal of Managerial Psychology*, 9(2): 17–21.

Kanter, R.M. (1990) *When Giants Learn to Dance*, New York: Touchstone, Simon and Schuster.

Kauffman, S. (1996) *At Home in the Universe: The Search for Laws of Self-Organization and Complexity*, London: Penguin Books.

Kauffman, S. (2006) 'The Evolution of Future Wealth. Technologies Evolve Much as Species Do, and that Unappreciated Fact Is the Key to Growth', *Scientific American.com*, November. Available online: http://www.sciam.com/article (accessed 4 July 2007).

Knowles, R.N. (2001) 'Self Organizing Leadership: A Way of Seeing What Is Happening in Organizations and a Pathway to Coherence', *Emergence*, 3(4): 112–127.

Knowles, R.N. (2002) 'Self Organizing Leadership: A Way of Seeing What Is Happening in Organizations and a Pathway to Coherence' (Part II), *Emergence*, 4(4): 86–97.

Knowles, R.N. (2002) *The Leadership Dance: Pathways to Extraordinary Organizational Effectiveness*, Centre for Self-Organizing Leadership.

Kotter, J.P. (1995) 'Leading Change: Why Transformation Efforts Fail', *Harvard Business Review*, March–April: 59–68.

Larsen, H.H. (2002) 'Career Management in Non-Hierarchically Structured Organizations', paper presented at 2nd International Human Resource Management in Europe Conference, Athens, October 2002. Available online: http://www.mbc.aueb.gr/hrconference (accessed 3 February 2003).

Law, A. (1999) *Open Minds*, London: Orion Business.

Levy, D. (1994) 'Chaos Theory and Strategy: Theory, Application and Managerial Implications', *Strategic Management Journal*, 15: 167–178.

Lewin, K. (1951) *Field Theory in Social Sciences*, New York: Harper and Row.

Lewin, R. (1993) *Complexity: Life on the Edge of Chaos*, London: Phoenix.

Lewin, R. and Regine, B. (1999) *The Soul at Work*, London: Orion Business.

Lovelock, J. (1989) *The Ages of Gaia*, Oxford: Oxford University Press.

Mabey, C., Salaman, G. and Storey, J. (2001) 'Organizational Structuring and Restructuring', in Salaman, G. (ed.) *Understanding Business Organisations*, London: Routledge.

Macintosh, R. and Maclean, D. (1999) 'Conditioned Emergence: A Dissipative Structures Approach to Transformation', *Strategic Management Journal*, 20: 297–316.

McMaster, M.D. (1996) *The Intelligence Advantage: Organizing for Complexity*, Newton, MA: Butterworth-Heinemann.

McKelvey, B. (1999) 'Avoiding Complexity Catastrophe in Co-evolutionary Pockets: Strategies for Rugged Landscapes', *Organization Science*, 10: 294–321.

McMillan, E. (1999) 'The New Sciences of Chaos and Complexity and Organisational Change: A Case Study of the Open University', unpublished thesis, Open University.

McMillan, E. (2000) 'Using Self Organising Principles to Create Effective Project Teams as Part of an Organisational Change Intervention: A Case Study of the Open University', in McCarthy, I. and Rakotobe-Joel, T. (eds) *Complexity and Complex Systems in Industry: A Conference Proceedings*, Warwick University, September.

McMillan, E. (2002) 'Considering Organisation Structure and Design from a Complexity Paradigm Perspective', in Frizzelle, G. and Richards, H. (eds), *Tackling Industrial Complexity: The Ideas that Make a Difference*. Cambridge: Institute of Manufacturing, University of Cambridge.

McMillan, E. (2004) *Complexity, Organizations and Change*, London: Routledge.

Marion, R. (1999) *The Edge of Organization*, Thousand Oaks, CA: Sage Publications.

Mintzberg, H., Ahlstrand, B. and Lampel, J. (1998) *The Strategy Safari*, London: FT Prentice-Hall.

Mintzberg, H. and Waters, J.A. (1989) 'Of Strategies, Deliberate and Emergent', in Asch, D. and Bowman, C. (eds) *Readings in Strategic Management*, London: Macmillan Education.

Moncrief, J. and Smallwood, J. (1996) 'Ideas for the New Millennium', *Financial Times*, 19 July.

Morgan, G. (1986) *Images of Organization*, Newbury Park, CA: Sage.

Nonaka, I. (1988) 'Creating Organizational Order Out of Chaos: Self Renewal in Japanese Firms', *California Management Review*, spring: 57–73.

Parsons, E. and Russell, C. (1995) 'A Programme for Organisational Change: New Directions at the Open University. A Case Study', Universities and Colleges Staff Development Agency, *Briefing Paper* 14.

Pascale, R.T. (1999) 'Surfing the Edge of Chaos', *Sloan Management Review*, spring: 83–94.

Pascale, R.T., Millemann, M. and Gioja, L. (2000) *Surfing the Edge of Chaos. The New Laws of Nature and the New Laws of Business*, London: TEXERE Publishing.

Pedler, M., Burgoyne, J. and Boydell, T. (1991) *The Learning Company*, London: McGraw-Hill.

Porter, M.E. (1985) *Competitive Advantage: Creating and Sustaining Superior per-formance*, New York: Free Press.

Prigogine, I. and Stengers, I. (1984) *Order Out of Chaos*, London: Heinemann.

Quinn, J.B. (1989) 'Managing strategic change', in Asch, D. and Bowman, C. (eds) *Readings in Strategic Management*, London: Macmillan Education.

Roberts, P. (1998) 'John Deere Runs on Chaos', *Fast Company*, 19: 164.

Salaman, G. (2001) 'The Emergence of New Work Forms', in Salaman, G. (ed.) *Understanding Business Organisations*, London: Routledge.

Sanders, T.I. (1998) *Strategic Thinking and the New Science*, New York: Simon and Schuster.

Semler, R. (1989) 'Managing Without Managers', *Harvard Business Review*, September–October: 76–84.

Semler, R. (1994) *Maverick!* London: Arrow Books.

Semler, R. (2000) 'How We Went Digital Without a Strategy', *Harvard Business Review*, September–October: 51–58.

Senge, P.M. (1992) *The Fifth Discipline*, New York: Doubleday.

Senge, P.M. (1994) 'The Leader's New Work: Building Learning Organizations', in Mabey, C. and Iles, P. (eds) *Managing Learning*, London: Routledge in association with the Open University.

Shakespeare, W. (1960) 'The Tempest', in Alexander, P. (ed.) *William Shakespeare. The Complete Works*, London: Collins.

Slocum, K.R. and Frondorf, S.D. (2000) 'Business Management Using a Fractally-Scaled Structure', in McCarthy, I. and Rakotobe-Joel, T. (eds) *Complexity and Complex Systems in Industry: A Conference Proceedings*, Warwick University, Warwick, September.

Stacey, R.D. (1993) 'Strategy as Order Emerging from Chaos', *Long Range Planning*, 26(1): 10–17.

Stacey, R.D. (1995) 'The Science of Complexity: An Alternative Perspective for Strategic Change Processes', *Strategic Management Journal*, 16: 477–495.

Stacey, R.D. (1996) *Strategic Management and Organisational Dynamics*, London: Pitman.

Stacey, R.D. (2003) 'Learning as an Activity of Interdependent People', *The Learning Organization*, 10(6): 325–331.

Stacey, R.D., Griffin, D. and Shaw, P. (2000) *Complexity and Management. Fad or Radical Challenge to Systems Thinking?* London: Routledge.

Stewart, G., MacLean, D., and MacIntosh, R. (2000) 'Applying Complexity Theory in Organisations (Comparing Experiences)', in McCarthy, I. and Rakotobe-Joel, T. (eds) *Complexity and Complex Systems in Industry: A Conference Proceedings*, Warwick University, Warwick, September.

Stewart, I. (1997) *Nature's Numbers*, London: Phoenix, Orion Books.

Styhre, A. (2002) 'Non-linear Change in Organizations: Organization Change Management Informed by Complexity Theory', *Leadership and Organization Development Journal*, 23(6): 343–351.

Tamkin, P. and Barber, L. (1998) 'Learning to Manage', Draft Report, Institute for Employment Studies, University of Sussex.

Tetenbaum, T.J. (1998) 'Shifting Paradigms: From Newton to Chaos', *Organizational Dynamics*, 26(A): 21–32.

Toffler, A. (1983) *Future Shock*, London: Pan Books.

Waldrop, M.M. (1994) *Complexity*, New York: Penguin Books.

Waldrop, M.M. (1996) 'The Trillion Dollar Vision of Dee Hock', *Fast Company*, 5: 75.

Walsham, G. (1993) 'Management Science and Organizational Change: A Framework for Analysis', in Mabey, C. and Mayon-White, B. (eds) *Managing Change*, London: Paul Chapman.

Wheatley, M. (1994) *Leadership and the New Science*, San Francisco: Berrett-Koehler.

Winograd, T. and Flores, F. (1991) *Understanding Computers and Cognition*, Reading, MA: Addison-Wesley.

Wood, S. (2007) 'Standing in the Way of Control', *People Management*, Chartered Institute of Personnel and Development, 13, February: 40–42.

Index